PRESIDENTS
in CULTURE

FRONTIERS IN POLITICAL COMMUNICATION

Lynda Lee Kaid and Bruce Gronbeck
General Editors

Vol. 9

PETER LANG
New York • Washington, D.C./Baltimore • Bern
Frankfurt am Main • Berlin • Brussels • Vienna • Oxford

DAVID MICHAEL RYFE

PRESIDENTS
in CULTURE

The Meaning of
Presidential Communication

PETER LANG
New York • Washington, D.C./Baltimore • Bern
Frankfurt am Main • Berlin • Brussels • Vienna • Oxford

Library of Congress Cataloging-in-Publication Data

Ryfe, David Michael
Presidents in culture: the meaning of presidential communication / David Michael Ryfe.
p. cm. — (Frontiers in political communication; v. 9)
Includes bibliographical references and index.
1. Presidents—United States—History. 2. Presidents—United States—
Language—History. 3. Communication in politics—United States—History.
4. Political oratory—United States—History. 5. Rhetoric—Political aspects—
United States—History. 6. Mass media—Political aspects—United States—History.
7. United States—Politics and government. I. Title. II. Series.
E176.1.R98   973'.09'9—dc22   2004018818
ISBN 0-8204-7456-8
ISSN 1525-9730

Bibliographic information published by **Die Deutsche Bibliothek**.
Die Deutsche Bibliothek lists this publication in the "Deutsche
Nationalbibliografie"; detailed bibliographic data is available
on the Internet at http://dnb.ddb.de/.

Cover design by Lisa Barfield

© 2005 Peter Lang Publishing, Inc., New York
275 Seventh Avenue, 28th Floor, New York, NY 10001
www.peterlangusa.com

Printed in the United States of America

To my mother, who always thought I could

Table of Contents

Tables

Figures

Acknowledgments

A PROJECT this long in the making incurs a great many debts. I wish to thank the Department of Communication at the University of California, San Diego and the School of Journalism at Middle Tennessee State University for their support. I have also benefited from the financial assistance of several organizations, including the John F. Kennedy Library Foundation, the Joan Shorenstein Barone Center on Politics, the Press, and Public Policy at Harvard University, and the Faculty Research and Creative Activity Committee at Middle Tennessee State University.

No two individuals have been more helpful to me during the course of this project than Michael Schudson and Daniel Hallin. Each read every version of the manuscript from beginning to end. Indeed, their insights permeate the text, making it better than it otherwise would be. More than that, they exemplify an intellectual generosity I am not worthy to receive, but can only hope to emulate. As a student, I cannot have wished for better mentors.

I wish to say a special word of thanks to Robert Horwitz. Though he juggled (and still does) an untold number of graduate students, Robert always made time for me. In meetings and correspondence, he took my ideas seriously—sometimes before I did. Such encouragement may seem a small thing, but to a young author gripped by doubt, it can mean all the difference in the world. It certainly did to me.

Librarians at the Franklin D. Roosevelt, Dwight D. Eisenhower, John F. Kennedy, and Jimmy Carter presidential libraries, as well as librarians at the Library of Congress, provided invaluable help during my brief stints in their archives.

Several scholars read and commented on parts of the manuscript during its long march to completion. They include Samuel Kernell, George Lipsitz,

Jeffrey Tulis, Roderick Hart, Paddy Scannell, Daniel Dayan, Elihu Katz, John Durham Peters, Bartholomew Sparrow, and Jill Edy. I thank them all.

Many others provided a timely word of encouragement in correspondence and conversation, and several deserve explicit mention: Stephen Skowronek, Stephen Ponder, Bruce Miroff, Elvin Lim, and David Zarefsky. I have learned a great deal from the work of these individuals, and even more from their generosity of spirit.

As the reader will soon learn, my arguments about presidential communication traverse the boundaries of political science, rhetoric, history, sociology, and communication. While such interdisciplinarity is widely celebrated as an ideal in all of these disciplines, I have learned that in practice it is a much tougher road to hoe. As editor for Peter Lang's series in political communication, Bruce Gronbeck has made the going easier. I greatly appreciate his insights and perspicacity.

Several essays related to this project have been published elsewhere. They include "Franklin D. Roosevelt's Fireside Chats," in the *Journal of Communication*; "'Betwixt and Between': Woodrow Wilson's press conferences and the transition to the modern rhetorical presidency," in *Political Communication*, and "Political Media Events and Mass Publics: A study of letters written in reaction to FDR's fireside chats," in *Media, Culture and Society*. I thank the editors for including my work in the pages of their journals, and the anonymous reviewers for helping me to clarify and sharpen my arguments. I also thank the parent publishers of these journals, Oxford University Press, Taylor & Francis, and Sage Publishers, respectively, for permission to include parts of the essays in the chapters that follow. One other early essay, "Presidential Communication as Cultural Form," appeared in Roderick Hart and Bartholomew Sparrow, editors, *Politics, Discourse and American Society: New Agendas*. Rod has been an unflagging supporter of my work and for that I cannot thank him enough. Moreover, I consider meeting Bat Sparrow one of the highlights of attending Hart's 2001 conference on New Agendas in Political Communication. Bat has remained a friend ever since. I thank Rowman & Littlefield for granting permission to republish a small portion of this essay.

Finally, my wife Jill has seen me through the entirety of this project. In a decade of conversations during meals, nights out, weekend trips, car rides, and vacations, the amazing birth of our child, Dylan, and countless other small episodes that make up the fabric of two lives entwined, she has kept me sane and grounded. Without her, this book would never have seen the light of day.

Introduction

Meaning in Presidential Communication

BY ALMOST any measure, presidential communication is an important element of modern American presidential politics. In terms of sheer time, modern presidents devote more attention to communication than ever before. Indeed, since the presidency of Franklin D. Roosevelt (FDR), each successive president has devoted more attention to the activity than the last.[1] The fact that the apparatus of presidential communication in the White House Office (WHO) has grown exponentially in the post–World War II years is another register of its importance.[2] Today, presidents have as many aides devoted to communication as to any other single activity. One might argue for its importance in still other ways. Presidential communication has been at the center of the growth of mass mediated politics in the last century. A moment's reflection shows that most every significant anecdote in the history of media politics—from Woodrow Wilson's "Creel Committee" during World War I to FDR's Fireside Chats to the Kennedy-Nixon televised debates to Ronald Reagan's "line of the day"—involves the presidency. And culturally, Americans simply expect presidents to communicate often and at great length about every public issue of the moment, no matter how far removed from the formal concerns of the office. We think nothing of the fact, for instance, that recent presidents have used parts of their State of the Union addresses to come out in favor of school uniforms and against the use of steroids in baseball.

For any or all of these reasons, it is difficult not to believe that presidential communication matters. It is such an obvious fact of modern American politics that it barely warrants discussion. The thornier questions are how and why it matters. It is a curious trick of language that while we can all agree that presidential communication matters, we can and do disagree—often vociferously—about precisely what this means. Scholarship on presidential communication demonstrates the point. Since the 1980s, the scholarly community has worked broadly within two theories of presidential communication, which conventionally are labeled the "public" and the "rhetorical" presidency.[3] Both of these theories spring from the premise that presidential communication matters. Yet, accepting this notion, they disagree quite profoundly on such basic issues as what presidential communication is, how it works, and how to measure its effects.[4] Ironically, in the act of agreeing that presidential communication matters, adherents to these theories succeed in saying vastly different things about why it matters.

One might chalk this up to a frustrating habit of scholars. Ensconced in the Ivory Tower, they have the luxury of theoretical debates. In fact, however, the broad purpose of this book is to show that the same kind of disagreement plays out in the actual practice of presidential communication. I wish to argue that struggles over the meaning of presidential communication—what it is (or ought to be); what its purpose is (or ought to be); and how it is (or ought to be) practiced—are part and parcel of the practice of presidential communication. For example, at the turn of the twentieth century both reporters and the progressive presidents they covered agreed that presidential communication mattered. However, as I show in chapter two, they meant something very different in saying so. Similarly, post–World War II presidents have often turned to FDR as a model communicator. Every presidential library I have visited contains at least one memo written by a presidential aide imploring his or her president to address the nation in the manner of FDR. Yet, in chapters three and four I demonstrate that FDR and the public he addressed understood what he was doing in very different terms than postwar presidents. Today, the idea that presidential communication is important wins near unanimous assent. Yet, as I show in chapter five, we disagree profoundly about what presidents ought to say, how they ought to say it, and what ultimately it ought to mean. In short, though Americans can agree that presidential rhetoric matters, what they mean by this notion has been a source of contention throughout the last century.

Each of the following chapters details the terms of this contention at a particular moment in the last hundred years. The result is not exactly a history of presidential communication. The chapters do not provide a chronology of events or offer analyses steeped in the minutiae of historical detail. One might instead think of them as an analysis of the rhetoric *about* presidential rhetoric. I mean by this something like Terence Ball's description of critical conceptual history: "What distinguishes critical conceptual history ..." he writes, "is its attention to the *arguments* in which concepts appear and are used to perform particular kinds of actions at particular times and at particular sites. Histories of political concepts are, in short, histories of political arguments and the conceptual contests and disputes to which they give rise."[5] Similarly, in these chapters I survey arguments over the meaning of presidential communication, the conceptual terms on which they have been waged, and how these terms have changed over time. Since at least the early 1900s, observers have agreed that presidential communication matters. These chapters detail the various terms on which Americans have fought over this conventional wisdom in the last century.

Before moving on to the chapters, though, perhaps, I should do a bit of conceptual ground clearing. If the extant approaches to presidential communication disagree on much, they share at least one assumption, namely, that presidential rhetoric arises out of the intentions and interests of individual presidents. Obviously, I beg to differ. To my mind, presidential rhetoric itself is subject to social construction. Its meaning arises in context, not in individual intentions. Even what counts as a presidential "interest" or "intention" is historically conditioned. Put more simply, I wish to argue that presidential communication is a cultural act. In the rest of this introduction, I elaborate on this idea and situate it with respect to the public and rhetorical models of presidential communication.

Presidential Communication as an Object of Study

Let me begin with what may seem like a banal point: any examination of presidential communication must have some sense of it as an object of study. Before any analysis can take place, that is, one must stipulate that presidential communication *is* a certain kind of activity. It is only from such a vantage that the practice can be recognized as a coherent activity. As I say, the point may seem so obvious as to be dull. But such mundane choices profoundly shape intellectual inquiry. They help to determine the kinds of questions scholars ask, the kinds of evidence they gather, and the kinds of evaluations they deem appropriate. With this thought in mind, I would like to briefly peruse the two most important scholarly approaches to presidential communication.

The Public Presidency

Richard Neustadt announced the first in his landmark study of presidential power.[6] Neustadt observes that modern presidents—for him, those from FDR forward—have been asked to be more vigorous legislative leaders, but have few formal powers to accomplish this mission. Absent these powers, they have naturally gravitated toward the one, albeit informal, power they do possess: the power to persuade. According to Neustadt, the exercise of presidential power looks something like this: presidents come to office with particular experiences and personalities; per force they must develop and seek to implement a legislative agenda; they have two essential resources for achieving this goal: their personal reputations within the Washington Community (essentially, assessments of them by inside-the-beltway political observers), and their popular prestige among the public at large (i.e., public approval). By leveraging reputation and approval, presidents strive to convince others—primarily members of Congress—that what they wish to have done is what ought to be done. Written in 1960, and revised over the next three decades, this deceptively simple theory placed communication at the heart of presidential politics. In so doing, it launched a new branch of presidency studies, fundamentally reorienting the field toward a greater consideration of rhetoric and public opinion.[7]

Notice, however, that it is a particular construal of communication. As Neustadt bluntly states, for him "the power to persuade is the power to bargain."[8] It is, in other words, a strategic resource invested in individual presidents.[9] As such, Neustadt—and those who follow in his footsteps—conceive of presidential communication essentially as a bargaining instrument useful for the accrual of presidential power. It is, one might say, a means to achieve a predetermined end. Like any such definition, this one has had certain consequences for inquiry into what became known as the "public presidency." Most obviously, in this formulation communication is all substance and no form. Neustadt cares little about *how* presidents seek to persuade. One will find little attention to rhetoric as rhetoric in Neustadt's work. Instead, he cares a great deal about the fact of presidential communication, more precisely the fact that presidents increasingly pursue policy ends through rhetorical means. And he cares a great deal about determining the conditions under which this form of presidential leadership is likely to work.

We see the consequences of this conception more clearly in Samuel Kernell's influential update of Neustadt's theory.[10] Kernell begins his study with the observation that the environment of Washington politics has changed considerably since the 1960s. At the time Neustadt devised his theory, the centers of power in Washington were relatively few in number, and political coalitions were relatively stable. This, Kernell argues, was an environment of institutional pluralism, and it was especially conducive to the kind of presidential bargaining observed by Neustadt. However, over the next forty years, a great many more, and more independent, centers of political power have arisen, and coalitions have become much weaker and ephemeral. Kernell identifies many sources for this transformation: weakened political parties; an expansion of federal bureaucracies under the province of the Executive Office of the President (EOP); a reduced power of Congressional leaders to control its policy agenda; the growth of interest groups surrounding the policymaking process; and the emergence of mass media, particularly television, as a primary vehicle for presidential communication. This new "individualized pluralist" environment presents presidents with a more complicated field on which to bargain, so much so that presidents increasingly have preferred to "go public" than to bargain with Congress.

This term—"going public"—refocuses the study of the public presidency in important ways.[11] For Neustadt, presidential power operates on a two-tiered track: a first along the line of the president's reputation within the Washington Community, and a second according to the president's public prestige. Neustadt referred to FDR as the archetypal bargaining president because it was FDR who first enhanced his inside-the-beltway bargaining with the occasional public address. In Kernell's "going public" model, public opinion has eclipsed reputation as a primary resource of presidential bargaining. "Modern presidents," he writes, "rely upon public opinion for their leadership in Washington to an extent unknown when Neustadt predicated presidential power on bargaining."[12] Thus, the bargaining model in Kernell's formulation becomes essentially a one-track process, that of cultivating public opinion. It is a theory that stresses far more than Neustadt an image of presidential leadership as a nonstop public relations campaign.

At the same time, the "going public" model retains Neustadt's definition of communication, and thus his sense of the "problem" presidential communication presents to scholars. At its most basic level, this definition invites scholars to approach communication as something akin to a pure flow of information: presidents have agendas; they communicate these agendas to citizens; citizens respond (or not); and other political actors strategically situate themselves in relation to this response (or not). Neither the medium nor the manner of communication matters, except to the extent that these elements influence the perceived accuracy of presidential messages. This approach also casts presidents as independent, rational decision makers. On its view, presidents are possessed of predetermined interests and confronted by a strategic environment. Armed with an array of political weapons, their task is to strategically deploy these weapons according to careful calculations of risks and rewards. Finally, this conception of communication casts the public as consumer of presidential information: citizens receive, cognitively process, and decide wither or not to "buy" information conveyed by the presidents. Taken together, these conceptual orientations offer scholars a particular problem to solve: under what conditions can presidents strategically use communication to move public opinion in ways that are favorable to their initiatives?

Ironically, after two decades of research, the findings are unequivocal: going public rarely works. Since its enunciation in the early 1980s, researchers have found little correlation between presidential communication, public approval, and legislative outputs. On rare occasions, presidential rhetoric seems to have positive effects on public opinion.[13] For the most part, however, these effects are minimal and short-lived.[14] The great majority of the time presidential rhetoric does not affect public opinion at all. It does not command the public's attention, at least for any great length of time; it does not move public opinion in discernible ways; and even when it does, it rarely leads other political actors to recalculate their strategic actions. In short, the "going public" model of presidential politics has not been borne out by the empirical evidence.

This finding raises a new problem: why do presidents continue to invest great personal and institutional resources in an activity that rarely succeeds?[15] This question, I think, points to the conceptual limits of the going public model. Having defined presidential communication in individualistic, strategic terms, the model quite naturally produces individualistic, strategic answers to this question.[16] On its view, presidents must either be irrational or mistaken to engage in this activity. Perhaps they have misjudged opportunities presented by the political context. Or perhaps they have an inflated sense of their rhetorical skills. Whatever the specific reason, within the terms of the model an explanation must have something to do with the personal miscalculations or misjudgments of presidents.

No doubt this approach offers some insight into the puzzle. On occasion, a president may simply miscalculate the costs and benefits of going public. As a general explanation, however, for why, despite all evidence to the contrary, every modern president has felt the need to go public—and every president feels this need more than the last—it seems narrow and uncharitable. Presidents are smart people surrounded by intelligent aides. They also have great incentives to distinguish themselves from their predecessors, and to succeed in their legislative endeavors. Given all of this, it seems unlikely that every modern president would repeat the same mistake, and do so more egregiously than the last. Indeed, it is far more likely that the model itself simply fails to capture the peculiar rationality of presidential communication.

The Rhetorical Presidency

A second tradition in the study of presidential communication offers a different set of resources for thinking about these issues. Like the literature on the public presidency, it begins with the observation that presidential rhetoric has increased substantially in the last century. And like this other literature, it traces the root of this pattern to a changing institutional environment. But it conceives of this environment in different terms from those of the public presidency literature. Ceaser et al. set the terms of this perspective when they trace the rise of the "rhetorical presidency" to three factors: "1) a modern doctrine of presidential leadership, 2) the modern mass media, and 3) the modern presidential campaign. Of these three, doctrine is probably the most important."[17] The "doctrine" to which Ceaser et al. refer is simply stated: the presidency is supposed to be the primary legislative catalyst in American politics, and rhetoric is its central tool in playing this role. In part in response to his observations of Theodore Roosevelt's "bully pulpit," Woodrow Wilson first championed this doctrine in his scholarly writings, and then argued for it strenuously while in office. Since that time, it has become, as Jeffrey Tulis argues, the "unquestioned premise of [modern] political culture."[18]

At first glance, this emphasis on doctrine rather than strategic context may seem a minor difference from the going public model. After all, both the public and rhetorical presidency models eventually reach the same conclusion: presidents go public as never before. Indeed, the two models are sometimes conflated into a singular theory of presidential rhetoric. But in stressing the role of ideas, the rhetorical presidency model develops a unique sense of presidential communication as an object of study. Perhaps most importantly, it stresses the structural context of presidential communication far more than the public model. Consider the question of why presidents go public despite much evidence for its utility. As we know, the public presidency model suggests that presidents are simply misjudging or miscalculating the costs and benefits of engaging in this activity. For the rhetorical presidency model, however, going public may be perfectly rational even when it is not especially useful for individual presidents. On its terms, all modern presidents must go public because the *idea* of presidential rhetoric has been institutionalized as a taken-for-granted norm in modern politics.[19] This expectation, in other words, exercises a certain force on presidential behavior. Even if it is not a winning strategy, and even when particular presidents express discomfort with it, presidents go public because not to do so risks seeming "unpresidential."[20] For Tulis, this idea—that the presidency ought to serve as a primary source of legislative and deliberative energy— represents nothing less than a "second constitution" in American politics—a layer of understanding about how the constitutional system is supposed to work that has been overlaid on to the original, founding conception.

This refocusing of presidential communication also leads scholars of the rhetorical presidency to emphasize the symbolic dimension of presidential rhetoric. Consider the question of what presidents can hope to achieve by going public. We know that they rarely move public opinion or achieve particular policy outcomes. But according to the rhetorical presidency model, this is not the point of going public at all. By going public, presidents serve an important systemic function. They propose and campaign for policies because Congress and every other political institution is ill-equipped to do so. Going public then, is designed less to cause policy outcomes than to initiate and define policy agendas. Individual presidents may go public to win legislative victories. However, the larger purpose of going public is institutional—the political system demands that presidents set and frame public and policy agendas.

On this score, modern presidents appear to be extraordinarily successful. Since at least the 1970s, we have known that public opinion tends to follow media agendas: issues reported in the news tend to be identified by citizens as more important or salient than issues not reported in the news. Indeed, the earliest research found a nearly perfect correlation between the news and public opinion. The greater the coverage, the more citizens were apt to report an issue as important.[21] We have also known that news media routinely favor official sources, and that none is more official, or more favored, than the president.[22] Together, these facts give modern presidents a power and prominence enjoyed by no other political actor. It does not mean that they can rhetorically determine legislative outcomes. However, it does mean that presidents are capable—far more than other political actors—of determining which issues will be placed on public and policy agendas, and how subsequent discussions will be framed. The research is unequivocal on this point: presidents set the terms of political discourse far more, and far more often, than other political actors.[23] This gives them a decided, though not decisive, advantage in framing how these issues will be discussed.[24]

Because they are concerned with issues of agenda-setting and framing, scholars of the rhetorical presidency devote a great deal of attention to the form of presidential rhetoric. It is in the form of what they say that presidents signal how they wish others to interpret public issues. As David Zarefsky puts it, because "the president is the principal source of symbols about public issues the function of presidential definition is primarily to shape the context in which events or proposals are viewed...."[25] In other words, presidential rhetoric matters because it defines political reality. This is its primary, systemic function. In their rhetoric, presidents invite others to debate some issues rather than others, and to discuss these issues in some ways rather than others. Rhetorically then, presidents construct a context in which other political actors maneuver. Given this understanding of presidential communication, it is not surprising that scholars of the rhetorical presidency pay a great deal of attention to the terms on which such contexts are constructed.

In their analyses of how presidents frame issues, rhetoricians will sometimes claim that such symbolic choices actually determine the fate of particular policies.[26] Indeed, as Stuckey and Antczak observe, much like the going public model, the literature on presidential rhetoric tends to conflate it with the personal political and legislative goals of presidents.[27] The great bulk of studies in this tradition focus on a single speech given in a particular context. And, much like the literature in the public presidency tradition, it defines its task as one of ascertaining whether or not a speech has succeeded in achieving a president's short-term political goals. Why have rhetoricians taken this tack? One explanation is simply that, as rhetoricians, they believe in the power of oratory. Another is that much of this work is rooted in a tradition of rhetorical criticism. Because this tradition prefers close readings of authorial intentions in texts outside of their wider social context, it reinforces an image of the president as a lone calculator of self-interest.[28] Consider, for instance, Medhurst's description of presidential rhetoric: "the most basic principle of rhetorical theory," he suggests, "is that the speaker or writer must begin with a thorough understanding of the rhetorical situation." In large part, this means that rhetors must "attempt to assess the current configuration of forces in the rhetorical situation ... then, having made that assessment ... [try] to adjust the discourse to the situation...."[29] This image of the president-as-rhetor conjures a definition of the "problem" of presidential communication that looks curiously like that offered by the going public model: has a particular president accurately assessed a given rhetorical situation and used rhetoric to achieve his predefined aims?

Such claims mischaracterize how symbols work. Though one might find examples from time to time, as a general matter symbols are not causal agents. As Clifford Geertz puts it, "culture is not a power, something to which social events, behaviors, institutions or processes can be causally attributed; it is a context, something within which they can be intelligibly— that is, thickly—described."[30] This does not mean that one cannot investigate symbols empirically. For scholars of the rhetorical presidency, presidential rhetoric "works" when it succeeds in setting policy agendas, and when its frames of those agendas resonate with audiences. All of this can be, in Geertz's words, "thickly described." For instance, it is possible to examine the terms on which a president announces a policy, track the extent to which the policy infiltrates the public and policy agenda, and determine whether or not others discuss it through the president's terminology—whether, that is, his reality becomes their reality. But if it is empirical such analysis cannot be predictive. Rather, it shows how patterns of symbols produce the possibility of meaningful action, how such patterns set the terms on which presidents and other political actors determine their roles, values, and obligations. It shows, in other words, how presidential rhetoric acts as a form of culture.

Of course, a good many scholars have taken Geertz's point to heart.[31] However, at least as regards presidential communication, none of this work has produced a theory of presidential communication on the order of the public or rhetorical presidency models. What is needed is a truly cultural model of presidential communication, one that imagines the meaning of the act of presidential communication itself to be socially constructed.

The Cultural Presidency

In developing this new model, perhaps it is best to begin with a claim that every observer agrees upon: modern presidents are expected to go public. What does this mean? Advocates of both the public and presidency models assume it means that presidents must seek to persuade. This assumption leads them to view the "problem" of presidential communication as one of determining the conditions—rhetorical or otherwise—in which presidents are most likely to successfully persuade others.

Stephen Skowronek offers another view.[32] According to him, the central problem of presidential leadership is not persuasion, but authority. Skowronek imagines the presidency as something on the order of a bull in a china shop, willing to break things to get its way. It is the office's institutional role, he argues, for the presidency to be a "blunt, disruptive force" in the political system, forever upsetting the status quo to impose its will.[33] Given their short time in office, presidents do not have time to persuade others to go along with their plans. Instead, they come to the White House motivated to act decisively. Their problem is not persuading others, but getting others to accept their proposed actions.[34] They must, in other words, seek a legitimacy for their actions which only others can provide. On this view, presidential communication looks more like a form of accounting than of persuasion. Can presidents provide accounts of their actions (or potential actions) that seem authoritative to others?

This conception orients us to the normative and ontological conditions of presidential communication. To the extent that presidents are "blunt" and "disruptive," they necessarily upset expectations for their behavior. As Scott and Lyman note, this is precisely the condition most likely to elicit accounts.[35] Faced with a president intent on imposing his will, others naturally ask: why are you doing (or not doing) this? Such questions imply not only that some presidential action is incorrect, but that it is wrong in an ethical or moral sense. Critics question this president's motives, not merely his proposals. Faced with this reaction, accounting for his behavior becomes a constitutive dilemma for this president. A good account must define political reality in such a way that the president's motives appear beyond reproach. Accounts, then, necessarily are grounded in ontological and normative definitions of context.[36]

As a form of accounting, presidential rhetoric only makes sense against a backdrop of assumptions about roles, purposes, obligations, and responsibilities that are appropriate in public life. These assumptions extend to the act of presidential communication, and even to how presidents come to understand their intentions and interests. Presidents do not define reality—words do—and these words arise in context, not out of individual intentions or interests. In other words, presidential communication is cultural through and through.

A cultural approach to presidential communication raises a host of new questions: what exactly is the "context" of presidential communication? Where do contexts come from and how do they work? Are presidents simply constrained by contexts, or do they have some freedom of maneuverability? Do contexts of presidential communication change, and if so, how might we track these changes?

As a way into these issues, I would like to suggest that the "idea" of the rhetorical presidency is essentially a kind of social rule.[37] It is what we mean when we say that, as a general *rule*, observers expect presidents to go public. But what kind of rule is this idea? Douglass North offers one definition. He writes that social rules "are perfectly analogous to the rules of the game in a competitive team sport.[38] Like the rules of a game, social rules determine what one can do—the kinds of moves one may make in a given situation—and when violated they mandate some form of punishment (as when a foul is called in football). According to this definition, the rule that presidents should go public is a guide to action. On assuming office, presidents confront rules that constrain and channel their behavior. Going public is one such rule. This is the sense in which Tulis argues that modern presidents are required to lead through rhetoric.

This conception seems quite reasonable, and in fact accords with how both the public and rhetorical presidency models understand the practice of going public. However, I think it mischaracterizes the nature of social rules, and more specifically, the nature of going public, in important ways. At a basic level, for instance, it tends to conflate what are in fact different types of rules.[39] I have in mind the distinction between "constitutive" and "regulative" rules. Here is Searle on this difference:

> Regulative rules regulate antecedently or independently existing forms of behavior; for example, many rules of etiquette regulate interpersonal relationships which exist independently of the rules. But constitutive rules do not merely regulate, they create or define new forms of behavior.... Regulative rules characteristically take the form of or can be paraphrased as imperatives, e.g., 'When cutting food, hold the knife in the right hand,' or 'Officers must wear ties at dinner." Some constitutive rules take quite a different form, e.g., 'A checkmate is made when the king is attacked in such a way that no move will leave it unattacked."[40]

What Searle seems to be saying is that certain kinds of rules define objects (situations, roles, etc.), so that without those rules the objects would not exist. Other kinds of rules direct behavior toward or within predefined or independently existing objects (situations, roles, etc.). A constitutive rule tells us what an object is; a regulative rule tells us something about an object. Constitutive rules are ontological; regulative rules are epistemological.

In this regard, it is apparent that, as a "second constitution" of American politics, going public is a constitutive rule of the modern presidency. This is so in the sense that it fundamentally redefines the presidency as a rhetorical office. Before the advent of this new rule, presidents may have used rhetoric to achieve their ends. But this was not viewed as a constitutive duty of the office. Nineteenth-century presidents, that is, were not expected to go public. The rhetorical presidency illuminates this dramatic change in our conception of the office. Since the early twentieth century, the presidency has been encumbered with a new ontological and normative vision. On the basis of this vision, presidents have assumed a new role in the political system, and with this new role has come new obligations and values.

The distinction between constitutive and regulative rules allows us to see a further point: *as a constitutive rule of the modern presidency, the idea of going public is all form and no substance.* The rule that presidents ought to use rhetoric says nothing about what counts as a "good" use of the rule. How do we know when a president has "gone public?" How do we know when he has gone public well? Conventional wisdom about the practice of going public must be worked out on the ground between presidents and others. It is in the process of this working out that regulative rules—how to perform acts of going public and how to evaluate these acts—emerge. Tulis' argument then, that the modern presidency is a rhetorical presidency, only takes us halfway to understanding this "idea." Granted that the idea now forms a constitutive rule of modern public life, we still know little about what it actually means in practice. To gain this understanding, we need to know more about the regulative rules which guide presidential rhetoric.

To this end, Jürgen Habermas' *Structural Transformation of the Public Sphere* is a useful starting point.[41] In this volume, Habermas tracks the emergence of a "category of bourgeois society," which he calls alternately the public sphere, or publicity. Before the seventeenth century, publicity was contained in the body of the sovereign, an individual who literally embodied the group he or she ruled. However, at this time, a new set of institutions began to emerge in European society. In cafés, salons, reading clubs, taverns, subscription libraries, and newspapers, bourgeois individuals began to fashion a new idea of publicity as public opinion. Famously, Habermas argues that this new idea constituted a "structural transformation" of public life, fundamentally redefining the public sphere. The argument has received quite a bit of commentary.[42] For our purposes, it is most important to note that, much like the idea of the rhetorical presidency, the idea of publicity as public opinion says nothing about what counts as legitimate opinion. Regulative rules had to be worked out by actual individuals in social contexts, between, for instance, actual letter writers, newspaper readers, and participants in café discussions. These rules, in other words, arose among the inhabitants of what Habermas calls the "institutions of the public sphere."[43]

Neustadt is on to a similar observation about the modern presidency when he notes that a president's "prestige" is rooted in perceptions of the "Washington Establishment." By this, he means to capture the influence of political "insiders"—all of the actors and observers who encircle national politics—in shaping perceptions of presidential actions. We might broaden the point and link it to Habermas' theoretical formulation. Regulative rules for what counts as a legitimate instance of going public arise out of what I will call "institutions of political life" (or what Neustadt calls the "Establishment"). Inhabitants of these institutions develop what are sometimes called "vocabularies" or "grammars" within which expectations about the practice of presidential communication arise.[44] These expectations structure presidential behavior to the extent that actors—including presidents themselves—invest both human (i.e., people, skills, knowledge) and nonhuman (i.e., capital) resources in them.[45] Presidents entering office within a particular structural environment confront a set of expectations which set a context for understanding their behavior (i.e., set criteria for what will count as legitimate or appropriate instances of going public).

Before summarizing this model, two other issues are worthy of attention. The first concerns the nature of agency within this cultural model. I have suggested that regulative rules form a structural context for presidential communication. Does this mean that presidents must simply follow these rules (i.e., abide by these expectations)?

The short answer is no. Presidents retain a measure of personal agency. Given the great body of literature that stresses the personal strengths of individual presidents, it would be surprising, and unconvincing, to suggest that presidents simply bear structural rules. But how might we conceptualize the relation between context and agency? Here, it is helpful to step back a bit to reconsider the nature of constitutive rules. As an idea of presidential leadership, the notion that presidents ought to go public opens a space of possibility for certain forms of presidential action. To accept the legitimacy of this rule is to open the possibility of sensibly acting as president. Within this space of possibility, regulative rules grow up within institutions of political life as conventional wisdom grows about how they ought to go about this activity.

Importantly, these rules are learned and understood as "things that presidents do" rather than as explicit rules of behavior. On entering office, presidents are not given a manual listing all of the rules they are expected to follow. Rather, they learn these rules by performing them. The observation is similar to Wittgenstein's description of how one might teach a game to a child. When teaching a game, Wittgenstein (1958) writes, "One gives examples and intends them to be taken in a particular way...."[46] (¶71). After every iteration, a teacher reacts favorably or not, offers a new example, engenders a reaction from the pupil, and the cycle begins again. "If the child is thereby induced to do the right thing ... and repeatedly," Pitkin concludes the point, "he has 'learned' what there is to learn."[47] (p. 48). So too, with presidents. Presidents learn how they ought to go public by engaging in the activity and repeatedly doing "the right thing."

Paradoxically, what this means is that presidents have little need of regulative rules to go public. In other words, rules for going public do not exist prior to actions, and therefore cannot be said to be their "cause." Let me explain what I mean. Suppose that you win the presidency and have just taken office. You have a legislative agenda and a deep desire to see it enacted into law. As a professional politician with long experience in the prevailing institutions of political life, it is doubtful that you will experience a sense of uncertainty. In other words, you will not assume office and immediately cast about for rules to follow. Rather, you will do just what you know how to do. You will do this because the rules of how to go public are embedded in how in fact it is done. Wittgenstein is useful again on this subject:

> "How am I able to obey a rule?"—if this is not a question about causes, then it is about the justification for my following the rule in the way that I do. If I have exhausted the justifications I have reached bedrock and my spade is turned. Then I am inclined to say: "This is simply what I do." [48]

What Wittgenstein's aphorism suggests is that regulative rules for going public serve as resources for the justification of, rather than as causes of, action. This accords with our sense that presidential communication is normative and ontological. As a general matter, presidents go public in the ways that are seen as appropriate in their time and place. More explicit rule following is only necessary when doubt has been raised about how presidents ought to act. Before doubt, presidents are simply going public.

This conception opens an aesthetic and rhetorical dimension to going public. Scholars of the modern presidency focus on the skills and personalities of individual presidents for good reason. Presidents have the freedom to go public in any way they see fit, or not to go public at all. Nowhere is it written down that presidents must engage in this activity. The idea of going public does not force them to act. Rather, going public is an assumption or expectation. Inhabitants of the institutions which encircle national politics expect that presidents will go public, and that they will do so in ways that conform to prevailing assumptions about the activity. When presidents push the boundaries of appropriateness, they risk running afoul of these assumptions. However, whether in fact they have violated these assumptions must be worked out. The question, this is to say, is open. An answer either way requires a justification. This justification will attempt to show that this way of going public comports with conventional assumptions. Whether or not this justification works depends upon the ability of the president to carry it off, that is, to get these inhabitants to accept that the action conforms to shared judgments about presidential communication. The point is that rules for going public do not exist except insofar as they establish a relationship between people. The claim to reasonableness is always also a claim to community, and thus is always a cultural artifact.

A second issue worthy of discussion concerns the matter of historical change. Habermas alerts us to the fact that structural transformations of public life can and do occur. They happen when the institutions of public life change. On these occasions, new institutions inhabited by different kinds of people introduce, and invest resources into, new ideas. Sometimes—as with the rhetorical presidency—this process reconstitutes political life in fundamental ways. Other times it introduces new standards (i.e., regulative rules) for thinking about an old idea. In either case, the result is a structural transformation of presidential communication, in the assumptions and expectations brought to bear on presidential rhetoric. Since the early twentieth century, the rhetorical presidency has served as a constitutive idea of modern American political life. But as the mix of institutions in American political life have changed, so too have ideas about how the rhetorical presidency ought to be conducted. Thus, while the idea of the rhetorical presidency has enjoyed great support in the last hundred years, its meaning has changed several times in the ensuing decades.

Organization of the Study

Broadly, the chapters that follow survey changes in how Americans have understood the rhetorical presidency over the last century. Much of this work involves an analysis of actual interactions between presidents, news media, and ordinary Americans. Why pay such close attention to these kinds of interactions? Because evidence for the existence of cultural assumptions can only be found in close analyses of the practice of presidential communication. Geertz makes the general point: "Behavior must be attended to, and with some exactness, because it is through the flow of behavior—or more precisely, social action—that cultural forms find articulation.... [W]hatever or wherever symbol systems 'in their own terms' may be, we gain empirical access to them by inspecting events...."[49] In other words, it is only through a close analysis of forms of presidential interaction—press conferences, nation-wide broadcasts, town hall meetings—that assumptions about presidential communication become visible. Or, put more precisely, these assumptions arise out of arguments about how these forms ought to be practiced.[50] Thus, detailed examinations of forms of presidential communication comprise the heart of each chapter. Close inspection of these interactions shows the often dramatic differences in the way the rhetorical presidency has been understood across the last century. This examination also reveals moments of tension when its meaning has been contested. At such moments, presidents must negotiate a difficult minefield, choosing among competing ways of accounting for their behavior, and dealing with the unhappiness and misunderstanding that inevitably follows.

I locate interpretations of the rhetorical presidency in distinctive institutional environments of political life across this century. Chapter one considers the meaning of presidential communication during the progressive period, a moment when churches, schools, newspapers, and women's groups exercised considerable influence in American political life. Chapter two discusses how the meaning of presidential rhetoric was changed by the emergence of new media industries in American public life. In chapter three, I survey the impact of new administrative and bureaucratic institutions on presidential communication during the Cold War. Finally, in chapter four, I examine the meaning of presidential communication in the post–Cold War, a time when New Social Movements (NSMs) have shifted our understanding of what it means to go public in significant ways. Each of these moments contains its own unique vocabulary for presidential rhetoric, and presidents have confronted them in their own unique ways. To illuminate this process, I have chosen to study both routine and emergent forms of presidential communication: "swing-the-circle" trips and newly institutionalized presidential press conferences in the progressive period; newly emergent nation-wide broadcasts during the New Deal; televised press conferences and nation-wide broadcasts in the post–World War II period; and a form of presidential communication unique to the last thirty years, presidential town hall meetings.

To avoid needless repetition, and to retain a focus on the meaning of presidential communication (rather than its chronological history), I have not considered every president—or every decade—in this study. Presidents Taft, Harding, Coolidge, Hoover, Truman, Johnson, and Nixon are not included, and the 1920s and 1940s are ignored. Taft contributes nothing to our understanding of progressive presidential communication which is not also evident in the rhetoric of Presidents Roosevelt and Wilson. A better argument can be made for including Presidents Coolidge and Hoover—and more generally for analyzing presidential communication of the 1920s. It seems to me, however, that the New Deal, particularly Roosevelt's use of radio, gets at issues raised by the demise of progressivism and the rise of mass culture in a way that a study of Coolidge and Hoover only hints at.[51] For a similar reason, I ignore the 1940s. President Truman initiated Cold War rhetoric, but its organizational form—and thus its preferred rhetorical resources—only became apparent in the 1950s. Perhaps the presidency of Richard Nixon is the biggest lacunae in what follows. Over the 1950s and 1960s, Nixon had a hand in most of the significant movements in presidential communication. However, to my mind he merely advances themes first initiated in the presidency of John F. Kennedy. Moreover, President Reagan carried these themes forward in ways that illuminate far more about the meaning of modern presidential communication than Nixon's presidency. Thus, while it might be preferable to include Nixon, his absence from this study does not produce great gaps in our understanding of presidential communication during the Cold War.

Schematically then, what follows is organized into four chapters on, respectively, presidential rhetoric in the eras of progressivism, the New Deal, the Cold War, and the post–Cold War. Within each chapter, I provide an overview of the institutional environment of the time, along with close analyses of forms of communication (press conferences, nation-wide broadcasts, town hall meetings) used by the following presidents during each period: Presidents Roosevelt and Wilson (progressivism); Roosevelt (New Deal), Eisenhower, Kennedy, and Reagan (post–World War II), and Carter and Clinton (contemporary). My analysis supports the notion that, in the last hundred years, the rhetorical presidency has served as a constitutive understanding of modern American political life. At the same time, Americans have often disagreed on precisely what this means. These chapters go some way toward helping us understand the terms of these disagreements. In so doing, they deepen our understanding of what we mean when we say that the rhetorical presidency has served as a second constitution in American political life.

Chapter One

"The Vital Connection": Progressive Presidential Communication

THEODORE ROOSEVELT and Woodrow Wilson anticipate much of modern presidential communication.[1] Roosevelt, for instance, was our first media/political celebrity. "In newspaper language," historian James Pollard writes, "he was a natural."[2] As president, he devised many modern techniques for manipulating the news. For instance, Roosevelt was the first president to realize that news columns were more important than editorials. To control the news, he invented the "leak," discovered Monday as a slow news day, created the unnamed White House source, and devised opportunities (ancestors of the "photo-op") to dramatize his actions.[3] Wilson capitalized on many of Roosevelt's inventions, and created a few himself. He took great strides in organizing and managing publicity bureaus in the various Executive departments; he employed the first presidential press secretary (if not in name then in practice), Joseph Tumulty; he delivered dramatic public messages before Congress that dominated the news columns for days after; and he created the first modern propaganda campaign during World War I via his Committee on Public Information (CPI).[4]

However, knowing all of this still leaves much unexplained. Why, for instance, did reporters cover Roosevelt's every move, but rarely detail his policy initiatives? Why did Roosevelt view this fact as demonstrating a lack of personal character among reporters? Why did Wilson institutionalize the press conference, and then refuse to answer most reporters' questions? Why, despite vast differences in experience and temperament, did both presidents often use biological metaphors when speaking of politics, turn to religious allusions when describing the role of the presidency in public life, prize individual character above all else, and imagine American history in evolutionary terms?[5] None of these aspects of their rhetoric seem particularly modern. Indeed, in some ways they directly contradict contemporary assumptions about presidential communication.

My point is that it is important to situate Roosevelt and Wilson's conception of the rhetorical presidency within the progressive culture from which it flowed. Progressivism is a hotly contested concept among historians. From about 1902 to 1920, it permeated American culture to such an extent that its boundaries are difficult to draw. More than a few historians have wondered if the term ought not to be discarded.[6] But as Eldon Eisenach notes, it is possible to say that progressivism grew up within a distinctive set of institutions—women's groups, journalism, the church, new corporate forms of business, professional associations.[7] Moreover, within this milieu, political actors may have disagreed greatly, but they expressed these disagreements within what Daniel Rodgers calls a "distinct cluster of ideas [or] social languages."[8] Publicity, public opinion, persuasion, and the news— terms commonly associated with modern presidential communication—were part of this cluster of ideas. But these terms gained meaning only in relation to other progressive touchstones, especially to religious, moral, and organistic conceptions of society. Within this progressive vocabulary of public life, it was possible for Roosevelt and Wilson to embrace publicity and the news, and at the same time to understand these activities in dramatically different ways from modern presidents. In other words, what Roosevelt and Wilson meant by insisting on the value of presidential rhetoric can only be understood in the context of the progressive culture in which it took root.

Roosevelt and Wilson's interactions with reporters are a particularly valuable prism for viewing the progressive style of presidential communication in action. When historian Richard Hofstadter famously described the "progressive mind [as] characteristically a journalistic mind," he referred more to muckrakers and the few national magazines for which they worked than to the news industry generally.[9] While reporters embraced publicity, public opinion, and certainly the news, they placed less value on religion and morality. Moreover, they did not accept the organistic conception of society that lay at the center of Roosevelt and Wilson's rhetoric. Thus, when the two presidents met reporters, a great deal of conflict and negotiation took place. In this negotiation the contours of a distinctively progressive understanding of presidential communication become apparent.

In what follows, I focus on two typical episodes of Rooseveltian and Wilsonian leadership of public opinion: Roosevelt's "swing the circle" trip down the Mississippi river in early October, 1907, and Wilson's press conferences during his first term. In these case studies, I show Roosevelt and Wilson articulating a similar understanding of presidential communication. Both conceive of public opinion in evolutionary terms, as an evolving mass of habits and beliefs. Both view the presidency as a model of this opinion, and therefore place a great deal of emphasis on personal character and intuition; both view persuasion as a kind of socializing process, capable of transforming the attitudes and beliefs of ordinary citizens into public opinion rightly understood. And both imagine the news as a passive conduit through which the process of modeling and refining public opinion might take place. The terms they use to express these views—publicity, public opinion, and the news among them—may be similar to modern conceptions of going public. To this extent, the two presidents do indeed anticipate modern presidential communication. But missing the distinctively progressive origins of their rhetoric risks distorting their sense of why presidential communication mattered.

A Progressive View of Political Communication

As a style of thought, progressivism was built up in response to dramatic change. Historians have told the story of the forty years between 1880 and 1920 in great detail.[10] For our purposes, it is enough to say that progressives at every level of society were anxious about the economic, political, social and technological changes that were transforming the country into a modern society. Inhabiting dominant institutions in political life—churches; women's groups; new administrative bureaucracies; and the like— progressives felt a particular responsibility for responding to these changes. In the act of this response, they conjured a new set of terms for dealing with social change.

Publicity and its cognates, exposure and investigation, constituted one group of these terms. Like no previous generation, progressives shared an interest in discovering how their society operated. "Muckraking" journalists led the way. Between 1903 and 1912, nearly two thousand "muckraking" articles published in popular national magazines exposed the prevailing system of business and politics.[11] But muckrakers were joined in the drive to expose society by social scientists, social and political reformers and even pragmatic philosophers. Whether a champion of the powers of journalism or of science, most were driven by the religious notion of revelation, of revealing the essence of modern society; and most were hopeful that scientific methods might illuminate social truths.[12] In this way, publicity, exposure, and investigation connect progressive activities as diverse as muckraking, John Dewey's philosophical analyses of experience, scholarly studies of political machines, Police Commissioner Theodore Roosevelt's midnight walks through the streets of New York City, and Jane Addams' investigations of urban slums.

The impulse to reveal was closely linked to a desire to educate. "The real vehicle for improvement," Herbert Croly writes, "is education. It is by education that the American is trained for such democracy as he possesses."[13] Like many progressives, Croly believed that sheer exposure amounted to little. Investigation that did not lead to action was useless. One publicized and investigated to "lift up" public opinion, to educate and refine it, to raise its consciousness and direct its purpose. As sociologist Edward Ross put it, if one desired to move beyond parochial, self-interested opinion, "the remedy is not to discredit it, but to instruct it."[14] For progressives, publicity, education, and public opinion were intimately wedded: one investigated to educate.

However, if progressives believed in the necessity of educating the public, they did not see this as merely a process of persuasion. Of course, they valued persuasion. But they thought of persuasion within nineteenth-century "organic" theories of the state to imagine "true" public opinion as a living, evolving mass of character, habits and experience.[15] For them, public opinion was a social tissue capable of growing, of coming to consciousness. Drawing on strands of Liberal Protestantism and German Idealism, progressives shared a belief that this organic national character was in the process of realizing itself, of becoming whole.[16] As Woodrow Wilson put it, "Democratic institutions are never done; they are like living tissue, always a-making."[17] However, positive growth was not inevitable. "The plutocracy," Walter Weyl wrote, by which he meant corporate businessmen, kept public opinion "confused and self-contradictory ... uninformed and hysterical...."[18] Fractured along geographic, racial and class lines, and fed misinformation by corporate elites, the public remained disorganized and, lacking common purpose, ineffective. True public opinion was organized and purposeful. Variously called "public sentiment," a "public conscience," "rational assent," "reflective consciousness and purpose," "public will," or "organic social judgment," it approximated something like Rousseau's General Will: an informed, morally right judgment of authentic public interest.[19] When progressives spoke of education then, they imagined it in terms of this refined collective purpose.

How did they propose to educate the public toward this collective purpose? On one level, progressives advocated a mundane notion of education, i.e., increasing the knowledge and intellect of average citizens. But they also harbored a wider educational vision. For them, education was a matter of socialization as much as knowledge. For instance, in his democratic model of education, Dewey paid less attention to the particular things children ought to be taught (i.e., what every child should know), than to the environmental conditions within which they should interact. Believing that democratic education was a "social process," he proposed that schools model democratic ideals of participation, open-mindedness, flexibility, and adaptability. By instilling these "habits of mind," Dewey hoped that schools would condition children to recognize themselves as democratic individuals, and to recognize these traits in others.[20] To Dewey as well as other progressives, this was not a paternalistic activity because, as Kloppenberg observes, progressives "believed that the state should manifest the values of autonomous individuals conscientiously fulfilling their social responsibility."[21] That is, believing that environment shaped psychology, Dewey and other progressives wished to build institutions that modeled democratic sensibilities.

This view of education was shared widely in progressive circles. Reformers at every level built institutions—from settlement houses to museums to schools—designed to socialize individuals in particular ways. This interest in modeling democratic habits led progressives to adopt a peculiar notion of leadership as well. For instance, drawing on this idiom, both Roosevelt and Wilson understood presidential leadership as a kind of modeling activity. "Whatever value my service may have," Roosevelt once wrote, "comes ... more from what I am than from what I do.... [T]he bulk of my countrymen ... feel that I am in a peculiar sense their President, that I represent the democracy...."[22] Wilson defined leadership in a similar way, as "the freedom to attempt the great role of living thus as models for the mass that fills a democracy...."[23] Of course, both men accepted that leadership was an act of persuasion, of arousing the public conscience, as Roosevelt often put it. But it was also, and perhaps more importantly, a matter of modeling. Thus, Roosevelt could respond to Lincoln Steffens' charge that he accepted "honest crooks" so long as they were on his side and represented him, in this way: "But I represent the common good."[24] Wilson could also champion the Presidency over the Congress, because it is the "vital link ... [with] the thinking nation...."[25]

This exalted view of presidential leadership is linked to the essentially moralistic character of progressivism. Political actors in this culture disagreed about many things, but they tended to engage one another through a shared vocabulary of motive; this is to say, they tended to view political activity in moral, religious, and personal terms. Thus, Roosevelt and Wilson shared Frederic Howe's suggestion that he "was one of the chosen," a leader with a duty to "pass what [he] had learned to others." Like Howe, Roosevelt and Wilson tended to think of their civic activities as a kind of "priesthood of service."[26] At times rooted in a religious conviction, at others in the appeal of scientific expertise, progressives of all stripes believed in the power of individual leadership. As George Mowry concludes, the progressive mentality was "imbued with a burning ethical strain which at times approached a missionary desire to create a heaven on earth. It had in it intense feelings of moral superiority over both elements of society above and below it economically. It emphasized individual dynamism and leadership."[27] On the one hand, this meant that progressive leadership was often leadership by personality. On the other, it meant that progressives coupled their impulse toward grass roots democracy (civic education) with political centralization. That is, just as they sought to expand the participation of individuals in public life, they created new forms of authority like commissions, agencies, and managers, and enhanced older forms of executive authority like the presidency, that highlighted the role of individual leaders.[28]

What Is Publicity For?

Taken together, the terms I have outlined—publicity, exposure, investigation, religion, civic education, science, public opinion, public interest, morality, and leadership—constituted key elements of the progressive vocabulary. Certainly, this list is not exhaustive.[29] But it captures enough of the progressive cosmology to offer a useful comparison with the way that reporters thought of the news. Given that progressives connected publicity to leadership, it is not surprising that they held a great fascination for the new instruments of communication. The telegraph and telephone, magazines and newspapers, constituted a network of media capable of publicizing, hence educating, on a national scale. As Robert Park put it: "The social agencies are every day experimenting with the principles of a slowly growing science of life.... To make this legislation effective, it must have the support of the community. One way to educate the community is through the press."[30] For Park, as for other progressives, the press may have been a "secondary" form of social control, but in the absence of primary forms like family and religion, it served as a modest socializing influence on heterogeneous communities.

Unfortunately, reporters only partially satisfied the progressive interest in civic education and social control. In his post-progressive phase, Walter Lippmann identified the key dilemma: "news and truth are not the same thing.... [T]he function of news is to signalize an event, the function of truth is to bring to light the hidden facts ... and make a picture of reality on which men can act."[31] Lippmann recognized, as progressives did not, that newspapers sold a commodity (audiences), to buyers (advertisers), and that the news merely linked the one group to the other. Thus, the news is always partial, tending to publicize obvious and ignore hidden aspects of society, and, therefore, to distort rather than refine public opinion. For Lippmann, the news could not possibly educate and direct public opinion.

Why had progressives thought that it could? This is a difficult question, but surely the close association of publicity with the news is part of the answer. Like progressives, reporters were out in society, recording and documenting people, places and events. And like progressives, reporters wished to attract mass publics to their writings. For many progressives, it must have seemed as if newsmen were animated by the same interests and desires as themselves. For the most part, however, they were not. Where progressives linked publicity to concepts like education and leadership, reporters made different associations. For reporters, publicity linked most closely with the news. Into the early 1900s, most reporters were paid according to the space their reports garnered in the newspaper.[32] In turn, editors based their allocations of news space on the relative newsworthiness of stories. Thus, reporters had an incentive not to publicize anything and everything, but to publish the news.

Of course, they had a notoriously difficult time defining this term. At a minimum, though, they understood that the news was truly new; news was defined by time and place: it happened in the present moment, and took place in specific locales.[33] This emphasis on time and place separated news from fiction. Urged on by competition with other reporters (and their editors), big-city reporters scoured their cities to "get the facts" of the stories they covered. This zeal for facts meshed with the wider progressive interest in realism and empiricism. In the new "science" of journalism, reporters saw themselves as "scientists uncovering the economic and political facts of industrial life more boldly, more clearly, more 'realistically' than anyone had done before."[34] As they saw it, their job was to gather the facts.

However, reporters did not conflate news with facts. Simple dates, times, places, and descriptions did not constitute the news. Rather, news stories were human interest stories, reports that dramatized and personalized events.[35] Facts lay at the base of news to be sure, but they were dressed up in the guise of sensationalism and human interest. In this sense, the news was closer to the genre of fiction than to scholarship.[36] It was human interest that gave the news its "symbolic character," and that marked it as other than a strict informational form. Thus, where progressives saw publicity and exposure as a kind of revelation, reporters saw it in terms of the news: highly stylized, dramatic, sensationalized, if factual, accounts.

Though concerned more with news than civic education, journalists nonetheless developed a sense of duty with respect to the readers who consumed their stories. But this sense of duty was rooted more in a budding sense of professionalism than in morality or religion.[37] In the early 1900s, journalists had only just begun to view themselves as professionals. It was only in the 1850s, when the "one man band" era of the newspaper industry gave way to specialization, that reporting became distinguished from editing and other activities.[38] However, even then reporters were poorly educated and underpaid. It wasn't until the 1890s, when the column-space system began to be replaced by salary-based compensation, that news reporting gained prestige.[39] At this time, a few journalists became public figures in their own right. Nelly Bly, Henry Morton Stanley, and Richard Davis, among others, received public adulation for their journalistic exploits.[40] And the industry and profession became more organized. In 1885 reporters established the Washington Gridiron Club, and in 1887 newspaper owners created the American Newspaper Publishers Association. Such associations not only codified journalistic norms, they established a new degree of legitimacy for the profession.

At the heart of the new sense of professionalism lay a set of techniques, a new beat system for producing the news, and a new self-conception. Where once reporters presented a strict chronology of events, by the 1880s they were digesting the essentials of events in a summary lead paragraph.[41] During the same period, reporters began to interview public figures on behalf of their reading public.[42] They employed these new techniques in an emerging beat system, in which individual reporters were assigned to specific locales: city halls; police stations; court houses. Stationed at these sites, reporters developed the sense that, as the Alsop brothers were later to put it, their legs were more important than their brains.[43] This is to say that for reporters, professionalism involved "leg work": working the beat, following leads, cultivating sources, and being first on the scene. Immersed in a world defined by the beat and the newsroom, journalists also began to associate professionalism with a particularly cool, detached demeanor. Witnesses to the best and the worst of human behavior, journalists began to stress their detachment from the human scene, to emphasize facts over emotion, neutrality over partisanship.[44] Schudson characterizes this self-conception as a "contempt for the critical, and generally moralistic, efforts of editorial writers ... [and an eagerness] to accept that position that wishes should submit to facts, soft dreams to hard realities, moralism to practical politics, and religion to common sense."[45] Unlike progressive reformers, reporters believed that once they had gathered and publicized information, their duty was done. Professionalism, that is, distanced journalists from precisely the educational vision embraced by progressives.

This professional self-conception did not emerge all at once. It began in the 1880s and continued to grow through the 1940s. But it had developed enough by the early 1900s to mark a divide between journalists and progressive reformers. This divide is nicely illustrated by an anecdote related to David Graham Phillips' 1906 muckraking expose, entitled "Treason of the Senate."[46] Reporters in Washington, D.C., embraced the professional ethos earlier and more strongly than journalists in most other cities. Far from their home newspapers, covering a small political world, Washington reporters developed strong ties among themselves, and to the sources on whom they relied for the news.[47] Far from conceiving of themselves as "earnest Christian[s] trying to apply Christian principles to ... very definite and serious problem[s]," as one muckraker described himself, Washington reporters practiced the art of news brokerage.[48] This is to say, they were in the business of trading, circulating, and hoarding the news. So it came as quite a shock when Phillips landed in town and turned a spotlight on Washington politicians and the journalists who covered them. Phillips argued that many senators were corrupt and that journalists knew this but refused to indict their sources. The story caused a maelstrom of criticism and protest. Citizens wanted to know why reporters had not revealed this corruption. Editors and publishers pushed their reporters to meet Phillips' challenge. However, reporters were indignant rather than contrite. When a group of muckrakers and concerned citizens proposed a "People's Lobby" to monitor the activities of Congress, one reporter responded that the press gallery "already constituted a people's lobby of one hundred and fifty 'professional observers,' who were 'weighing, doubting, scrutinizing, suspecting' every congressional action."[49] Here, the reporter's professional sensibility conflicts with the moral outrage of progressive reformers. He was a "professional observer" doing his job ("weighing, doubting," etc.) On his view, his professionalism naturally set him apart from the average citizen.

This is not to say that the vocabulary of news wholly conflicted with that of progressivism. These idioms were not idealized, pristine abstractions. Rather, they were wholly ordinary vocabularies, produced and reproduced in social interaction. Rooted in different social practices, they nonetheless were capable of being combined and used in innovative ways. Indeed, given that both involved a concern for publicity, exposure, and investigation, and for an informed citizenry, they lent themselves to precisely this kind of commingling. Despite this flexibility, however, they were distinctive idioms. While not imposing themselves, they pushed individuals toward different self-conceptions and worldviews. A progressive reformer imbued with the sense of being a "chosen one" held a very different self-conception than a journalist who viewed his job as a detached quest for the story. A progressive leader intent on modeling right conduct might naturally have recoiled from the dramatized presentation of personalities offered by the daily newspaper. And a progressive reformer desirous of refining the collective will might easily have been flabbergasted at a journalist's unwillingness to go beyond reporting the facts. All this is to say that expectations and assumptions were negotiated, not imposed.

Progressive presidential communication took shape amid this combustible mix of expectations and assumptions. In the two case studies that follow, I show how Roosevelt and Wilson drew from progressivism to account for their actions, and the way that reporters translated these accounts into news.

A "Fundamental Fight for Morality": Roosevelt's "Swing the Circle"

Perhaps no one blended progressive principles with a fascination for newspapers better than Theodore Roosevelt. Though historians have been reluctant to bestow the label on him, it is fair to say that Roosevelt was a preeminent progressive leader.[50] As president, he advocated two of the most important progressive causes: civil service reform and corporate trust reform. During the 1912 presidential campaign, he carried the banner of the progressive party. Not surprisingly, Roosevelt drew upon the progressive idiom to champion these causes.[51] He spoke of "efficiency" in government; he praised the American "national character," which he defined as "that assemblage of virtues, active and passive, of moral qualities."[52] He believed that the national character evolved, not in a war of all against all, but through the development of a "general feeling among the members ... such that the average individual [will] work for the ultimate benefit of the community as a whole."[53] For him, leadership involved modeling this moral vision. As he put it to Lincoln Steffens, the real need in public life was not merely a fight against privilege, but "the fundamental fight for morality."[54]

At the same time, he was a great champion of the news, and perhaps the preeminent newsmaker of his generation. As Police Commissioner in New York City in 1895–96, he allowed Jacob Riis and Lincoln Steffens unprecedented access to government activities.[55] Newspapers made him the most famous combatant to participate in the Spanish-American war, and propelled him toward the governorship of New York. As governor, he held daily press conferences. And as president, he devised many of the modern techniques by which presidents make news. By the time he left office, Roosevelt had made so much news over such a long a period of time that he had become the quintessential icon of his age.[56]

It is precisely in Roosevelt's iconicity that one finds the tension between his progressive understanding of presidential communication and the news. Where Roosevelt understood his rhetorical activities as an opportunity to lead by modeling core values, reporters saw in them the epitome of a news persona. Both models and personae are role-playing characters, but they are oriented to different ends. For progressives, modeling took place within a wider environment of socialization. Models represented the best virtues in order to educate and socialize. In contrast, in the news personae existed in an environment of play rather than socialization. Their efforts were entertaining more than educational, playful more than revelatory. When reading about personae, readers were invited to enjoy a tale rather than to learn a lesson. Of course, differences between modeling and acting can be exaggerated: learning and entertainment are not completely distinct. Still, the terms were ultimately linked to different vocabularies of political life, and therefore to different assumptions and expectations about the meaning of presidential rhetoric. In the space between these expectations and assumptions one finds a negotiation over the meaning of Roosevelt's iconicity.

Roosevelt's "swing the circle" trip down the Mississippi River in October 1907 demonstrates the terms on which this negotiation took place. In part, Roosevelt's trip merely continued a longstanding executive practice. Presidents since George Washington had gone on speaking tours of essentially the same kind.[57] But several things marked Roosevelt's tours as unique. For instance, his trips were designed to promote executive rather than party or congressional policies. Indeed, as the first "rhetorical president," Roosevelt undertook the tours precisely to go over the heads of an uncooperative Congress. In this way, during his tours Roosevelt aggressively modeled himself, and the executive branch generally, as the primary representative of the national public interest. Roosevelt's advocacy also took a typically progressive form: a moral appeal for the value of scientific expertise. For instance, during his 1907 tour, Roosevelt sought to gain grassroots support for waterway and conservation proposals by forming expert commissions and framing the issue as a moral crusade for the public interest. Also in typical progressive fashion, Roosevelt conceived of his role on these tours as educating the public and forming a collective purpose. That is, he saw himself as the "steward" of the public interest.[58] Finally, he sought to fulfill this role by making news. In the case of the 1907 tour, Roosevelt's Director of the Forest Service, Gifford Pinchot, used reporters' interest in Roosevelt to induce news coverage of the president's conservation initiatives. Thus, in Roosevelt's swings around the circle, one finds a meeting of progressive desires and the idiom of news, a meeting that centered exactly on Roosevelt's symbolism.

The particular swing around the Mississippi River valley I examine here was instigated by Pinchot and other leaders of the Inland Waterways Commission.[59] Arranged to take place in October 1907, Pinchot and the Commission invited Roosevelt to make a trip down the Mississippi River with it and the Mississippi Valley Improvement Association. Roosevelt linked the trip to the dedication of the William McKinley Memorial in Canton, Ohio, and a two-week hunting vacation in the Louisiana canebrakes. On a trip that began September 30th and ended October 23rd, Roosevelt gave seven speeches: a dedication of the William McKinley memorial in Keokuk, Iowa (October 1st); speeches given during his trip down the Mississippi river in St. Louis, Missouri (October 2nd); Cairo, IL (October 3rd); and Memphis, TN (October 4th); and three speeches, given in Vicksburg, Mississippi (October 21st), the Hermitage near Nashville (October 22nd), and Nashville, Tennessee (October 23rd).[60]

In his speeches Roosevelt championed specific policies: federal regulation of corporations; the Panama Canal; land-grant universities; and most importantly, conservation, land use and an inland waterways system. He did so within a particularly progressive organic conception of the nation. For instance, Roosevelt began many of his speeches with a bit of history to show how the people and geography of the Mississippi Valley region were connected historically and geographically to the nation. He described Cairo,

Illinois (pp. 1405–1406), as the geographic "heart" of the nation whose people "are distinctively American in all their thoughts, in all their ways of looking at life; and in its past and its present alike it is typical of our country." People and geography constituted a kind of interconnected body, physically in the sense that environmental conditions in one region affected those in others, but also materially, in that the interests of people in one region were intimately connected to those of others. "In the long run," he argued in five of the speeches, "we shall go up or go down together" (Keokuk, p. 1385; St. Louis, 1394; Memphis, p. 1423; Vicksburg, p. 1445; Nashville, p. 1463). Roosevelt also turned to organic terms to propose a progressive view of federalism (i.e., of the Constitution's separation of federal and state responsibilities). To claims that his initiatives usurped state power, he argued that the Constitution was a "living organism" (St. Louis, p. 1398), which the framers intended to be "an instrument designed for the life and healthy growth of the nation" (Vicksburg, p. 1452). Within this conception, Roosevelt viewed trends like corporate and political corruption and environmental degradation as "unhealthy" (Keokuk, p. 1381; St. Louis, 1391). Not surprisingly then, for Roosevelt federal action was not merely constitutionally lawful, it was necessary to preserve the continued viability of the nation.

If the conditions of American society had changed, however, and its "health" was threatened, Roosevelt assured his audiences that the spirit of the nation remained unchanged. Each American generation confronted unique problems, Roosevelt maintained, "but the spirit in which those problems must be met cannot be changed." That spirit lay in "the man who has the stuff in him to make a good citizen" (Hermitage, p. 1459). Or, as he put it in Memphis (p. 1440), "Good laws can do much good ... but there is infinitely more need of a high individual average of character." Character, like efficiency, were key aspects of Roosevelt's defense of his proposals. In his speeches, Roosevelt associated it with duty and discipline, bravery, honesty, and a strong work ethic, but most importantly, with morality. Character for him meant the ability to recognize right and wrong, and a disposition to fight the one in the name of the other. "There are many wrongs to right," he told his Cairo audience (pp. 1408–1409), "there are many and powerful wrong-doers against whom to war; and, it would be base to shirk from the contest, or to fail to wage it with a high, a resolute will." Though new social conditions required new administrative initiatives, these actions must be motivated by unchanging moral verities. "We can realize our future only upon a condition," Roosevelt argued, "that we conduct our policy as among

ourselves in accordance with the immutable laws of righteousness..."
(Vicksburg, p. 1456).

This turn to morality was rooted in a basic progressive desire to imagine
political actions as inherently and wholly good and desirable.[61] Progressives
wished to develop solutions to pressing social ills, but to do so in a way that
was motivated by fundamental, hence unchallenged, moral principles. Or, as
Roosevelt put it to his Nashville audience (p. 1470), "Our whole movement
is simply and solely to make ... the golden rule of some practical moment...."
Often, Roosevelt and other progressives translated this desire into the
language of science and administration. Thus, for instance, he criticized
(Vicksburg, p. 1446) prior legislation and uses of the Mississippi Valley
waterways system not as immoral, but as wasteful and a "misapplication of
effort." And he described his Inland Waterways Commission (Memphis, p.
1430) not in terms of the high character of its members, but in terms of its
ability to create a "single comprehensive scheme for meeting all the demands
[on the waterways system]." For Roosevelt, as for other progressives, science
and morality were dedicated to a similar search for truth.

His own job, as he saw it, was to educate the public to recognize the
meeting of interest and morality in the idea of the nation. We are not, he
claimed, a society that pitted self-interests against one another. Instead, the
"healthy" evolution of the nation—the national interest—demanded the
recognition that individual interest ultimately was rooted in the larger
national interest. Roosevelt's thinking went something like this: the nation
constituted an interconnected whole; developments in one area necessarily
influenced conditions in another; to the extent that individuals were
connected in this manner, efforts to develop the nation necessarily benefited
individuals as well; thus, actions taken in the national interest were morally
right because they conformed to the long-term interests of both the nation
and individuals. Roosevelt's task was to convince individuals to recognize
this fact of living in a modern complex society. "I am striving," he told his
Memphis audience (p. 1436), "to accomplish what I can ... because the
welfare of the nation imperiously demands [it].... It is action in the interest of
all the people...."

How was he to make this case to the public? That is, what did he think
his speeches might accomplish? As he described it in Nashville (p. 1465),
Roosevelt saw his role as making "the average citizen ... get into his soul the
belief that he will not only receive justice, but that he will have a part in
meting out justice." At another time, he suggested that he must make people
"alive to their own interests" (Keokuk, p. 1374). In part, getting feelings into

the souls of average citizens and making them alive to their [ultimate] interests was a matter of persuasion. Thus, for instance, Roosevelt routinely tried to persuade his audiences that honesty and dishonesty were the same whether they were found in businessmen or working men. Additionally, he argued for a flexible view of the Constitution in support of greater federal intervention in the economy.

Such leadership, however, was also a matter of modeling. As he put it in his dedication to President McKinley (Canton, p. 1367), a president is great not because he persuades, but because he serves as an "unconscious example to his people of the virtues that build and conserve alike our public life...." In this context, a moment in his speech at Canton is particularly telling. Roosevelt was engaged in a typical effort to distinguish honest from dishonest men. At one moment, he received a rousing applause when he promised to discourage and punish dishonest businessmen. As the crowd thumped its support, Roosevelt stopped:

> Wait a moment; I don't want you to applaud this part unless you are willing to applaud also the part [promising to punish ignorant and hostile actions against honest wealthy men] I read first, to which you listened in silence.... I want you to understand that I will stand just as straight for the rights of the honest man who wins his fortune by honest methods as I will stand against the dishonest man who wins a fortune by dishonest methods.

Roosevelt then proceeded to read the first statement over again and demand that the audience applaud as loudly as they had for the second statement. Here, Roosevelt leads by, as he put it, "standing" for something—in this case, for the idea that honesty should be applauded, and dishonesty punished, at all times. His tour down the Mississippi was peppered by many such dramatized gestures: in St. Louis he refused an umbrella or to change his clothes before delivering his speech during a torrential rain; in Keokuk he delayed his speech for a few minutes while he motioned for a farmer, his wife and children to step from behind the ropes and take seats at the front of the enclosure; and in Cairo he extemporized from his speech to proclaim (as he often did) that his ancestry was half Northern and half Southern, "and I should be ashamed of myself if I were not as much the President of the Southern as of the Northern states." On these occasions, Roosevelt dramatized his "standing for" the best virtues, honesty and integrity, of manliness, of charity and justice, and of an integrated nation—ultimately, of the American character.[62]

It was this sense of presidential communication as a kind of modeling that sets progressive conceptions of presidential communication apart from later usages. Indeed, perhaps Roosevelt's most important message, amid the millions of words he spoke and wrote in his long public life, was his insistence that displays of individual character were more important than mere persuasion. For him, what one said was far less important than what one was. This is the meaning of his constant refrain that good government depended not on institutions or policies, but on "individual character." Further, it explains his comment to Lincoln Steffens that he embodied, rather than simply represented, the common good. If the common good was rooted in national character, and there was no distinction between national and individual character (i.e., they contained the same attributes), then to the extent that he embodied these attributes, Roosevelt could rightly claim to *be* the common good. Finally, for Roosevelt, character also solved the dilemma of extreme heterogeneity in American society. The possession of character meant not only displaying these virtues to others, but also recognizing those virtues in others. It provided the kernel of recognition that held a heterogeneous, complex society together. Whatever else divided them, Roosevelt believed that men of high character immediately responded to one another. Thus, in a curious way, by embodying quintessential American virtues, Roosevelt made other forms of persuasion superfluous.

Viewed in terms of the transition from nineteenth- to twentieth-century conditions, one might say that Roosevelt sought to account for twentieth-century policies within a nineteenth-century vocabulary. "The image Roosevelt achieved politically," historian Richard Collin argues, "can be explained in part by a feeling that he could move America from the nineteenth century to the twentieth century in a relatively painless way."[63] Or, put more succinctly by Henry May, Roosevelt offered Americans "the old moralities with pepper added."[64] Like progressives generally, Roosevelt met the challenges of a modern complex society within an idiom that sought to impose social order by asserting a moral order. That is, he met the problems of the new century by translating them into the terms of the old. Corporate reform, railroad reform, conservation—these and other policies Roosevelt advocated in terms of sin and righteousness, sickness and health. Though efficiency, science and administration figured prominently in his reforms, these terms gained meaning within a larger progressive cosmology in which the nation strove toward a righteous future.

A Man of Action: Roosevelt and the News

Despite their supposedly hard-boiled cynicism, many reporters who covered Roosevelt were mesmerized by his personality. "Almost without exception," Nicholas Roosevelt recalls, "newspapermen assigned to cover him became and remained hero-worshipers."[65] One certainly gets this sense from William Allen White's description of his first meeting with Roosevelt: "I had never known such a man as he...." White writes, "he overcame me ... he poured into my heart such visions, such ideals, such hopes...."[66] Though more circumspect, one nonetheless detects in David Barry's description of Roosevelt's personality as "so fascinating, so appealing ... so overpowering, so alive and altogether unique..." something of the hero-worshiper.[67]

But this personal reaction was less important to Roosevelt's relationship with the press than certain institutional realities. Put simply, reporters were in no position to challenge Roosevelt's efforts to lead public opinion.[68] As George Juergens suggests, "A ... moral of the Roosevelt years is that the President received the kind of publicity he did because he dealt with a still immature and relatively impotent press corps."[69] In the days of the party press, a president could always count on opposition editors being critical. In the days of the professional press, presidents faced a strong, institutionalized corps of reporters. Roosevelt's presidency came between these periods. In this interim, he exercised a profound power over reporters who were still struggling to define their roles and responsibilities.

For instance, reporters never really interviewed the president.[70] Instead, upon meeting them, Roosevelt simply started talking—and never stopped. If Roosevelt was never interviewed, and thus never abided by the modern obligation to answer reporters' questions, he also kept strict control over how reporters could use his torrent of words. He did this in a number of ways. For instance, he chose the reporters he would see and those he would not.[71] Reporters Roosevelt favored were allowed into his "newspaper cabinet" and his daily press meetings; those he did not were cast into the "Ananais club" and denied access to the president. He also kept an iron grip on the kinds of news reporters publicized. TR's military aide Archie Butt reports that TR "saw the newspapermen freely, but they understood that they were only to print what he authorized them to use, and if they did anything else he would not allow them near the White House or office, and he has been known to have them dismissed by their papers."[72] This went so far that Roosevelt proposed stories to reporters and even wrote their leads.[73]

More broadly, Roosevelt established publicity bureaus throughout the Executive departments to promote his various policies. When he left office in 1908, departmental press aides could be found in agencies as diverse as the Bureau of Soils, the Bureau of Biological Survey, the State Department, the Census Bureau, the Bureau of National Roads, the Smithsonian Institution, and the Post office. None of the Executive departments was more active in this area than the Department of Forestry under Gifford Pinchot. Pinchot wrote presidential speeches, coordinated publicity releases in support of forestry initiatives, contacted newspapers, helped to form the first presidential commissions on the environment, and involved Roosevelt in many of these activities.[74] Compared to this publicity apparatus, White House reporters were far less institutionally or professionally established.

Therefore, even if reporters were not personally inclined to support the president, they were in no position to challenge his control of the news. Given this fact, it comes as no surprise that Roosevelt's swing down the Mississippi River was a publicity coup. Roosevelt and Pinchot worked very hard to ensure its success, and afterwards they were not disappointed. "This excursion...," Roosevelt wrote in his *Autobiography*, "gave our inland waterways a new standing in public estimation."[75] Pinchot agreed, describing the trip as a "huge success."[76] Surveying press coverage of the trip, historian Stephen Ponder claims that the trip not only was an "important experiment in publicity" for the White House, it also was "one of his most successful public appearances."[77]

A glance at the coverage of the trip in my sample of seven newspapers appears to confirm this conclusion. During the principle days of the swing, October 1st to October 5th, some coverage appeared in these newspapers on all but four occasions. *The New York Herald Tribune* went furthest, splashing five and six column headlines across its front page twice during the five day period. But all of the papers gave the trip heavy play, and most published a transcript of the speeches with pictures and synopses of their main points. In total, during this five day period, the newspapers published forty-six stories totaling 335.5 column inches, which averages to a little more than one seven column inch story per paper per day (see Table 1.1).

However, a closer analysis of this coverage tells a slightly different story. If in one sense journalism's institutional immaturity allowed Roosevelt unparalleled control of the news, in another sense it blunted his message. As Michael Schudson has argued, journalism's institutional maturity coincided with the development of new conventions of news reporting. These conventions include: the summary lead and inverted pyramid structure; a view of the president as the most important actor in any event in which he takes part; a focus on single events rather than patterns; the use of quotes as a way of highlighting the most important aspect of speeches or documents; and an effort to determine the meaning of a political event in a time frame larger than that of the acts themselves.[78] Through the use of such conventions, modern reporters mark themselves as independent interpreters of the political scene.

Table 1.1: Newspaper Coverage (in column inches) of Roosevelt's Swing Down the Mississippi River

Newspaper	Oct. 1st	Oct. 2nd	Oct. 3rd	Oct. 4th	Oct. 5th	Total
NYHT	29.5	11.25	9	11	14	74.75
KCS	5.25	19.75	—	13.25	22.5	60.75
CT	8.0	5.25	4	12.75	5.25	35.25
NYT	12	8.0	6.25	6.0	14	46.25
WES	6.5	—	—	4.25	—	10.75
LAT	15.75	10.25	7.25	6.25	12.75	52.25
WP	17.5	9.5	8.5	7.5	12.5	55.5
Totals	94.5	64.0	35.0	61.0	81.0	335.50

Given the transitional nature of journalism at the time, it is not surprising that reporters covering Roosevelt's tour used these conventions unevenly.[79] For instance, reporters for the *New York Herald Tribune* and the *Chicago Daily Tribune* employed modern conventions. In his coverage of Roosevelt's speech dedicating the McKinley memorial, the *New York Herald Tribune* reporter used a summary lead: "With the dedication of the beautiful memorial to his predecessor, the late President McKinley, President Roosevelt began to-day his extensive trip in the West."[80] Here, the president is the main protagonist in a lead paragraph that conveys who, what, where, and when. The *Chicago Daily Tribune* reporter went further to frame the story in terms of a phrase Roosevelt uttered in the middle of the speech: "President Roosevelt, during his address at the dedication of the McKinley mausoleum today, administered a mild rebuke to his audience on account of failure to applaud a certain sentiment."[81]

In contrast, a reporter for the Associated Press (AP) wire service used a more traditional news form. The following is the lead paragraph from *The Washington Post*:

> The nation paid homage to-day to the memory of William McKinley when the splendid monument which marks his last resting place was unveiled in the presence of an assembled throng such as Canon never saw before, and with the President of the United States as the principal speaker. It was the tribute of a grateful nation, both in word and in deed, to a "good citizen, a brave soldier, a wise executive," and more than 50,000 persons representing all walks of life and every part of the country participated in the ceremonies dedicating the monument, the loving gift of a million Americans whose contributions aggregating $800,000 provided the splendid tomb in

which rest the bodies of the third of the martyred Presidents, his wife, and their two children.[82]

Here, the frame of the story centers on people participating in a tribute to their great leader—not on Roosevelt and his speech. And the story is told in colorful language that stresses the atmospherics of the occasion rather than the meaning of the event in a larger political frame (such as Roosevelt's effort to promote his waterways proposal).

Table 1.2: References to Roosevelt's Speeches and Waterways Proposals in Newspaper Coverage (in column inches)

Newspaper	Day	Oct. 1st Col. Ins.	Oct. 2nd	Oct. 3rd	Oct. 4th	Oct. 5th	Total
NYHT	Speeches	1.5	5.5	—	1.5	—	8.5
	Waterways	—	1.5	.25	1.25	—	3.0
KCS	Speeches	—	—	—	—	2.25	2.25
	Waterways	—	1.0	—	—	—	1.0
CT	Speeches	1.5	.5	—	1.5	—	3.5
	Waterways	—	—	.5	.75	—	1.25
NYT	Speeches	—	4.75	4.0	3.5	2.75	15.0
	Waterways	—	.75	.5	—	—	1.25
WES	Speeches	—	—	—	—	—	—
	Waterways	—	—	—	—	—	—
LAT	Speeches	—	2.0	—	—	—	2.0
	Waterways	—	.5	—	1.5	1.0	3.0
WP	Speeches	—	.5	3.0	—	—	3.5
	Waterways	—	—	—	—	—	—
Totals	Speeches	3.0	13.25	7.0	6.5	5.0	34.75
	Waterways	—	3.75	1.25	3.5	1.0	9.5

If one counts the subject matter in the 46 stories devoted to Roosevelt's trip during this five-day period, it is clear that reporters preferred premodern narrative conventions.[83] Of the 335.5 column inches in the forty-six stories devoted to the trip, only 34.75 column inches, or 10% of the total, actually referred to Roosevelt's speeches (see Table 1.2). Take, for instance, the AP report on Roosevelt's visit to the Inland Waterways Convention in Memphis, Tennessee, on October 5th. Pinchot and Roosevelt intended the convention to be the culmination of the three-day trip. However, as published in the *Los Angeles Times*, the AP reporter began his story describing "bands playing, children singing and enthusiastic men shouting...." He went on to detail the president's arrival at the Auditorium and the speech by the convention's president, W.K. Kavanaugh. Of the nearly 13 column inches devoted to the story, none referred to Roosevelt's speech much less detailed or analyzed his arguments. The same is true for the coverage in the other six newspapers in the sample. Indeed, although the newspapers published 81 column inches on the occasion, only five inches contained information on Roosevelt's speech. Even more telling, only 1.0 of those inches discussed Roosevelt's waterways proposal.

What does this mean? It means that Roosevelt made news, but his intended message often was lost in the ensuing coverage. Reporters described the crowds and the weather, the steam ships and the guests of honor, Roosevelt's appearance and his actions. But they hardly discussed his waterways proposal or highlighted his effort to model common virtues. For example, in its coverage of Roosevelt's appearance in St. Louis, the *Chicago Daily Tribune* described, in order, the rain, crowds, Roosevelt's wet clothes, the luncheon, more crowds, and then, eight paragraphs into the article, concluded with a brief description of Roosevelt's speech:

> In his speech, which 10,000 heard and cheered, the president declared it the nation's duty to restore the Mississippi river to its proper place as a great artery of commerce, and termed the proposed fourteen foot channel from the lakes to the gulf a "national task." He warned against plans which might "entail reckless extravagance or be tainted with jobbery," but urged a liberal waterway policy.

This traditional, chronological form of news reporting dampened Roosevelt's control of the news. Rather than concentrating on Roosevelt and the political meaning of his speech, reporters preferred to describe the scene as it unfolded, from Roosevelt's entrance to his departure. Within the day's pageantry, his speech, at least in the news coverage, played a minor role.

However, if in some ways modern news had not quite matured in 1907, it was far enough along to allow reporters to identify Roosevelt as newsworthy. This meant that while his speeches made little news, Roosevelt himself played a major role in the news coverage.[84] In part, this was due to the chronological nature of the reporting. Roosevelt was always arriving or leaving. During events, he met people, spoke, and left for the next occasion, where he met more people and delivered another speech. Thus, in the news coverage, Roosevelt was always leading, speaking, rebuking, pleading and warning. For instance, included in the headlines on Roosevelt's speech at

McKinley's tomb were: "Roosevelt speaks at McKinley's Tomb," "Gentle Rebuke by President," "Roosevelt Leads Parade of Boats," and "On Way to West."[85]

But the meaning of Roosevelt's actions went beyond mere chronology. Reporters did not just report Roosevelt's actions; they sensationalized them. In so doing, Roosevelt became a news character defined by action. That is, the president's newsworthiness was defined by his propensity to strike the demonstrative pose. Few cameras, for example, pictured him standing still. Instead, they showed him on a boat, in a car, or on a horse.[86] A cartoon that appeared in the *Chicago Daily Tribune* on October 1st captures this theme.[87] Printed on the front page, five column inches across and four columns wide, the cartoon contains three panels. In the first, a line of people, including a cameraman, sit on bleachers waiting for the president. In the second, a whirlwind barrels through the scene from right to left, at the end of which is the caption, "De-Light-Ed." In the third panel, the people recover from the whirlwind. As one person says, "Hooray, I saw him," and another that Roosevelt bowed to him, the cameraman exclaims that he "caught him" in his camera's frame.

In part, newsmen were drawn to frame Roosevelt in this way because it comported with their sense of the news as new. Each day, Roosevelt promised to do something new, and this made him imminently newsworthy. As *The Los Angeles Times* reporter put it at the beginning of Roosevelt's trip, "The president's adventures and daily success will be regularly communicated to this station...."[88] And in part, Roosevelt's actions matched reporters' conception of the news as conflict. For them, what was most important in Roosevelt's actions was not only that they were new on a daily basis, but that they challenged others. Thus, for instance, reporters framed his speeches in terms of his fight against railroads ("President Urges Rail Curbs"), and against those who criticized his decision to send a naval fleet on a trip around the globe ("Must Hit to Win Fights—Roosevelt"). His speech in Nashville was notable for his declaration that he would "not let up" on prosecuting corrupt businessmen and that Wall Street "cannot move him." In the pages of these papers, Roosevelt did not just act, he urged and declared, fought rather than retreated, gave no mercy, hit hard and was cheered for doing so.

Nothing seemed to define Roosevelt as a fighter better than his propensity to hunt. Newspapers gave more coverage to Roosevelt's bear hunt than to his swing down the Mississippi River. Of the 203 news stories on Roosevelt's trip written from September 23rd to October 23rd, fifty-six were devoted to the bear hunt, compared to forty-six stories on the waterways trip. Indeed, hunting fit Roosevelt's news persona so well that it became the primary trope through which newspapers framed the meaning of his trip.

This is most clear in the twenty-three cartoons featuring Roosevelt that accompanied the news coverage. Most of these cartoons appeared in *The New York Herald Tribune* and *The Chicago Tribune*, but only *The Kansas City Star* failed to publish at least one. For a reading audience with limited literacy skills—especially in the big cities—cartoons often conveyed more meaning than news stories. In this context, it is telling that the first mention of Roosevelt's trip in *The New York Herald Tribune* consisted of a 6.5 column inch, six column wide cartoon titled, "President Roosevelt Ready for the Canebrake Hunt."[89] In this cartoon, Roosevelt, in rough rider outfit and carrying a shotgun, meets a snake, a bear, a cougar and a jack rabbit. Each of the animals holds up a sign: "Immune. I'm a Practical Varmint," "Immune. Grand Father of the Teddy Bear," "Immune. Testified Against Fakirs," and "Immune. A Friend of John Burroughs." Here, Roosevelt's political actions are defined in terms of his propensity to hunt. Many other cartoons make the same equation. Roosevelt is shown in rough rider outfit aiming his gun through the canebrake at an octopus labeled "Standard Oil," with the caption, "Oh, Why Are All the Creatures Immune But Me?"; He is depicted carrying a "big stick" on the trail of a "big law breaker"; in a cartoon captioned "The President's Dream of a Successful Hunt," he is portrayed in rough rider outfit standing over a fallen bear labeled "Bad Trusts"; and he is shown, again in rough rider outfit, steering a steamboat down the Mississippi River through a series of hazardous tree limbs rising up through the water, labeled "Harriman Interests," "Railroad Trusts," "Beef Trusts," and "Standard Oil."[90] In tandem with headlines highlighting Roosevelt's rebukes, retorts, and proclamations, the effect of these cartoons was to transform Roosevelt into something very much like a modern cartoon action character.

Much in this portrayal flattered Roosevelt's sizeable ego. But in more reflective moments, he condemned the depiction. His reasoning was consistent with his progressive view of presidential rhetoric. To Roosevelt's mind, his effort to lead public opinion, on this trip and during his presidency generally, hinged on the notion that underneath superficial differences of interest, men of all classes shared a common national interest. He stood for this common interest. As long as newsmen reported on his efforts to do so, Roosevelt applauded them. But they veered into "sensationalism" when they described his fights as mere entertainment, with no larger purpose or importance. As he wrote to George Otto Trevelyan, politics was not a "game," and any person who treated it as such was "but one degree less noxious to his country than the man who attempts to make something out of his public life for his own personal advantage."[91] Typically, Roosevelt viewed the issue in moral terms: reporters who sensationalized stories were "liars." "So far as in one article or another corruption and fraud are attacked," Roosevelt stated to another correspondent, "the attack has my heartiest sympathy and commendation; but hysteria and sensationalism never do any permanent good and in addition I firmly believe that to the public ... the liar is in the long run as noxious as the thief."[92] The analogy of sensationalism to theft is telling. It suggests that when reporters framed their stories in terms of simple conflict, they robbed the public of an opportunity to see public life as a particular kind of conflict, one between good and evil, the national interest versus self interest.

The two ways of viewing Roosevelt's rhetoric were never fully reconciled. Newspapers dutifully printed speeches in which Roosevelt cast his actions in resolutely moral terms. Beside these speeches, the same newspapers printed cartoons like the one that appeared in *The Washington Post* on October 3, 1907. In this cartoon, Roosevelt is portrayed as a "schoolmaster" in the "School of Political and Industrial Honesty."[93] He is shown sitting at a desk clutching several "switches" labeled "The Law" and "Public Approval." In front of him are seated a group of men hiding behind texts labeled "Honest Business Methods in R.R.," "Honest Finance," "No Oppression of the Weak," and "Clean Politics." In such cartoons, Roosevelt's effort to "stand for" honesty in business and politics becomes the stuff of entertainment rather than education.

Thus, one finds great tension in the coverage of Roosevelt's month-long trip. On the one hand, Roosevelt sought to lead by example; on the other, newsmen transformed his efforts into entertaining tales of action and conflict. When reporters engaged in this practice, Roosevelt responded in a typically progressive way: he first labeled them immoral and unethical, and then devised new "techniques" for managing the news. For instance, knowing that reporters would sensationalize his hunting trip, he banned them from his compound and then allowed select reporters to visit periodically so that he could give them the news.[94] Of course, reporters camped outside the canebrake published every tidbit of news; and cartoonists had a field day with the spectacle. One cartoon, titled "Where the President Was Last Seen," featured several reporters and cameramen waiting anxiously for the president to emerge from the canebrake. Cartoons depict local men rounding up bears, many resembling the famous "Teddy Bear," to be shot by the president before the cameras. Others showed bears (in rough rider outfits) panic as Roosevelt's steamboat heads toward the canebrake.[95] As the president had difficulty in finding, much less shooting a bear, cartoons showed bears laughing, nailing signs to trees claiming to have left for Wall Street, and taking roll calls. Another, captioned "If He Could Only Find One," showed a hunting guide with a paper signed by Roosevelt giving him a postmaster commission.[96]

This tension between moral leadership and entertaining tales of conflict was basic to the interaction between Roosevelt and reporters. In his speeches, Roosevelt sought to stand for a common national interest rooted in a fundamental moral order. Reporters translated Roosevelt's stand into a cartoonish image of a man engaged in heated battles with his enemies (both political and animal). To the extent that Roosevelt was a unique personality meeting reporters at a particular stage in journalism's development, their interaction was distinctive. But, as we will see in our discussion of Woodrow Wilson's press conferences, the tension was endemic to political communication as a whole during the progressive period.

Sawing Wood: Wilson Institutionalizes the Press Conference

Compared to Roosevelt, Woodrow Wilson thought and wrote a great deal more about the proper form of presidential leadership. Indeed, as he assumed office, he had written about American politics, particularly the presidency, in more detail than any president since James Madison. Although he may have embraced the progressive political program late in life, and only then half-heartedly, his writings betray a characteristically progressive view.[97] Like other progressives, he defined democracy in organic terms, as a "stage of development ... built up by slow habit."[98] And like other progressives, he believed that underneath the polyglot of mass opinion lay a true common purpose rooted in the moral character of the nation.[99] It was the duty of leaders, he argued, to discover this common purpose and model it for the nation. Taking his cue from Roosevelt, Wilson came to believe that only the president could fulfill this leadership function. In *Constitutional Government in the United States,* he argued that the president "takes the imagination of the whole people. He is the representative of no constituency, but of the whole people."[100] As such, the president was morally bound, on Wilson's view, to refine mass opinion into a national will. Thus, like Roosevelt, Wilson conceived of true politics as a search for a national interest above and beyond self-interest.[101]

Unlike Roosevelt, however, Wilson had little interest in the news. In his writings, Wilson devoted very little thought to the role of newspapers in a democracy. In scattered places, he applauds newspapers for helping to transform society into a kind of "school," and for extending the reach of public opinion by bringing issues to national attention.[102] In others, he suggests that newspapers' "discussion of affairs [is not] of a kind that is necessary for the maintenance of constitutional government" because the stories they produce are merely part of the jumble of mass opinion.[103]

Given this view, it is not surprising that Wilson saw very little value in catering to newsmen. As Governor of New Jersey, he adopted a policy of "pitiless publicity," and met with reporters routinely. However, when he became the Democratic presidential nominee in 1912, his attitude toward newsmen changed. In fact, on the very night he won the nomination, Wilson bristled at the reporters assembled around him. A reporter on the scene, Oliver Newman, describes what transpired after Wilson apologized for not having enough chairs for the reporters:

> "Well Governor," remarked a New York police reporter. "You've got the first page now. Hang on to it. You've got the edge on Teddy and we want a lot of good stuff from you."
>
> Another chimed in: "We are all on space down here, Governor, and the more we can play you up the more we can increase our checks at the end of the week."
>
> The Governor looked over at the first man and smiled: he thought it was a joke. He did not smile quite so broadly at the second man. (p. 367)

Newman stood in the middle of the pack of journalists and watched Wilson's face grow

> graver, stern, and more serious. I knew that he was thinking of his nomination in the most serious manner, and he felt that a most serious obligation and responsibility had been placed upon him ... and I could see that he was thinking in his mind, and he afterwards confirmed it, as he looked around this room and listened to these questions, that he was thinking: "My God, is my destiny in these hands?"[104]

Here, it is clear that Wilson took the possibility of becoming president very seriously. Put in the terms of his writings, he imagined himself as campaigning to become the nation's moral leader, someone charged with the responsibility of discovering the nation's common purpose and standing for that purpose before the public. To his mind, the newsmen surrounding him seemed intent on trivializing his position.[105]

Thus, unlike Roosevelt, rather than attempt to use reporters for his own purposes, Wilson tried to ignore them. Frank Stockbridge, Wilson's publicity manager during the 1912 campaign, recalls that during a swing through the Western states, Wilson balked at preparing speeches in advance so that they could be telegraphed to local reporters and publicized before he arrived ("I can't write for a stenographer"). He was also very reluctant to let himself become a "personality" whom reporters would want to cover: "It took a great deal of explaining," Stockbridge writes, "to make him see the difference between himself as a local news feature and himself as a man with a message."[106] Though he did at times demonstrate a certain degree of reflection on his inability to get along with reporters, as when he confided to a group of journalists that though he would like to very much, he simply couldn't "make himself over" to please reporters, he generally believed that reporters corrupted politics with their cynicism, and were as much a part of the problem of politics as its solution.[107]

It is not surprising then, that when Wilson agreed to conduct regular press conferences at Joseph Tumulty's (his private secretary) request, he did so only because they seemed to him an efficient way to spend as little time with reporters as possible. However, the very fact that Wilson saw fit to institutionalize his meetings with reporters indicates that the newsmen could not be ignored. By 1913, more reporters were covering the White House than ever before. In a process spanning over 15 years, Washington reporters slowly began to see the presidency as a prime source of news. McKinley had given them a table in the White House; Roosevelt had given them a room. In his press conferences, Wilson gave them legitimacy. The form of the press conference itself carried with it all the assumptions embedded within the interview format from which it was derived. In this form, reporters had a legitimate right to ask questions of the president as representatives of a third party—the public. Reporters capitalized on their newly won status by founding the White House Correspondents Association soon thereafter, in 1914.

Although Wilson may have wished to ignore reporters, by 1913 it was impossible for him to do so. During his first three years in office, he met the press regularly.[108] Like Roosevelt's swing the circle trip down the Mississippi River, Wilson's conferences offer an opportunity to glimpse the interaction of a president firmly possessed of a progressive view of presidential rhetoric with reporters intent on transforming him into a newsworthy persona.[109]

The clash of expectations was immediate. For his first press conference, on March 15, 1913, Wilson entered the Oval Office and found himself surrounded by more than 100 Washington correspondents. The unease was almost visceral. One reporter described Wilson as appearing "embarrassed" and reserved.[110] Edward Lowry recalls that the new president seemed almost stunned into silence at the number of newspapermen who filled his office. "There was a pause," he writes, "a cool silence, and presently some one ventured a tentative question. It was answered crisply, politely, and in the fewest possible words. A pleasant time was not had by all."[111]

Wilson tried again the next week. Sixteen years later, in a letter to Ray Stannard Baker, journalist Richard Oulahan could only recall that Wilson "made a speech which astonished us (journalists) very much in that he argued that it was of no great importance what political Washington thought and he advised us, therefore, to bring to the attention of the Executive Government and Congress what the country was thinking...."[112] Oulahan's memory is remarkably accurate. Verbatim, Wilson asked the journalists to go into a "partnership" with him, to "tell Washington what the country is thinking," rather than telling the "country what Washington is thinking."[113] Here, Wilson asks journalists to assume their proper place, that is, to bring to him the jumbled mass of public opinion so that he may have the opportunity of digesting and refining it. Oulahan's reaction to this request also accurately reflects that of the journalists as a whole: "Of course, it was impossible for us to follow that formula."

Instead, journalists approached Wilson with the tools of their profession. That is, they approached him as a potential source of news. For instance, the first press conference for which there is a transcript, dated May 8, 1913, begins with this question: "Can you tell us anything about currency legislation, Mr. President?"[114] It continues: "will there be a currency committee organized?" "will the house go into recess?" will there be "final action on the tariff bill in this session?" These questions suggest that reporters were seeking to fit the presidency into their regular task of tracking the legislative process in Washington. They wanted Wilson to provide them with information that might help them anticipate future political events, and transform him into a man of action in conflict with others in Washington. What will happen next? How will you (the president) respond?

This is to say that reporters were functioning in their routine manner as *news brokers*. The use of "tag questions" or long prefaces to questions nicely illustrates this routine. To generate news, reporters often brought information learned from other sources to the president and asked him to respond. For instance, on June 5, 1913, this exchange occurred:

Reporter: That makes it a fair assumption, does it not, that the Stanley bill is not an administration measure?

Wilson: I do not know which Stanley bill. Is there a new one?

Reporter: There is supposed to be a Stanley bill introduced in the House and to cover the Attorney General's plan.

Wilson: Well, I hadn't heard anything of it. This is the first I have heard of it.

Here it is evident that the reporter knows about an impending Congressional action and that he is searching for potential conflict between Wilson and the Congress. Many other questions have this same basic form. "Mr. President," a reporter begins on April 2, 1914, "there is a story today to the effect that you had given your approval to a bill by Mr. Crosser of Ohio for the municipal ownership of street railways in the District?"[115] Again, the reporter is probing for advance notice of an impending action, only this time the source for that action is not a Congressman, it is another newspaper story. As news brokers, White House reporters sought to barter with the president, and when he was reluctant to trade, to force him to respond to third-party sources. This kind of questioning served a dual purpose. It allowed them to take an active role in generating news just as it protected their much-coveted stance of neutrality.[116] At least implicitly then, these question types sought to connect the presidency with the system of sources, contacts, and leaks that composed reporters' understanding of the process of political deliberation in Washington.

It is apparent that, unlike Roosevelt, Wilson did not control the questions or the newsmen who asked them. There was no Ananais Club in Wilson's White House, and all White House reporters were free to attend these meetings. Wilson did, however, control his answers. And as Table 1.3 shows, he rarely satisfied the reporters' thirst for news. For instance, over the twenty press conferences in my sample, Wilson was asked 630 questions, or an average of 33 questions per conference. Of these 630 questions, the president flatly refused to answer fifty. That is, he indicated that he could answer the question, but refused to do so. To another ninety-three questions, he pleaded ignorance: he simply did not have enough information to answer the question. So, to 143 of the questions asked of him, or 22 percent of the total, Wilson was utterly unhelpful to the reporters. To another 178 of the questions that he did answer, Wilson gave a one-line response, and to 103 of the remaining questions, he gave a two-line response. Even when he did attempt to answer a question then, 280 of his answers (or 44 percent) were very short one- or two-line responses. Altogether then, to the 630 questions asked of him, 67 percent of Wilson's answers were either unresponsive, uninformative, or cursory. Even when he was asked for his direct opinion, as in the seventeen questions in which reporters' sought to elicit his point of view, Wilson remained adamantly mum. He declined to give his opinion on all seventeen occasions.

Table 1.3: Types of Answers Given, By Category, Wilson Press Conferences (n = 630)

Type of Answer	Number	Percentage
Unresponsive Answers	50	8.0
Pleadings of Ignorance	93	15.0
1-Line Answers	178	28.0
2-Line Answers	103	16.0
Rest of Answers	206	33.0

Implicit in the form which press conferences take—presidents standing before reporters and answering their questions, is the assumption that reporters have the "right to manage the organization of topics" and to expect answers to their questions on those topics.[117] It is clear from these numbers that Wilson did not respect this assumption. Rather, most often he refused to respond, gave a cursory answer, or pleaded ignorance.

This lack of respect was often taken as a lack of respect for individual reporters. After all, Wilson's frustration was acted out on particular reporters, not on an abstract news culture. But Wilson's answers to obviously "political" questions suggest something more was at work than personal antagonisms. These questions had nothing to do with public policy; instead, they sought to substantiate Washington gossip, instigate conflict between Wilson and another political actor (most often Congress), or were unusually personal. For example, on June 5, 1913, Wilson was asked this question: "It is suggested that you are persuaded that this stock-market flurry is caused by sinister influences and that you are going to suggest an investigation of Wall Street methods in that regard." The phrase "it is suggested" indicates that the question is motivated by gossip from another quarter. The use of "sinister" frames the issue as a potential conflict between Wilson and Wall Street. Wilson's response: "No sir, that is entirely without foundation. I have all my life been so innocent that I have never known what flurries were founded on. That is something too dark for the lay mind." To a similar question, "Do you regard an extra session [of Congress] as [possible]?" a question which in its design implies an impending conflict with Congress, Wilson gave this answer: "I don't go on a hypothesis. 'Sufficient unto the day is the evil thereof.'" And Wilson cut off this question, "Did you read the remarks in Congress today with reference—" before it could be finished, with "I read everything that is intended for the salvation of my soul."[118] When asked how well he liked the presidency on his six-month anniversary in office, Wilson responded: "I have no opinions about myself or my own administration. I am sawing wood." Finally, when asked if he was going to participate in the impending state elections, he answered, "I haven't been invited yet." A reporter then said, "We can fix that up, Mr. President." To which Wilson coldly replied, "I wasn't fixing."[119]

These questions have in common an explicit interest in the mechanics of politics: which actor is doing what and how will other political actors respond. Issues of public policy are completely absent from them. They are in many ways the archetypal questions of a news culture: they emphasize public officials in (potential) conflict over particular issues at specific times and places. Roosevelt simply would have dismissed them, or even dismissed the reporter who asked them. After institutionalizing the press conference, Wilson had no such luxury.

Instead, he routinely accounted for himself and his actions in the terms of moral adages and folk wisdom. That is, he simply refused to account for his actions in the terms preferred by reporters. In the face of the obvious political nature of their intent, Wilson cast himself as a naive Christian, a patient person who is "sawing wood." In his reliance on such moralisms, Wilson demonstrates his reliance on a progressive vocabulary of motive. Within this vocabulary, politics is (or ought to be) conducted by individuals who are responsible to their internal moral code of conduct. These kinds of questions obviously challenged Wilson's moral code. Thus, when reporters asked about the mechanics of politics, Wilson responded with the morality of politics. To Wilson, the reporters seemed immoral; to the reporters, Wilson seemed unprofessional.[120]

Wilson's problem, of course, was that, by 1913, Washington news was defined by just the kind of political machinations that interested the reporters. Leo Rosten's comment that in Washington gossip functions "as a source of information and a framework for political analysis," though made twenty-five years later, is still no less true for Wilson's era.[121] Political gossip was, and is, the lifeblood of Washington news. As journalists became independent agents, separate from party or editorial control, their status as professional political observers was enhanced. Knowledgeable and accurate reporting on political activities became a symbol of journalistic professionalism, and an important aspect of objective reporting. As independent professionals, journalists were no longer political advocates; instead, they were political scorekeepers. In part, the twentieth-century news culture has been defined by this new journalistic role.

Was Wilson Newsworthy? Coverage of the Press Conferences

Given the obvious antagonism between Wilson and the press, and Wilson's utter refusal to become a news persona, one might assume that his press conferences rarely made news. A simple count of my sample does not bear this out. Only on 33 of 160 possible occasions did Wilson's remarks during his press conferences appear on the first page of these papers. On another thirty-five occasions, remarks made at the conferences appeared on other than page one. In all, the press conferences appeared 43 percent of the time in these papers. These numbers are more or less steady for papers across region and political persuasion. This is a relatively high number, given the character of Wilson's answers during the press conferences, and the fact that, except for *The Washington Post* and *The Washington Evening-Star,* all of the newspapers were based elsewhere. Although three of the other papers maintained Washington bureaus (*The New York Times*, the *New York Herald*, and the *Chicago Tribune*), all of them were more concerned with local affairs than Washington politics. Even with these limitations, the conferences appeared in the papers nearly half the time.

Confined to an analysis of headlines, and a simple count of column inches, these numbers are in line with Elmer Cornwell's observation that the presidential image has expanded greatly in the twentieth century.[122] On this view, whatever the personal inclinations of particular presidents, the image of the presidency has seen a steady, inexorable climb in the news media. However, a closer look at the actual content of the stories in which the press conferences are mentioned tells a slightly different story. En total, 650.25 column inches were devoted to stories in which the press conferences were mentioned in the eight newspapers. Of this total, only 199.25 column inches, or 31 percent, actually involves material from the press conferences. This number gives a slightly different cast to the newspaper coverage. It is true that the press conferences appeared in 42 percent of the papers in my sample. But actual material from the press conferences is used in only 31 percent of the total of these stories. In fact, like Roosevelt's swing down the Mississippi River, though Wilson's press conferences often appeared in the newspapers, they very rarely made news.[123]

The question, of course, is why this dearth of news? I have already suggested that Wilson did not use the press conferences as a vehicle to make news. Certainly, the rule that he could not be directly quoted obviously hindered reporters from writing newsworthy stories based on the content of the press conferences. It is also true, however, that reporters had not yet fully adopted the convention that presidential words and actions were by definition newsworthy. In Congress, a body of 535 legislators, reporters saw greater opportunity for finding news than at the White House. In other words, Congress was more apt to produce more of the kind of political news favored by Washington reporters. This hints at the institutional context of politics in the early 1910s. At this time, the presidency was still comparatively weak, and the parties and the Congress relatively strong in the American political system. The president was not yet the center of the political world, and the coverage reflected this fact.

Although the press conferences did not make much news, the news they did make is revealing of the news idiom in which they were produced, and Wilson's response to this idiom. This coverage displays a constant search for news—that is, for human interest, conflict and sensationalism—and hints at a few of the techniques reporters used to generate such stories. It also gives some indication of the kind of presidential performance most likely to make news.

For instance, on December 22, 1914, Wilson was asked about recent newspaper discussions concerning appointments. He answered:

> So I see. It has been chiefly in the newspapers, let me say. I have learned with a great deal of interest that there is a fight between me and the Senate. I wasn't aware of it. The Senate has a perfect right to reject any nominations it pleases. I have no criticism. You may be sure that nobody can get up a row on the matter of patronage. We are engaged in a very large affairs in this government, much larger than patronage. You won't find any harangues in this office on the subject.[124]

Here Wilson signals several things: it is the newspapers, and not himself, that are instigating a conflict with the Senate; furthermore, speaking for himself, he would never "get up a row" over the question of patronage, which is a relatively minor matter. The *New York Herald's* lead story of the next day ("Senators See Hint of Peace in Patronage Fight") reflects the fact that reporters rarely took Wilson's view of the matter at face value. Instead, they went to the Senate (in this particular case, to Congress more generally) to get reactions to Wilson's comments. "This talk of peace," the *Herald's* story reads, "and reference to the offices still on the patronage counter caused only mild amusement in the Senate.... Some members of the Senate, however, professed to see in President Wilson's statement the possibility of a reconciliation."[125]

Here Wilson takes a stand that in itself is not newsworthy. There is no news in the headline, "Everything is O.K. Wilson Says, Nothing Has Changed." By bringing Wilson's comments to the Senate, however, reporters are able to fabricate a sense of political movement: Wilson makes a statement and the Senate responds. With movement, there is potential conflict. Much of Washington reporting is composed of leg work designed to circulate statements such as these to produce responses that hint at confrontation.[126]

It should be noted that despite his lackluster performance in press conferences, Wilson was capable of dramatic action. Like Roosevelt, he often sought to let his actions speak louder than his words. For instance, he was the first president since Thomas Jefferson to deliver a five-minute message in person before Congress. The message itself said little; the action spoke volumes. Wilson enjoyed making these kinds of statements, as his several appearances on Capitol Hill to discuss legislation attest.

Wilson's actions toward reporters on these occasions illuminate the relative importance he ascribed to the kind of publicity reporters could provide. For example, on the afternoon of June 5, 1913, Wilson made an unexpected trip to the Capitol to deliver a list of diplomatic selections. The story made the front page of *The Washington Post* and *The New York Times*, each of which emphasized the dramatic nature of the surprise visit. However, Wilson did not advertise the trip at that morning's press conference and never responded to reporters' queries on the subject. On another occasion, Wilson was to deliver a message to the Foreign Relations Committees of both houses concerning the situation in Mexico on the evening of August 25, 1913, and the same message before the whole Congress the next day. In his press conference on the morning of the 25th, he downplayed his message as a simple "summary of the situation," and refused to elaborate any further until the message was complete and delivered. Of course, the lead story of the papers the next day was about Wilson's message to the two committees, the gist of which had been ascertained through interviews with individual Congressmen after it had been delivered to them.

This style of public leadership is not so far removed from Roosevelt's as it first appears. Of course, Roosevelt never missed an opportunity to frame the meaning of his actions to reporters. But he, like Wilson, also sought to lead by example—by standing for particular principles and values. Both intended for the meaning of their actions to be contained in the actions themselves. To Roosevelt's mind, when he stopped his speech to upbraid the audience for not clapping at the appropriate time, he was not grandstanding for the newsmen. It would have been unseemly and insulting to make the accusation. Neither was Wilson when he spoke before Congress. Of course, both Roosevelt and Wilson expected reporters to publicize their actions; but because they assumed the meaning of their actions was intrinsic, they felt no need to make further explanations.

Moreover, even on those occasions when Roosevelt did seek to frame his actions for reporters, he was generally no more successful than Wilson at coaxing the newsmen to frame them other than as newsworthy events. Coverage of Roosevelt's swing down the Mississippi River looks remarkably similar to that of Wilson's press conferences: many column inches devoted to the events, but little coverage of the president's words themselves. It is true that reporters went further to frame Wilson's utterances in terms of Washington politics, but this is probably due to where the events took place (Washington, D.C., versus the Mississippi River), and the relative accessibility of alternative sources, than to any meaningful distinction in the way reporters approached the two presidents.

That being said, it remains the case that Wilson's reluctance to engage with reporters made life more difficult for them than it had been during the Roosevelt administration. Roosevelt sought much more personal control over the news, going so far as to write headlines and leads. For reporters inclined to accept such handling, it made getting the news nearly effortless. But even for reporters who sought greater independence from the president, his constant orations always gave them news. In contrast, Wilson rarely gave reporters newsworthy comments. Therefore, when covering him, reporters had much greater freedom to rely on the interpretations of other authoritative sources, or on their own judgments about what the actions meant.

This can be seen on Wilson's trip to visit John Lind, his emissary to Mexico, in Gulfport, Mississippi, on January 3, 1914. Though Wilson told reporters that he would meet Lind onshore, he instead met him aboard the U.S.S. *Chester*. During an impromptu press conference held the day after the visit, Wilson minimized the meeting's importance and refused to give out details. He met with Lind "for no special reason," he said, just to have a "conversation" about the situation in Mexico. "Nothing specific was discussed" and Lind was already on his way back to Mexico.

This reticence put reporters in a bit of a bind. Such a dramatic action as leaving Washington for a nearly clandestine meeting with his emissary to Mexico had to be of some significance. But what did it mean? "Just why the nation's Chief Executive decided not to permit Mr. Lind to have any 'shore leave,'" the second paragraph of *The New York Times* story of the next day began,

> and took upon himself the inconvenience of being transshipped four times at sea, is
> not explained. President Wilson volunteered no explanation, but some think that he
> did not wish the special envoy to be subjected to the questioning of newspaper men.
> Another theory is that the President wished to show Mexico that there was no
> change in the American policy and no actual interruption of Mr. Lind's mission.[127]

Obviously, here reporters are spinning theories amongst themselves, always a tenuous situation for a profession that valued its neutrality. This particular occasion was unusual in that it occurred outside Washington, away from reporters' other sources. This was not the case on another occasion, in which two stories, one concerning the currency situation and the other the Mexican situation, were in the news. During his press conference on October 23, 1914, the president was asked about the recent proposals for nationalizing the banking system of Frank Vanderslip, president of the National City Bank of New York. He refused to comment. He was also asked several questions about the situation in Mexico, which he asked to be "excused" from answering.

On this occasion, however, reporters could turn to other sources to interpret Wilson's silence. In a story about the Vanderslip plan, the *Chicago Daily Tribune* reported the president was informed of Mr. Vanderslip's attitude and that he refused to comment. The next paragraph began: "His [Wilson's] silence was not without significance, inasmuch as he declared a week ago that he would not consider the O'Gorman plan for a moment because he regarded it in conflict with the declaration of the Democratic platform...." The story then went on to present interpretations of Wilson's views from other sources. Wilson's silence on the Mexican situation elicited this headline in *The San Diego Union*: "With Ominous Silence in Washington, Huerta States Position Defiantly to the World." How did *The San Diego Union* know that Wilson's silence was "ominous?" Because "official Washington" interpreted it that way.[128]

These examples demonstrate why reporters clashed with Wilson much more overtly than with Roosevelt. Wilson refused to honor the idiom of news on more occasions. David Lawrence described Wilson's theory of news as one in which "nothing is news until it [is] completed ... that only conclusions or decisions [are] of interest to the public."[129] Elmer Cornwell notes that the president did not so much meet with reporters as offer himself for questioning to them.[130] Although he once told George Creel that he "prepared for the conferences as carefully as for a Cabinet meeting," compared to subsequent presidents, he prepared very little.[131] He did not study possible questions or memorize answers as most presidents after him have done. On most occasions, he also did not prepare an opening statement. Instead, he merely presented himself before the reporters, confident in his capacity to solve political problems regardless of what the newspapers printed. To Wilson, when reporters refused to engage him on this level, they acted immorally. That is, they trivialized the serious responsibilities of public leadership put upon him.

Wilson's refusal to address reporters in their preferred terms meant that they had to work harder—do more leg work—to fashion his actions into newsworthy events. This made them cantankerous and unkind toward the president, but it did not prevent them from making Wilson newsworthy. Indeed, in one sense Wilson's reticence gave them greater independence to frame stories in newsworthy ways. Still, in terms of their growing sense of themselves and their role in national politics, Wilson's recalcitrance seemed unprofessional. To their mind, they were trying to help him publicize his initiatives to an interested reading public. His refusal to help them do this— and particularly the moral terms on which he criticized them—seemed old fashioned and even irresponsible. If not through the newspapers, then how was Wilson to marshal public opinion behind his policies?

Having laid out this interpretation of Wilson's interactions with reporters, it is time to qualify it. In his press conferences, it is clear that Wilson had little interest in publicizing his initiatives or in the needs of newsmen. But Wilson did not completely foresake interest in publicity and the news. In this regard, the role of his personal secretary, Joseph Tumulty, is significant. Tumulty took on much of the burden of interacting with reporters. It was Tumulty who held daily press conferences, who interpreted Wilson's actions for the reporters, who kept a clipping file of Wilson's press coverage, who smoothed over ruffled feathers when Wilson irritated the reporters, and to whom Wilson turned when he wanted an accurate barometer of public opinion as measured by the newspapers. John Blum describes his efforts:

> Tumulty devoted endless hours to analyzing American sentiment. With no public opinion polls to aid him, he had to rely on his reading and private sources of information. Every day his staff clipped the leading newspapers and magazines from all over the country, arranged the clippings topically, and pasted them on long sheets of yellow paper. Each evening Tumulty took this "Yellow Journal" home, studied it carefully, evaluated the importance of every item, and, when appropriate, wrote memoranda based on his findings to Wilson or to a responsible department head."[132]

If Wilson received positive press coverage, it was often due to the efforts of his secretary. Tumulty played to the rhythms and needs of the reporters in ways that Wilson refused to do.

Moreover, Wilson had great interest in the mechanics of publicity. As early as 1914 he proposed the creation of a "national publicity bureau." During World War I, this idea grew into the Committee on Public Information (CPI), headed by George Creel, a former journalist and publicity agent for various politicians.[133] Wilson charged the CPI with producing propaganda to get the American people behind the war. Naturally, Creel transformed Wilson into a persona to make these appeals. Most CPI advertisements carried Wilson's words and image. And the effort as a whole stimulated the institutional networks of advertising and public relations, bringing together dense networks of these professionals to work on a common cause.[134]

The fact that Wilson himself steered clear of personal involvement in these activities did not lessen their impact.[135] Nor did it discount the fact that despite his personal attitude toward the news, Wilson responded to its requirements. Like progressives generally (including Roosevelt), Wilson was both fascinated and repulsed by the news culture flowering around him. As employed by reporters, Wilson thought the news was too sensationalized, too entertainment-oriented, and likely to result in the further degradation of American society. However, as a medium of communication, Wilson was alive to the possibility of news. Through executive publicity agencies manned by professional specialists, he sought to channel its potential in ways that conformed to his moralistic view of politics. The result was a curious blend of moralism and professionalism.

Beyond Progressive Presidential Communication

Roosevelt and Wilson had different personalities and embraced divergent political programs. But in borrowing from a reservoir of progressive meanings, they shared a distinctive understanding of presidential rhetoric. On their view, going public involved persuasion; however, more fundamentally it depended upon the modeling of basic American virtues. To the extent that presidents "stood for" principle, their actions spoke for themselves. If it is understood as a kind of persuasive salesmanship, this understanding of going public has little in common with modern conceptions of going public. Rather, Roosevelt and Wilson understood publicity as an act of making fundamental truths visible. This sense of presidential communication grew out of the organic, moral worldview of progressivism. Ironically, then, they were after a rhetorical presidency that had little to do with rhetoric itself.

Reporters tended to fill the resulting void of publicity with tales of sensationalism and conflict. In the terms of the news, Roosevelt and Wilson became personae, their efforts to lead by example a form of entertainment. The result, ironically, was a great deal of news coverage that paid precious little attention to the substance of either president's words. Both Roosevelt and Wilson interpreted this result in similarly moral terms: reporters were simply unworthy men who lacked character. But both continued to harbor a grander, more noble vision for the press, one in which it truly educated and socialized rather than pandered to the public. Animated by this vision, they developed new "techniques" and institutions for managing the news, like the news leak and the publicity agency.

We might understand this ambivalence toward the news as one part of a larger progressive reaction toward mass culture.[136] The progressive interest in education and socialization drew reformers to newspapers, movie houses, advertising agencies, and public relations agencies. But their moral view of society made them recoil at the use of such powerful instruments of communication for mere profit. They were greatly enamored of the new expertise in these industries, and equally distressed at the way these experts catered to the most base emotions of their audiences. Through the 1910s, progressives continued their attempt to fuse social and economic regeneration with moral regeneration, that is, to wrap the forces of an increasingly corporate, professionalized, consumerist, nationally oriented society in the gauze of a late-nineteenth-century moral outlook. The contradictions endemic to this effort constituted a great cultural tension of the period.

It is difficult to overstate the importance of World War I in transforming the terms of this tension. During the war, new, denser social networks were built between professional publicists, business, and government.[137] Within these networks, professional propagandists turned to new psychological ideas and theories of the masses to provoke Americans to support the war.[138] These state-sponsored propaganda campaigns demonstrated the malleability of public opinion, but also how mass publics could be moved to irrational heights of emotional frenzy. Progressive confidence in the innate rationality of individuals, and the inevitable progress of American culture, was deeply shaken by the experience, as elites recoiled from the prejudice and violence unleashed by the Wilson administration's propaganda campaigns.[139] In the process, dimensions of the progressive idiom that stressed a socialized, refined collective purpose receded just as its fascination with science, administration and professionalism increased. Participants in political debates of the 1920s were less inclined to favor organic metaphors of social evolution than a general dispersion of science.

The famous Dewey-Lippmann debate over democracy and public opinion in the mid-1920s demonstrates how much the progressive vocabulary had changed by this time. Like Wilson, Lippmann began the debate by arguing that the modern world was characterized by an enormous quantity of information that led to a polyglot mix of public opinions.[140] Unlike Wilson, however, for Lippmann this was not principally a problem of moral and political leadership; rather, it was an epistemological dilemma. For the postwar Lippmann, the public did not compose an organic whole, tied together by common habits and history; rather, individuals were fragmented and alienated, susceptible of being moved in any direction. He argued that individuals have "pictures in their heads" which they distill into "stereotypes" that prevent them from making informed, rational decisions about public issues. The solution, as he saw it, was the creation of bureaus of expertise composed of highly trained professionals paid to sift through the mass of information produced by modern society.

Dewey adhered to a stronger sense of cultural cohesion, and in this he came closer to the older Progressive vision. He believed that a lack of information made people uncoordinated, not apathetic. "It is not that there is no public," he writes against Lippmann. The problem is that "There is too much public, a public too diffused and scattered and too intricate in composition."[141] But again, for Dewey the problem was no longer one of morality, education and leadership. Rather, it was an "intellectual" problem," a "problem of method" rather than of culture.[142] With Lippmann, Dewey believed that it was necessary to privilege the scientific method of inquiry in public affairs. He writes: "Application [of science] in life would signify that science was absorbed and distributed; that it was the instrumentality of that common understanding and thorough communication which is the precondition of the existence of a genuine and effective public."[143]

As the terms of Dewey and Lippmann's debate imply, by the 1920s progressive institutions, i.e., settlement houses, muckraking journals, and the like, had been transformed. With this change, the moral and religious tenor of progressive thought changed as well. Organic conceptions of society lost favor; a stress on individual character and morality came to seem naïve, a product of a more innocent time. It is not that progressivism disappeared—it remains a residual reservoir of American political culture to this day. Rather, it is that, by the 1920s, it no longer seemed to address adequately the problems and possibilities of American public life. In the midst of this transformation, it became more difficult for presidents to account for themselves and their actions in progressive terms. In their search for new terms, they fastened on an emergent vocabulary of mass culture. At least since the 1890s, mass media, by which I principally mean advertising agencies, film studios, and radio networks, had been fashioning new ways of addressing mass publics. In the midst of the Depression, a time when progressive institutions had withered and other traditional institutions like the church, business, and political parties had lost favor, media organizations enjoyed a new power in American public life. It should come as no surprise that presidents began to experiment with this new cultural resource. As they did so, the way in which they imagined presidential communication changed as well. Franklin D. Roosevelt's fireside chats—the subject of our next chapter—illuminate this meeting of presidential communication and mass culture.

Chapter Two

"The People Are with You and What Else Matters?" Presidential Communication in a Media Culture

"THE RHETORICAL PRESIDENCY and the rise of mass communications," a recent textbook informs its students, "grew in tandem, especially after Franklin D. Roosevelt's (FDR's) arrival in the White House...."[1] As we learned earlier, this dating of the rhetorical presidency has its roots in the public presidency model initiated by Richard Neustadt. For Neustadt, FDR's ability to hoard, manipulate and wield presidential power—often through the new instruments of mass communication—represents a watershed in presidential history.[2] Neustadt thinks so much of FDR's leadership style that he devotes a great deal of his text to comparing every subsequent president against the model FDR innovated. Others have followed Neustadt's lead. Theodore Lowi credits FDR with initiating a "revolution" in American politics.[3] Fred Greenstein identifies FDR's tenure in office as the "breakthrough" of the modern presidency, a time when the traditional office gave way to a new, more vigorous and aggressive presidency.[4] And, Samuel Kernell refers to FDR as a "paragon," a president who "established new standards" and "educat[ed] scholars and future presidents alike."[5] FDR's use of mass media does not encompass all of his contributions to the modern presidency, but Neustadtians agree it is a defining feature of his legacy.

If this is true, then FDR's fireside chats are exhibit A of the new, rhetorically minded presidency.[6] These broadcasts are remembered as a principal tool of his political efforts—it is no surprise that a man listening to a radio with a hand cupped to his ear accompanies the recently finished FDR Memorial in Washington, D.C.—and as a model for the modern public presidency that has flourished in the post–World War II period. However, despite, or perhaps because of their obvious importance, historians have reflected very little on what, precisely, made these broadcasts successful. The conventional argument goes something like the following. Radio, it is suggested, gave FDR unparalleled direct access to the public. This is true in two senses: the radio industry remained extremely deferential to the Roosevelt administration during his thirteen years in office; and radio allowed FDR to talk to the American public without the mediation of party or press.[7] Unrestrained by other political institutions, FDR capitalized on the potential of radio as an intimate medium. He couched his appeals in emotion rather than argument, speaking to the public in tones of "soothing conciliation." While many critics, like Kathleen Hall Jamieson, question whether the result can "properly be labeled public address," they acknowledge the power inherent to FDR's appeal: he succeeded by inviting his listeners to suspend their critical faculties in a focused concentration on how the broadcasts made them feel.[8]

Though much in this argument has the ring of reasonableness, close scrutiny reveals as many questions as answers. Arguably, the television industry of the 1950s was at least as deferential to the White House as the radio industry of the 1930s (and hence, might have offered similar opportunities to Eisenhower and Kennedy). More importantly, although neither party nor press mediated FDR's public appeals, the claim that radio was "inherently" an intimate medium assumes what in fact ought to be investigated. Why did radio privilege intimacy? In what form? Did it convey only intimacy? What is the significance of this intimacy for presidential communication? One wants also to question the notion that the public suspended its critical faculties during the chats. The assertion rests on anecdotal evidence scattered throughout the literature rather than on a sustained analysis of empirical data. Indeed, there have been no reception studies of the chats.[9] Taken as a whole then, the conventional view fails to answer the crucial question: what made the fireside chats so successful?

Answering this question requires a greater sensitivity to historical context. FDR assumed the presidency at a time when traditional political institutions like business, the parties, and churches, had lost favor. The Great Depression had robbed them both of material resources and political legitimacy. Media culture, by which I mean the symbolic resources of the advertising, film, and broadcasting industries, gained new power in this institutional vacuum. One can see the seeds of this growing influence as far back as the brief presidency of Warren G. Harding. But media culture proved particularly resonant in the 1930s, a time of "talkies," network broadcasting, and a New Deal administration intent on immersing American audiences in a wave of advertisements, newsreels, radio programs, documentaries, press releases. This institutional environment sets FDR's use of media culture in a unique context—a time after the demise of progressive institutions, but before the post–World War II emergence of the national security state.

Media culture also had a distinctive shape in the 1930s. Of course, media industries then and now are shameless for the way they borrow from other cultural forms. To this extent, media culture of the 1930s had obvious links with popular forms before and since. But it would be a distortion to conclude that the mode of address of media culture remains constant. In fact, to the extent that it remains in close contact with the needs and desires of its audiences, one would expect its mode of address to adapt as new social experiences arise. In this vein, we want to place the symbolic resources offered by media culture in the 1930s in their historical context as well. That context, I want to suggest, had much to do with a mode of address that I call "romantic realism." Both romanticism and realism have antecedents in earlier popular forms. However, it was the genius of early twentieth-century media industries to combine the two into a singular mode of address. That is, they combined a capacity to seemingly represent the world in fine detail (to depict the world in a realistic manner) with the romantic declaration that individuals mattered in modern life. In the Depression era, with widespread concern that the scale of modern life threatened to dissolve the capacity of individuals to act in the world, this posture served as an important meditation on the nature of selfhood in modern society.

The key to the success of FDR's chats then, lay in the combination of political context and symbolic resources made available by 1930s media culture. FDR turned to the reservoir of symbolic meaning offered by media culture because it had a resonance unrivaled at the time. As he did so, he invited listeners to adopt its attitude, to see the world through its prism, and, most important for our purposes, to understand the practice of presidential communication itself on its terms. A brief comparison to progressive presidential rhetoric illuminates the distinctiveness of FDR's rhetorical presidency. As I demonstrated in the last chapter, Theodore Roosevelt (TR) and Woodrow Wilson imagined the presidency at the center of public life— as a literal embodiment of public opinion—and placed great stress on its ability to model values that lay at the "heart" of the nation. In contrast, FDR occupied several different roles in the chats. By turns, he framed himself as a friend, father, counselor, salesman and religious figure. Where TR and Wilson sought to "stand for" preferred values, the chats show FDR as a flexible, shifting figure in the public imagination. Perhaps more importantly, FDR made the public the central protagonist of New Deal recovery efforts.

Where TR and Wilson placed themselves at the center of political life, FDR assigned that role to his individual listeners. Moreover, eschewing the organic thinking characteristic of progressive presidential communication, he encouraged his listeners to believe that together, as a mass public, they could make radical changes in public life. In short, in a way no twentieth-century president before or after has dared, FDR invited listeners to believe that they mattered. In FDR's chats, finally, we see a rhetorical presidency firmly rooted in the possibilities (and the limitations) of 1930s media culture. I suggest that the chats were successful not despite, but precisely because of their immersion in mass culture. In these chats, FDR crafted a practice of presidential communication that resonated profoundly with the romantic realism of mass culture—a set of institutions that enjoyed a unique legitimacy at the time.

In what follows, I briefly describe the institutional environment and symbolic resources of mass culture. I then interpret the fireside chats, and listener's reaction to them, in the context of the media culture from which they borrowed.

A Culture of Sound and Sight

"The decade of the thirties," Warren Susman observes, "was ... an era of sound and sight," a time when the words and pictures, sounds and images, of mass culture had a profound impact on American public life.[10] Of course, mass culture has a much longer genealogy. Depending on how one dates these things, one can argue that it emerged first in the penny press of the 1830s or the ten-cent national magazines of the 1890s. However, Susman's point, I think, is that it was in the 1930s that mass culture came to have a dominant influence on American culture. In part due to new organizational and technological developments (the development of "talkies," and the networked broadcasting system), and in part to the more sophisticated uses to which they were put, media culture saturated 1930s American public life in ways it had not in the past. And, Susman concludes, as it did so, it became a central aspect of a new search for an "American culture" more broadly conceived. That is, at a time when traditional social institutions were rapidly disintegrating, media culture was enlisted in a collective effort to "seek and define America as a culture and to create the patterns of a way of life worth understanding."[11]

Put another way, Susman's argument is simply that public actors in the 1930s turned to media culture as a way of framing and accounting for their political projects. This raises the question of what it means to use media culture (rather than some other cultural reservoir) in this way. Here we must look to the distinctive way that mass media organize social experience and address their audiences. Media producers had been experimenting with different ways of enticing the public to consume their wares at least since the late nineteenth century.[12] Because they possessed similar goals and confronted similar constraints, they developed a shared set of conventions, habits, and practices—a set of symbolic resources—for addressing mass publics. By the 1930s, these symbolic resources linked media producers into a common organizational environment.

Much like progressive culture then, it is fair to speak of a "media culture" by the 1930s. Much of this culture's resources were dedicated to solving a fundamental dilemma: then and now, media producers are inevitably at some remove from consumers. Mass culture is literally made in different places from where it is consumed (for instance, the movie studio versus the theater). Media producers also tend to think of themselves as different kinds of people (as professionals or experts) than media consumers. And pragmatically, producers use the cultural products they make for different purposes than consumers. Where producers mean to make a profit from media culture, consumers use it for other purposes like entertainment, diversion, or edification. The problem, in sort, is that media producers have little interaction with consumers, and even less control over how consumers interpret and use their products.

One response to this situation is obvious. If media producers cannot know what consumers wanted, perhaps they can teach audiences to want the things they are selling. This response led media producers into the terrain of demographic marketing research. Gilded Age magazines pioneered the use of gimmicks like mail-in games to learn more about their readers. In the twentieth century, media companies began to tie such practices to scientific polling so that they might target the interests and habits of their audiences in ever greater detail. This information did not allow them to "give consumers what they want," but it did help them learn what (and how) consumers might be made to want the standardized products they sold. In the 1930s, however, these technologies were in their infancy, if they existed at all. Scientific polling became widespread only in the 1940s. This left media producers of the 1930s with nineteenth-century tools like games and gimmicks—vulgar techniques that shed precious little light on the interests and desires of their audiences. Put bluntly, media producers during the long tenure of the New

Deal simply did not have the power to direct audience tastes in the way they would come to possess in later decades.

This fact had important consequences for the kinds of symbolic resources characteristic of 1930s mass culture. Most importantly, it meant that media producers had to respond to the interests, experiences, and desires of consumers. That is, if they could not reliably direct audiences to specific ends, then they had to reach out to where audiences lived their emotional lives. This pushed mass culture of the time more into the realm of art than of science. Movies went furthest in this direction (which perhaps explains why movie makers most tightly embraced an artistic identity). But even advertising agencies hired "creatives"—individuals whose job it was to fashion ads that connected with social experience.[13] When they engaged audiences in this manner, media producers lost control over what one scholar has called the "authorial voice" of media culture.[14] This loss of control put this culture into play as a symbolic resource, adoptable and adaptable for use by others in "authoring" themselves in the social world.[15]

Consider just one example: the movie star. The movie star was a creature of the Hollywood Studio System that dominated the movie industry in the 1930s and 1940s. As part of that system, movie stars acted as brand names for generic movies.[16] All Hollywood Westerns looked the same, for example, but John Wayne differentiated his movies by his status as a star. Given the economic importance of stars, it was not surprising that movie studios developed a highly rationalized "star system." This system involved calculated publicity campaigns designed to convince audiences that actors naturally possessed certain qualities.[17] Clearly, it had a manipulative character. Studios essentially lied to audiences when they suggested that stars possessed authentic qualities that set them apart from regular actors. But, as Richard Dyer argues, the star system of the thirties contained a kernel of possibility that is no longer present in contemporary Hollywood. Dyer writes that, although audiences recognized the publicity machinery that went into making stars, they attended to them because stars "enacted ways of making sense of the experience of being a person" in modern society.[18] Stars, that is, anchored audiences in "a world that is shared in common," not by providing models of behavior (as progressives once tried to do), but by articulating a shared set of values."[19] In this way, stars provided a point of access to a social world—an authorial voice—for addressing shared concerns. Their cultural value lay not in the way that they imposed meaning—their instrumental character—but in the way that they made meaning possible for and shareable by a mass audience.

Movie stars were one part of a wider vocabulary of "romantic realism" that characterized 1930s media culture. This vocabulary set a context in which Americans responded to the deep cultural skepticism and anxiety of the times.[20] Amid the grand changes of industrial society—massive immigration, the flight to the cities, the rise of a national consumer economy, the increase in pace and scale of modern life—individual subjectivity and agency seemed diminished. As Walter Lippmann suggested at the time, Americans were experiencing a "vast dissolution of ancient habits," the end result of which no one could predict.[21] A crisis of subjectivity erupted in this breach. Was it possible for individuals to know and understand, to exercise agency, in the social world? Media producers borrowed from longstanding aesthetic traditions—realism, romanticism and melodrama—to address these issues.[22] For much of the nineteenth century, these traditions worked in opposition to one another. It was the curious achievement of early twentieth-century mass media to blend them into a recognizable attitude or posture toward the world. This attitude involved a recognition of the self as something that mattered in the world—a kind of romantic declaration of individuality in the midst of the scale and pace of modern society. Conjuring worlds at least once removed from reality, and thus from society, the romantic ethos of media language stressed the power of individuals to make their own reality. It particularly asserted the role of spiritual values—honor, love, courage—in fashioning conditions of existence. Melodrama represented an emotionally heightened register of these themes. As Peter Brooks suggests, "melodramatic rhetoric, and the whole expressive enterprise of the genre, represents a victory over repression, [an effort to] break through everything that constitutes the 'reality principle....'"[23] Melodrama sharpened the romantic ethos into distinctive images of heroic individuals in battle with social conditions that connived to constrain them. Depicting Manichean contrasts between ideals of good and evil, the romantic tenor of media culture portrayed stereotypical characters involved in a dramatic enactment of social conflict rendered in intimate terms.

The romantic impulse of media culture was often far removed from the actual social world. It conveyed entertaining fantasies to audiences wishing to escape from the mundane, often harsh, reality of modern life. However, in part to distinguish its products from other forms of popular culture, and in part to satisfy audience demands, media producers linked the romantic ethos to the realist impulse that swept across American society in the last half of the nineteenth century. In so doing, 1930s media culture anchored the romantic sensibility more closely to the everyday social experience of audiences. Much of the media's realist appeal related to their technological characteristics.[24] Based on the photographic image, movie cameras obtained a cultural authority conveyed by presenting the world wholly and completely.[25] As a "moving" eye, the movie camera seemed an especially appropriate means for capturing the fluidity characteristic of modern life.[26] When movies added sound in the late 1920s, it became possible for them to etch *mis-en-scenes* of unapproachable realism.[27] In this regard, the "liveness" of broadcasting also obtained a certain realist appeal. Modern society seemed complex in part because things happened so quickly and simultaneously that it was difficult to interpret the flood of information or to make causal inferences. By taking audiences to events outside their environs, and doing so "live," as events unfolded, broadcasting offered audiences a sense of immediacy and command they once seemed to enjoy in slower, simpler times.[28]

Together, romance and melodrama geared media culture's mode of address toward intimacy, domesticity, and personality. Combined with realism, this ethos offered a serious meditation on the social experience of the modern self. The result was a sort of truth-telling dimension of 1930s media culture, not only in the sense that media representations literally corresponded to the world, but also in the sense that they revealed important aspects of social experience. For instance, advertising agencies turned to "sociodramas" in the 1920s—short, highly dramatized pictorial vignettes— that featured modern social encounters: a chance encounter on a street corner, a meeting with one's neighbor, or a first date. Depicted with a concern for detail that betrayed advertisers' investment in realism, these sociodramas approached consumers as particular people confronting the impersonality of modern life. Standing beside consumers (usually in the guise of a character or personality), they offered advice for how to navigate the terrain of modern social life in terms that mimicked a face-to-face dialogue. Offering this advice in an intimate exchange, and compounding it with the aura of realism, the ads conveyed the sense that they contained some essential truth about social reality.[29] The idiom of movies worked in much the same fashion. D.W. Griffith, a primary innovator of this idiom, pioneered narrative techniques that stressed character psychology.[30] In his magnum opus, *Birth of a Nation* (1915), he conveyed the drama of the civil war through the prism of two families, one Southern and one Northern. He motivated the plot not by action on a grand scale, but by the psychological development of its characters—the love felt between a Southern daughter and a Northern son; the unbridled ambition of a mulatto politician; the thirst for revenge of a brother.[31] Here, the grand realism of historical detail was linked to an argument about the underlying spiritual reality of the war—that Northern and Southern whites were bound by a common race, heritage and sentiment. Radio—the most hybridic of mass media—perhaps stressed this sense of intimacy most overtly.[32] In its daily programming—especially instructional programs, dramas, soap operas, and talk shows—it foregrounded individuals acting on and in the world, offering audiences instruction in the many ways that the self mattered in social life.

Romantic realism served as media culture's preferred mode of address in the 1920s and 1930s. This attitude conjured social experience as a domain of human fabrication, of self-creation: I, me, you, we, author, or authorize, the social world. To the extent that this posture demanded recognition—of myself and others as potential authors—one might also describe it as a democratic sensibility: I borrow a posture of selfhood from media culture that gains meaning through its recognition by others. By establishing a sense of commonality on this basis, media audiences might collectively authorize themselves. However, if this mode of address "redeem[ed]" individualism as agents of social life, as Paddy Scannell puts it, then the price paid for this redemption was responsibility.[33] Individually and collectively we assume responsibility for public life not because media have provided us some knowledge of the world, but because, through its vocabulary, we now acknowledge one another as agents of public life, and thus as standing in an intimate relation to words spoken and deeds done in that sphere.[34]

This, in any event, was the possibility of media culture in the 1930s. It is my contention that this possibility became a reality in FDR's fireside chats. FDR was able to capitalize on its potential because the dominant institutions of political life at the time—business, political parties, interest groups, churches, schools—had been severely weakened by the Depression.[35] Media culture stepped into the resulting breach. Borrowing the posture of romantic realism offered by this culture, FDR shaped his chats in ways that made the Depression apprehensible by ordinary people. Moreover, this posture opened an opportunity for listeners—individually and collectively—to recognize themselves as prospective agents of change. To the extent that listeners interpreted the chats through this lens, they came to see the Depression as a romantic tale of heroic conquest—with the "public" (i.e., themselves) as its principal protagonist. The chats, in this sense, succeeded because they "redeemed" individuals as people who mattered in public life.

The Fireside Chats[36]

Speaking in a New Key

FDR once famously proclaimed that he wanted to be a "preaching president," like his cousin Theodore.[37] In many respects, he was well suited to the role. As a boy, he had occasion to watch closely his cousin's use of the bully pulpit. And, as Undersecretary of the Navy, he had a prime vantage point from which to observe Wilson's rhetorical flourishes. But in 1933 FDR had powerful new tools at his disposal—including newsreels, movie houses, and broadcasting networks—tools that promised to dramatically alter the nature of the president's public sermons. FDR demonstrated a fascination with these tools very early in his political career. Already as Undersecretary of the Navy, he saw the value of newsreels for increasing the Navy's budgets.[38] His relationship with radio extended as far back as his 1928 "Happy Warrior" nominating speech for Al Smith at the Democratic Convention. As Governor of New York, he continually experimented with both radio and newsreels, delivering weekly radio reports to the citizens of New York and appearing in newsreels to support his candidacy for the Democratic nomination of 1932.

It was during his tenure as Governor of New York that FDR experimented with different approaches to addressing mass audiences via radio. In his weekly radio reports to the citizens of New York, he asked them to send him their opinions. As with the broadcast networks, the ensuing mail was carefully monitored, in FDR's case by his Secretary, Louis Howe, for how his appeals were going over with the public.[39] Over these four years, he fell upon the friend-next-door technique favored by professional radio announcers. Dave Garroway, a popular radio announcer, describes that technique as

> just rambl[ing] along, saying whatever came into my mind. I was introspective. I tried to pretend that I was chatting with a friend over a highball late in the evening.... Then—and later—I consciously tried to talk to the listener as an individual, to make each listener feel that he knew me and I knew him.[40]

Charles Mickelson (at the time, the director of publicity for the Democratic National Committee) recalls FDR doing much the same thing. In preparation for the chats, Mickelson recalls the president looking "at the blank wall, trying to visualize the individuals he was seeking to help: a mason at work on a new building, a girl behind the counter, a man repairing an automobile, a farmer in the field...."[41] Frances Perkins describes a similar scene.

President FDR, she writes, thought of his audience "in family groups. He thought of them sitting on a suburban porch after supper on a summer evening. He thought of them gathered around a dinner table at a family meal."[42] The result was a form of radio "fresh talk," a naturalized conversational form of talk that strove for a sense of intimacy and informality.[43]

To help him capitalize on the power of his newfound radio voice, the new president gathered around him men experienced in the arts of the mass media. Stephen T. Early and Col. Marvin Hunter McIntyre served as Washington Bureau Chiefs for newsreel companies (McIntyre for Pathe News and Early for Paramount News). Others, including Louis Howe, William Hassett, Charles Mickelson, and Lowell Mellett, were former journalists and publicity men. These men crafted the most successful peacetime publicity campaign in American history to that date. As FDR's press assistant, Early coordinated FDR's radio broadcasts, monitoring audience size and reception of his addresses, and hectoring uncooperative radio stations. Much like a movie studio publicity agent, Early also supervised other general publicity efforts such as mass mailings of FDR's photograph to government offices and projects around the country. Howe oversaw a Correspondence Section responsible for answering FDR's mail and organized a Division of Press Intelligence whose task was compiling a daily news and editorial opinion clipping collection. A summary and index of this opinion was produced daily and sent to 450 government officials in the form of a "Daily Bulletin." Each executive agency and department had its own publicity department staffed by former journalists whose task, according to Early's directive, was to "do [their] job just like [they] were working for a newspaper."[44] Besides promoting positive newspaper coverage of the New Deal, an important function of this coordinated activity was the projection of FDR's personality to the public. Much like advertising campaigns, it sought to convey a singular message: that the New Deal was taking positive, effective measures to help people, and the president was firmly in control of, and responsible for, this process.

Although they were occasional events—27 over 13 years, according to the editors of FDR's public papers—the chats were organized with much the same concern for efficiency and standardization as media products generally.[45] Like a Hollywood movie, the chats were the product of no one person, but were produced within a structured division of labor. Various groups of officials, from departmental officials to cabinet members to advisors who held no official government position, participated in their production. Each group produced information which was funneled to a central group charged with putting the pieces together. No detail was too insignificant. Special paper was brought for FDR's reading copy, so that no rustling could be heard on the broadcast, and the president wore a special bridge to reduce the whistle caused by his missing tooth. Care was taken to be as economical as possible, both in total words and in word length. President FDR himself read each draft, urging his writers to use short, simple statements, with no abstractions or what he called "weasel words." The chats rarely lasted longer than fifteen to twenty minutes. But like a Hollywood movie, the president liked for them to end on a proper "high" note. The resulting speech, James Ragland has argued, looked much like a "cue-sheet for a stage play. All the signals were clearly marked: the pauses by dashes, the words to be emphasized is underlined, the phrase marked for special treatment...."[46]

To distinguish the chats as special broadcasts, the time and reason for each broadcast was carefully considered. FDR's assistants ensured that these broadcasts never competed with popular radio shows like *Amos 'N Andy* or *The Jack Benny Show*. Most were broadcast on Sunday evening at 9:45 Eastern time, when a majority of Americans were presumed to be home. FDR's staff monitored conditions around the country that might influence his audience size. Knowledge of media markets was a necessary part of this job. Editorials, news reports, mail, and special correspondence were scrupulously studied for reactions to the talks.

In their organization and structure then, the chats clearly resemble the production and delivery system of the mass culture industries. Their goal—to sell New Deal programs—was every bit as instrumental as those of the mass media. And their production process—from conception to delivery—was every bit as standardized and economical.

Nothing indicates their instrumental character so well as their most oft-cited characteristic: the use of personal pronouns. In the very first sentence of the first chat, FDR began with, "I want to talk for a few minutes with the people of the United States about banking." Subsequent chats were defined by the series of I's, you's, me's, and we's that constituted their cast of characters. It is a rhetorical device described in somewhat ominous tones by John Dos Passos as FDR "speaking clearly and cordially to youandme, explaining how he's sitting at his desk there in Washington, leaning towards youandme across his desk, speaking clearly and cordially so that youandme shall completely understand...."[47] Here, Dos Passos catches the sense in which FDR's use of "I," "you" and "we" elides the boundaries between himself and the public: at times "we" refers to the government and at others to the American people. The confusion works to identify FDR and his policies with the nation as a whole. At the same time, it also encourages listeners to assume the position of "you" the citizen, a frame of reference that the president himself has constructed. As listeners identify themselves as this "you," they link themselves in an intimate fashion to government recovery efforts. In this way, FDR's use of personal pronouns served his larger political goals.

However, as with any instance of media culture, the chats never completely closed the gap between the president and his listeners. Indeed, the very fact that he left the character of "you" the listener ambiguous, so as to allow his many listeners to occupy the same position, indicates the relative openness of the chats' structure. This aspect of FDR's appeal is illuminated by a contrast with the progressives' desire to impose a fixed definition of American citizenship. For TR and Wilson, to be an American was to possess very definite characteristics. And they were not shy about defining these qualities in some detail. Not so for FDR. In the chats, he spoke only to "you." Qualifications to occupy this position went little beyond a willingness to assume the identity of this ambiguous pronoun. In this way, FDR managed to speak to Americans in all their heterogeneity by allowing them to define precisely what it meant to occupy this identity. Listeners retained the power to occupy that position, to occupy it on some occasions and not others, or to refuse its invitation.[48]

In trying to establish control over how audiences interpreted his message, FDR had little recourse to the conventional choice of modern politicians: demography. Although he turned to polling increasingly in his second and third administrations, in the early 1930s the science of surveying was still undeveloped. True, he had other kinds of data available from newspapers, the party, and the massive amount of mail he received, but these provided only distorted images of national preferences. It was very difficult, therefore, for the president to know with any great specificity how to shape public opinion. But if FDR did not have access to such instrumental information, he had a great understanding of his audience's social experience, particularly the anxiety, frustration and despair caused by the Depression. As he opened the chats to this experience, he drew upon the posture of romantic realism characteristic of media culture.

This is clear in the way he narrativized the nation's problems. FDR framed these problems not in terms of business cycles or economic theories (as President Hoover had done), but as a consequence of individual action and psychology.[49] For instance, in the first chat he describes the banking crisis as a problem caused by a few "incompetent or dishonest" bankers who speculated in unwise loans. Their dishonesty led to a "crisis of confidence" on the part of ordinary individuals, who rushed to get their money out of the banks. In this story, the Great Depression became a struggle of good people against the nefarious actions of bad people. Characteristically, FDR suggests that winning this struggle requires psychological—not institutional—change: the restoration of "confidence." To this end, he reports that the "patriotic" Congress has passed legislation to rehabilitate the banks and to monitor unscrupulous bankers, and he is "confident" that these measures will solve the problem. The rest of the chats elaborate the same theme. In the second chat, FDR describes the Depression as "a condition ... not a theory," one that threatens not the American economy, but "the peace and contentment of the individual and of his family." Even in his discussion of the drought (chat #8), a problem ostensibly caused by weather patterns and soil composition, FDR is at great pains to personalize the issue. Rather than describing the nature of the drought, its causes and consequences, FDR describes his trip through the Midwest, in which he "talked with families who had lost their wheat," and "saw cattlemen [who] ... have been compelled to sell all but their breeding stock"; he speaks of the "spiritual" connection between farmers and the rest of the nation, and of the readiness of the farmers to "fit, and not to fight, the ways of nature." Here again, a large-scale problem is rendered in melodramatic terms, as a challenge to the American character rather than a complex natural occurrence.

Put simply, within the romantic world constructed by the chats, individuals and their dispositions mattered. It mattered that a few people were greedy or unscrupulous; it mattered that FDR was confident and enthusiastic. Most importantly, public opinion mattered. The chats always frame the public as their central protagonist. "After all," FDR says to end his first chat, "there is an element in the readjustment of our financial system more important than currency, more important than gold, and that is the confidence of the people.... It is your problem no less than it is mine." Perhaps FDR's strongest claim in this regard is his suggestion that solutions to the depression rest in public psychology rather than in governmental measures. Statements like "It is your problem, your problem no less than it is mine," dot the entire corpus of chats. The "only instruments," he says in chat #3, which the government will use to fight unemployment "come from opinion and from conscience." Chat #5 urges the public to judge government recovery programs by "the plain facts of your own individual situation."

Chat #6 suggests that gains in trade and industry will be made "on the driving power of individual initiative...."[50] And chat #7 ends with the claim that "we have in the darkest moments of our national trials retained our faith in our own ability to master our destiny." Much of FDR's speaking time is spent detailing large-scale government programs, such as the National Recovery Act; but underneath these institutional behemoths always stands the moral force, pragmatism, and ambition of the American public. "I cannot guarantee the success of this nation-wide plan," FDR says chat #3, "but the people of this country can guarantee its success."

If FDR could not close the gap between himself and his audience through imposition, he sought to do so through invitation. He invited his listeners into a melodramatic narrative, which not only acknowledged their anxieties, but went further to cast them as the heroic protagonists of a historic drama. Of course, FDR tells his listeners, we face challenges. But we will prevail if we simply recognize them for what they are—challenges to the heart and spirit—and recognize in ourselves the capacity to overcome them. In this way, FDR's repeated declaration "to tell you," "interest you," "make it clear to you," and "make you understand," works as a device for portraying his listeners as the motive force behind New Deal initiatives. "You will watch the work in every corner of this Nation," he tells his audience toward the end of chat #7. "Feel free to criticize. Tell me of instances where work can be done better, or where improper practices prevail." To the extent that individuals identified with FDR's "you," they came closer to accepting his frame of the nation's problems as a romantic challenge to the spiritual resources of a nation. FDR's accomplishment was to link this romantic image to the wider collective effort of New Deal policies.

To this point, I have said little about FDR's role in the chats. If he framed his listeners as the stars of his melodramatic narrative, FDR portrayed himself as their costar. Like any movie star, he carefully cultivated his image. Through his time in office, he combined a large-scale dissemination of his image with carefully controlled revelations of private details of his life. His image appeared on posters at public works projects, in pictures at government buildings, in newsreels at the movie houses, in pictures in the newspapers and on walls in family living rooms. His voice and the voices of his cabinet and immediate advisors were heard over the airwaves almost daily. At the same time, FDR maintained extensive control over the dissemination of his image. Steve Early carefully monitored still photography and newsreel images of the president. As early as April 1933, he advised Will Hays, the Director of the Motion Pictures Producers and

Distributors of America, that "the President decidedly objects to his picture being used in either shorts or features...."[51] FDR's official policy mandated that his image was not to appear in any production which included professional acting talent, advertising, or any material which was not historically accurate. This policy extended to radio. Impersonators were prevented from mimicking the president's voice, and doing so meant a prompt reply from Early. Finally, FDR was the first president who constantly worried about overexposure. Often, he would become animated about some issue and begin to plan another fireside chat. "Nine times out of ten," Steve Early tells interviewer John Sharon, "we advised against his going on the air for we did not want the fireside chat to lose its appeal to the people."[52] The president states this basic idea in a letter to Ray Stannard Baker, who encouraged him to make more radio appearances:

> Whereas in this country there is a free and sensational press, people tire of seeing the same name day after day in the important headlines of the papers, and the same voice night after night over the radio. For example, if since last November I had tried to keep up the pace of 1933 and 1934, the inevitable histrionics of the new actors, Long and Coughlin and Johnson, would have turned the eyes of the audience away from the main drama itself....[53]

Here, FDR refers to the public as an "audience" and to the New Deal as a "drama"; he acknowledges that his public persona has much in common with other public "actors"; and he indicates an explicit, well thought-out theory for using his constructed personality to his advantage.

At some level, FDR understood that audiences relied on his image to authenticate the melodramatic narrative of the chats. That image was crafted on air during the chats, but also in other venues like newspapers, photographs, newsreels. Listeners in rapt contemplation of FDR's words were led to the social world outside the chats by these other layers of his image. In this way, the president's image served as a primary axis through which social experience entered the narrative world of the chats. FDR also capitalized on the liveness of broadcasting to accentuate the realism of the chats. When, precisely at 9:45 p.m., the radio announcer interrupted regular programming to declare, "Ladies and Gentleman, the President of the United States," listeners knew that FDR was speaking to them in the moment. Other gestures, as when FDR paused to take a sip of water, or, as in chat #7, to tell listeners about his vacation plans, reinforced the sense that this was the president talking directly to them.[54] These realist devices worked to bring FDR's melodramatic tale even closer to the realm of actual social experience. That is, like the president's image generally, they engendered a sense of confidence, of trust and assurance, in the president's words.

A certain flexibility in FDR's performance was also key to the chats' success. Unlike TR or Wilson, both of whom preferred to stand for particular values, FDR played many roles in the chats. Often, his performance has been described in terms of familiarity. One scholar writes that FDR "talked like a father discussing public affairs with his family in the living room."[55] On this view, the president related to the public much like a friend sitting across a kitchen table. Looked at more closely, however, it appears that, like movie stars or advertising personalities, FDR displayed a remarkable capacity to shift roles in the chats. At times, he presented himself as a kind of advisor. For instance, he often described his chats as "reports" to the public, and spent a great deal of time listing "specific measures," in point form no less, for alleviating economic and social problems. In this role, FDR is concerned to tell the public what has been going on in Washington, why it has gone this way, and what they (the public) should think about it. To this end, as in chat #1, he offers information: "let me state the simple fact that when you deposit money in a bank the bank does not put the money into a safe deposit vault"; he anticipates questions: "what, then, happened during the last few days of February and the first few days of March?" he acknowledges fears: "I know that many people are worrying"; and he offers his personal testimonial: "I am confident," "I can assure you," "I am certain that the people of this country understand."

At other times, FDR is more explicitly a salesman of the New Deal. In a "review" of New Deal programs (chat #5), he notes that legislation passed by his administration "provided for," "lent a hand," "strengthened," "made further advances," "took definite steps," "created," and "reorganized and simplified." Just as advertisers attempted to do, FDR laid out a context in which events should be understood, promoted his actions in regard to those events, and suggested appropriate public reactions: "The legislation which has been passed or is in the process of enactment can properly be considered as part of a well grounded plan," and in another place, "It is wholly wrong to call the measures … taken Government control of farming…." (chat #2) In these examples of informal radio "fresh talk," FDR is not just a friend, he is the public's counsel, and a personal spokesperson for New Deal legislation.

These devices worked to humanize FDR to his audience, to make him appeal authentic and genuine. Combined with the constant declaration of his intention to "be at all times honest" with the American people, to tell them in "simple" and "plain" English about his policies, the effect was to tie New

Deal policies to FDR's personal veracity. Like a movie star, that is, FDR's image became a fungible currency, rooted in his personal sincerity and authenticity, but multiple in its meanings. It is precisely its fluid nature that made FDR's image accessible to working-class urban immigrant and the small-town businessman, to the housewife and the southern black farmer. FDR's efforts worked not by meaning all things to all people, but by meaning something to every person.

Before moving on to a discussion of how listeners responded to the chats, it is worth taking a moment to ask why reporters played along. After all, FDR made exaggerated claims—his critics called them lies—about the New Deal, himself, and the heroic status of the public. These exaggerations were many and easily apparent. For instance, in the midst of a widespread banking panic, he calmly asserted (chat #1) that it was "safer to keep your money in a reopened bank than under the mattress." A few months later, he described the legislation passed during the first 100 days as a "granite foundation in a period of confusion." And in the midst of massive labor rebellions in 1934, a period when agitation was the norm rather than the exception, he asserted (chat #4) that "nearly all Americans are sensible and calm people. We do not get greatly excited nor is our peace of mind disturbed...." As one scholar of the chats notes, "one of the devices most consistently employed by the president was to state, as a fact, the existence of a situation or an attitude which he sincerely and fervently wished to be true."[56]

Many of FDR's closest advisors worried about his propensity to stretch the truth. Harold Ickes was particularly concerned. Ickes is quoted as once telling FDR, "You are a wonderful person but you are one of the most difficult men to work with that I have ever known ... you never get too hard but you won't talk frankly even with people who are loyal to you.... You keep your cards close up against your belly."[57] Others noted that he would invent stories to make a point, or to embellish his own past accomplishments to get people to think well of him. Patrick Maney describes a scene in which "One time a Democratic congressman told Harold Ickes that FDR would have difficulty in refuting Huey Long's charge that he, FDR, was a liar. 'Its pretty tough,' the interior secretary confided to his diary, 'when things like this can be said about the president of the United States and when members of his own official family and of his own party in Congress feel that his word cannot be relied upon. It hurts me to set down such a fact, but it is the fact, as I have had occasion to know more than once.'"[58]

The commonness of this reaction raises the question of why journalists did not cast a more critical eye on the president's speeches. Part of the answer is that journalists were no more immune to FDR's enchantments than ordinary people. Indeed, many rooted for him as loudly as any partisan.[59] But reporters also sensed that modern presidential communication required this sort of performance, that it had become essential to being a professional politician. Raymond Clapper wrote at the time that, in contrast to the publishers for whom they worked, reporters were "ninety-percent" for FDR for five reasons: (1) he maintained personal contacts with them; (2) he always gave them hard news; (3) he seemed to be for the underdog, a position reporters were likely to admire; and, (4) and (5), he was viewed as an expert at political craftsmanship, that is, a professional politician who knew how to play the political game. That is, reporters regarded FDR's radio performances as something like a method or technique rather than a lack of sincerity or honesty.[60] This sentiment was also held by radio men, who "regarded [FDR] with admiration and spoke of him as a 'real pro.'"[61] These assessments have in common a flattery of the professional status of reporters and radio men and of professionalism in general. Self-consciously professional men like reporters viewed FDR's ability to portray different public roles as an essential political skill, one sorely lacking in most politicians. To them, FDR seemed the model of a new professional politician, one who had mastered the necessary techniques for performing in a mass-mediated public culture.

In sum, I have suggested that as a distinctive practice of presidential communication, the fireside chats gained much of their meaning from 1930s media culture. In particular, they borrowed heavily from the romantic realist mode of address characteristic of media industries during this period. In the chats, FDR argued that the Depression was manmade—not a consequence of impervious business cycles or abstract theories. He rendered this manmade problem as a melodrama, a tale of good versus bad, of Americans wielding their spiritual resources against the evil actions of a few corrupt businessmen. Conveyed with the realism made available by broadcasting technology, this appeal invited listeners to recognize public life as part of their social world, as something that mattered to them and was susceptible to their influence. This is to say, as an instance of media language, the chats were loosened from FDR's specific political interests to become a more widely shared mode of address, a medium through which listeners might authorize themselves to speak for and about public life. In this way, they constituted a unique version of the rhetorical presidency.

Listening in a New Key

How did listeners respond to FDR's appeal? At the outset, I should note that many listeners found themselves simply unable to describe how the president's invitation affected them. "It is just marvelous," one listener wrote of the first chat, "and I find myself at a loss to tell how it affected me, without appearing fulsome."[62] Another wrote vaguely of feeling FDR's "presence, something tangible." While still another characterized the same feeling as an "intangible quality."[63] When describing the chats, listeners often were reduced to platitudes: the chats were "splendid," "magnificent," or "wonderful." Having never been addressed by their president in this manner, it appears that a good many listeners responded with confusion, vagueness, or sheer brevity. Some letters are no more than one or two lines of congratulations; others fill pages with disconnected ramblings or offer only the most mundane or vague observations.

And, of course, for the scholar wishing to use the letters in some sort of generalizable way, the fact that they represent a self-selected sample of individuals is a concern.[64] But these methodological dilemmas are mitigated by the fact that these letters offer the only evidence of its kind of the ordinary person's sensibilities toward the chats. As such, they offer insight into how listeners made sense of their listening experience. Despite the obvious methodological concerns, then, these letters are worthy of investigation because they illuminate important aspects of the cultural reception of the chats, and the feelings of ordinary people at being addressed in this manner.

Even with the brevity and incoherence of many of the letters, a few reactions come through clearly in these letters. It is clear, for instance, that the performance of the chats meant more to listeners than the policy information they conveyed. Of the 380 letters in my sample, over three-quarters (78 percent), refer to the chat or to FDR himself, while only 15 percent refer to his policies (see Table 2.1).

If listeners wanted to respond to policy-related issues, there was more than enough information in the chats to do so. Indeed, lists of specific New Deal policies and proposals represent a large part of the content of each chat. Yet those who wrote letters rarely discussed policy issues. Instead, most of their attention focused on the performance itself: how the words sounded and made them feel. And when they did not discuss the performance, letter-writers demonstrated an interest in FDR himself: his attitudes, his courage and his popularity. Even when FDR asked his listeners to judge the New Deal by the standards of their own situation (in chat #5, broadcast on June 28, 1934), an appeal which explicitly directed listeners to consider their relationship to New Deal programs, only 19 percent of the letters referred to such programs. This general trend becomes a little less true over time. Reaction letters to chats broadcast in the last half of 1934 through 1936 indicate more interest in specific policy measures, and no sample of letters reaches the high of the 75 percent focus on the performance set in responses to the first chat. However, as one would expect with a mass cultural form, it is fair to say that the public responded less to New Deal policies outlined by the broadcasts than to the performance and the performer.

Table 2.1: Referents of Public Reaction Letters, Fireside Chats (n = 380)

CHAT #	PERFORMANCE OF CHAT	FDR	NEW DEAL PROGRAMS	MISC.	TOTALS
#1					
# Letters	40	9	3	1	53
% Total	76	17	6	1	100
#2					
# Letters	30	16	4	6	56
% Total	53	29	7	11	100
#3					
# Letters	15	3	7	2	27
% Total	56	11	26	7	100
#4					
# Letters	23	14	5	3	45
% Total	51	31	11	7	100
#5					
# Letters	26	11	10	4	51
% Total	51	22	19	8	100
#6					
# Letters	26	20	8	7	61
% Total	42	33	13	12	100
#7					
# Letters	19	22	17	2	60
% Total	32	37	28	3	100
#8					
# Letters	12	10	4	1	27
% Total	45	37	14	4	100
Totals					
# Letters	191	105	58	26	380
% Total	50	28	16	6	100

Listeners' focus on FDR rather than his policy proposals indicates one way in which they were able to insert themselves into the narrative structure of the chats. FDR's message was one of community and common purpose. But the terms of this community were left open precisely to attract the attention of a diverse audience. It was FDR's persona that held this ambiguous, at times contradictory, message together. I have suggested that FDR adopted multiple roles in the chats. The public reaction mail indicates that listeners interpreted this role in their own way, appropriating FDR's persona to construct a personal understanding of community and their role within it.

For instance, some listeners saw the president as the second coming of George Washington or Abraham Lincoln, a father of his country ready to lead the nation out of its dire circumstances. To others, he was an "ordinary guy," a "friend," "one of us," a "real fellow," a man "not like those other men in the White House." Listeners described him as a "father" or a real "human" or as an "idol," a "superman," "a supreme being," a "gift from God," or a "Moses leading the nation out of the chaos of darkness." His image could be interpreted as at once a hero and a deity, a father and brother, a friend of the people and one who "encompasses all elements of man's social destiny"; to one letter-writer he seemed to be all of these things at once: a "President, Guide, Counsel, and Friend."[65]

Listeners could interpret the president in these diverse ways because, like any media character, his image circulated freely through media culture. Two twelve-year-old boys perfectly capture this when they write that "the other night we turned on the radio and found that you were speaking.... [W]e saw your picture in the Pathe News showing some of your visits ... and we have also seen you in the picture show...."[66] Like the films of movie stars, the chats were to a large extent vehicles for the projection of FDR's persona. Unlike TR or Wilson, FDR embraced this role. Indeed, he and his aides worked assiduously to ensure that he occupied this place in the public psychology. As a persona (rather than a model), FDR's image constituted a fungible currency through which listeners might construct a sense of community. For some, it was a political community; for others, a religious one; and for still others, it was a community in the image of the family. Rather than a homogeneous message of commonality then, FDR's depiction of himself and the public, and his frame of the Depression, were at least to some extent open to interpretation. Community could mean many different things. How listeners interpreted this message depended to some degree on how they interpreted FDR himself. Like media culture generally, FDR's chats worked because they were messages that could be fit into many different kinds of narratives constructed by listeners.

This is another way of saying that the form of FDR's performance mattered a great deal to his listeners and their constructions of the political community. What mattered most? Interestingly, simplicity and sincerity mattered. Two hundred and seven of the 380 letters in my sample (fifty-five percent) give some description of the chats. Thirty-three percent of the descriptions focused on FDR's "plain," "simple," style. "You spoke," many of these letters began, "in plain, everyday, humble English," "as man to man," in an "honest straight-from-the-shoulder message."[67] Others wrote of the chats as "plain" and "outward" talks that were examples of "forceful simplicity." They were "clear and lucid" speeches that, in the words of one man, did not "put the fodder too high on the racks."[68] For many letter-writers, the talks seem to have represented two things at once. On the one hand, the chats indicated, as one man put it, that "it is no longer the public be damned, but the public be informed." The public was now to be put "in the confidence" of the president, and not "talked down to." On the other hand, the talks were crafted on such simple terms that "even the lowly," "poor intelligences" and "foreign elements" could understand them.[69] The sense of speaking to both high and low in "good ordinary English" was taken by many listeners as an example of, in the words of one writer, "American sincerity." For years, another letter-writer wrote, "I had longed to hear an American talk like an American," a longing satisfied by the chats.[70]

This celebration of simplicity and plainness is rooted in a longstanding American preference for a "middling style" of political language.[71] However, it gained new meaning in the context of media culture. As Paddy Scannell argues, this middling style constitutes a "sociable" rhetoric that "transposes the norms of everyday interpersonal existence into public life." [72] This is to say, it transfers the "sociable" linguistic styles of interpersonal communication to mass mediated conversations. In so doing, it confuses a mode of address designed to speak to masses of people with more intimate, interpersonal forms of interaction—what Scannell calls a "for-anyone-as-someone" structure. In their concentration on such seemingly trivial qualities as the president's sincerity, letter-writers indicate how the chats made the public world *matter* for them personally, how that world had been put within their purview by the president's "sociable" mode of address. No president had ever before addressed a mass public in this for-anyone-as-someone style. By doing so, FDR quite literally invited his individual listeners to see their relation to public life in a new way.

Yet, having accepted this the critic might still respond that FDR *was acting*. That is, his rhetoric was practiced, preplanned to make listeners feel as if they were being drawn into public conversation. There is necessarily something artificial and dissembling about a rhetorical style that uses colloquial speech for manipulative ends. Moreover, there is something sinister in the fact that presidential communication became so closely entwined with a language that depended upon this illusion.

Two points can be made in response to this kind of accusation. First, listeners were necessarily distanced from FDR's appeal. Structurally, the public remained far removed from the production of the chats, and thus retained control over the moment of reception. While he worked hard to direct listeners to particular interpretations of the chats, FDR had little explicit control over their evaluations. Second, letter-writers were also keenly aware that the chats were performances. Letter-writers described the chats as "masterpieces," and "masterly essays," that composed "a new technique," or a new "kind of statesmanship." This technique inspired "hearty congratulations" and "applause" from his appreciative audience, who marveled at his "convincing tones," and "splendid radio voice." At times, letter-writers even referred to their letters as "fan mail" to the president. FDR himself was lauded as a "supersalesman" or "executive" whose messages would lead the country out of the Depression. Listeners clearly understood that FDR's appeal was practiced and preplanned. Contrary to vulgar forms of media criticism, FDR possessed little explicit control over how audiences interpreted his messages and his audiences were not dupes.

Still, it is at least a bit troubling to find that a majority of listeners interpreted the chats as sincere presentations. Of the 207 letters which offered descriptions of the chats, forty-six, or 22 percent, specifically used the word sincere. Another 21 letters described FDR himself in terms of sincerity, honesty or humanness. Sincerity is a quality of unfeignedness, of transparency and honesty. Letter-writers often turned to FDR's "plain words" as evidence that he was a "real, plain and honest ... fellow," or that his chats were "honest-minded," "heart-to-heart" talks.[73] They reported feeling a certain closeness to the president and his words, as if the psychological distance between them had been shortened. FDR, one man wrote of the first chat, "talked in terms of human understanding ... [that] has made him feel near to us all."[74] How is it that listeners could understand chats as performances and yet praise them as paragons of sincerity?

The letters offer only murky answers to this question. One possibility is that different reactions to the chats correlate with class distinctions. Perhaps wealthier, educated people focused more on the performative aspects of the chats while poorer, less educated people "bought in" to the performance and interpreted them as sincere and honest statements. Something like this interpretation has a long history in media studies.[75] With respect to letters written to FDR, Leila Sussman found that while middle and upper class people were more likely to write the president, less-educated letter-writers were more likely to write in the fan mail style.[76] My data lend some credence to this argument. In my sample, those who wrote fan-style letters were generally more emotionally effusive and less distanced from FDR's appeals. For instance, a woman wrote FDR to tell him "how greatly we all love and admire you for your splendid understanding and above all for your great humanity," and signed her letter, "One of your Friends."[77] Further, those who focused on FDR's technique often spoke in the tone of a disinterested observer. After describing chat #3 as a "masterful presentation," one man went on to suggest that such talks might form the "psychological basis for action that will solidify the masses of the people...."[78] Here, the letter-writer explicitly distances himself from the chat, assuming the role of someone who is not part of the "masses" and thus not in need of a psychological relationship with the president. While there is too little evidence in the letters to match these variables and types of responses precisely, something like this correlation may be at work.

However, many of the letter-writers in my sample exhibit an ability to hold contradictory beliefs simultaneously. This is to say, many listeners understood the chats *both* as performances and as sincere presentations. The same individual often described the chats as, in the words of one letter-writer, "masterly addresses" that also "thrilled" her with their tones of sincerity.[79] For these listeners, the chats were "gem[s], masterpiece[s] of a sort," that also had them listening with "the greatest fascination."[80] A man listening to chat #3 described it as a "masterpiece" that "was to us who are suffering the same as a cool shower of rain to a tortured land of aridness."[81]

Such examples indicate that the ambiguous nature of the chats may be doing important cultural work. In this regard, we might note that their curious blend of deception and realism has been a feature of American mass culture since the 1830s.[82] Of course, it has a much longer genealogy, stretching back to Western traditions of carnivalesque entertainment and still life painting. But in modern times it has been a signal element of American mass culture. Generally, historians explain its popularity as a form of "middle class play."[83] They mean by this that public discourse around episodes of deception was one way that middle-class urban Americans negotiated tensions that naturally arose from living among strangers in highly complex urban environments. We might understand FDR's chats in these terms. As a form of cultural play, performances of the kind FDR delivered in the chats seemingly cry out for verdicts. He was telling listeners what they wanted to hear! No, he was telling the truth! How one answered these questions was less important than the fact that they were debated and discussed. It was precisely through such discussion that listeners worked out the boundaries of truth in an ever-more complex mass society.

Something rather complex also emerged in the many expressions of feeling elicited by the chats. If anything is clear in the letters, it is that listeners responded to the chats with feeling. Indeed, they virtually ignored the policy information contained in the broadcasts. Of the 380 letters in my sample, 236 (62 percent) indicated some feeling toward the chats. Many of these reactions took the typical form of fan mail: "It [chat #3] so filled me with hope," one man wrote, "that I find it difficult to restrain from writing...." Others were "inspired," "filled with pride," "thrilled to the core," "moved to tears," and "spellbound."[84] Such reactions support the view that the chats were a highly personal, emotional form of communication that tended to arrest any inclination listeners might have had toward critical reflection of their message.

But letter-writers more often struggled to describe a collective rather than personal feeling in their letters. Of the 236 letters that indicated a feeling toward the chats, 75 percent discussed that feeling in collective terms as opposed to only 45 percent in terms of personal emotions. Radio figures prominently in these expressions of collective experience. "With thousands of other citizens of the country," one listener wrote, "I listened to your talk over the radio last night." Another wrote as "one of the millions of radio listeners." Though the experience of listening to the radio as part of a national audience was not new by 1932, listening to the president as part of this public did seem unique. A listener wrote that as she sat in front of her radio, she "kept thinking (in common with millions more) that is my president speaking, my president."[85]

Expressions like these indicate that listeners did not experience the chats solely as individuals in the privacy of their homes. Instead, they experienced a sense of listening along with others, of belonging to a larger whole. In some cases, the attribution of a collective feeling took the relatively simple form of the pronouns "we," and "us," as in, "*we* drank in every word," "*we* think as you think," "how thrilled *we* all were over your wonderful speech last night," "Your leadership—your personality, has aroused in *us* a feeling of patriotism and loyalty," and "*we* are all with you." (italics mine)[86] Others spoke in the voice of "the people" or "the public:" "People have gained courage and confidence"; "I am certain that the great mass of American people..."; "You may feel sure that the people of the nation are..."; and, "The people want this New Deal."[87]

At least in the interwar period, then, a time when people were first experiencing the sensation of being part of a simultaneously addressed mass audience, media culture produced a sense of commonness, not apathy. In their letters, listeners assumed the voice of the collective "we" not to confirm their homogeneity or apathy, but to assert a certain rhetorical power. Letter-writers faced a dilemma when they sat down to write the president: why should he take the time to read their letters? Some writers solved this problem by asking the president's secretary not to send their notes to him. These listeners wrote to express their feelings, nothing more. Others asked the president not to respond to their letters, the implication being that since no actual interaction with the president was expected, no justification for writing was necessary. However, the majority seem to have wanted the president to read their letters and respond to them. Why should he? In the chats FDR addressed individuals particularly and as part of a mass audience. Listeners responded in kind: as individuals and as embodiments of public sentiment.

Letter-writers expressed their representation of public opinion in two ways. On the one hand, they conceived of their letters as adding to the sum total of the actual opinions of many individuals: "I feel I must add my voice to the chorus of praises...." "I wish to add my appreciation to the many like expressions...." "May I add a word of appreciation and congratulation to those of the other hundreds of thousands...."[88] The rhetorical basis of such letters is their empirical accumulation. Alone, a single congratulation of a radio message is not likely to be very meaningful. Included with the praise of thousands, however, such letters gain rhetorical force. They are powerful precisely because they are part of a mass opinion.

On the other hand, letter-writers often employed a more complex notion of public opinion, one normally associated with elite use of the term. In his negotiations with other political elites, for instance, FDR often claimed that public opinion supported his positions. Such rhetorical manipulation of "the public" is not limited to elites. Many of the public reaction letters indicate that they were not so much feeling themselves to be part of a mass public as learning to talk in its terms, to manipulate and exercise its potential. One person claimed that, "My feelings are an echo of what the majority of the people in my section of Colorado feel." And another suggested his "utterance is not from me only as an individual citizen, for it is the potential, modest, still quiet voice within the thoughts and spirit of every living soul." Still another wrote confidently that just as he was "thrilled.... The whole country, I am sure, responded to your 'fireside address' in the same manner as I did."

Even those who did not enjoy the chat made claims of this kind: "I was disappointed in your talk ... and believe so were thousands of other people." Finally, such reactions sometimes veered into the Whitmanesque: "I am truly voicing the sentiment and trusting belief of multitudes...."[89]

In part, these statements illustrate the documentary point of view William Stott identifies as dominant in the 1930s.[90] Like filmmakers, reporters, and advertisers, these letter-writers are working from their inner selves outward, fashioning a public opinion out of their personal reactions and feelings. Their claim to legitimacy rests in the identification of their personal opinions with those of the masses. Too, these reactions demonstrate Warren Susman's claim that the 1930s were characterized by a new appreciation of and concern for the "American Way of Life."[91] According to Susman, Americans in the 1930s were more conscious of and interested in the nature of significant cultural patterns which tied individuals together. The effort to connect one's reactions with those of a mass public is in some sense an effort to identify oneself with such larger cultural patterns.[92]

But the Whitmanesque quality of the claim is also important. It is a strange thing to claim to speak for "multitudes," to carry an entire public's opinion within oneself. What can this rhetorical feat mean? In an essay on Walt Whitman—one of the most important of nineteenth-century American romantic writers—George Kateb argues that Whitman's writings elaborate a theory of democratic individualism. In "Song of Myself," Whitman writes that "what I shall assume you shall assume, / For every atom belonging to me as good belongs to you." Notice the similarity between this claim and those of FDR's letter-writers. Like Whitman, letter-writers suggest that what is inside them is also in others. Kateb interprets Whitman to mean that living in a democracy "encourages a certain recognition of likeness." We all have "potentialities," and as such we have the equal right to the recognition "granted by every individual to every individual."[93] Interpreted in this light, the claim to speak for multitudes is a claim of recognition: I recognize in myself a right to speak, to realize my potential as a bearer of public opinion, just as I recognize that right in others. It is, in other words, a claim to empathy with others as democratic citizens.[94] In addressing the public via the romantic realism of media language, FDR not only invited listeners as particular individuals to participate in civic life, he also encouraged them to recognize this right in others.

The general point I wish to make here is that FDR not only crafted the chats as forms of mass culture, but listeners interpreted them through this lens as well. The result was not privatism, apathy, or cynicism. Instead, the chats stimulated a vibrant bout of "sociability," and a sense that individuals could take charge of public affairs. References to conversations, debates and discussions instigated by the chats litter the letters. One individual wrote to describe the scene during the third chat: "There were between three or four hundred men in the room listening to what you had to say.... [W]hen it was ended I wandered from group to group exchanging a few words here and there to get their reaction." Another man described his "small sphere of action" in which he had several verbal conflicts with "men of selfish greed who make light of your so-called 'Brain-Trust.'" Still another wrote to inform the president that "the people of Buffalo with whom [he] came in contact [were] very pleased with [his] foresight and leadership." People wrote the president to describe conversations with family members and churchgoers; they wrote of "a large number of conversations with friends" and of news articles and editorials in local newspapers. They described speeches which they had given in response to the chats and outlined "argument[s] that we have to contend with [in] the opposition press and speakers...." In short, the chats inspired letter-writers to reflect upon their situation in common with others.[95]

The eruption of this national conversation gave letter-writers the sense that "something new and fine [was] taking place in American life." That something involved the creation of a new feeling, a feeling of being a citizen amid the masses, of being a mass citizen. Letter-writers expressed confidence that FDR's talks were instilling "in the minds of millions of people the confidence they have lacked," the confidence that their opinions and actions matter. Armed with a new standing in public life, letter-writers took responsibility for things that happened in the public sphere. They canvassed their communities, talked to their friends, people at the local grocery, and local business people, to gauge the tenor of public sentiment. One traveling businessman wrote FDR to express favorable opinions he had heard during his business trip in the East. Another wrote to inform the president that he "will keep [his] ears to the ground with 100% support." And still another notified the president that he was available to "to discuss [the] situation in the Central West at [FDR's] convenience."[96]

A faith in public opinion has always been a hallmark of American democracy. But never before had "mass opinion" seemed so tangible. Letter-writers expressed joy that the chats seemed to have swayed "the masses" to a new spirit of optimism. They were confident that these radio talks were having a "salutary and conservative influence upon the millions who heard [them]." They were "Happy to hear expressions of cooperation from everyone with whom I have come into contact...." And they reported to the president that "Everywhere [they heard] praise for [his] address."[97] Even when they were less certain of the prospects for FDR's success, they expressed these feelings in terms of mass opinion: "I am not so sure of the clear thinking of the masses as you are, but if anything will hold them against the fight to defeat you, it will be your personal talks over the radio." In short, letter-writers expressed a new sense of power in their role as a mass public: "The people are with you," one man concluded, "and what else matters?"[98]

Presidential Communication as Mass Culture

The conventional wisdom about the fireside chats is, in some sense, right. As instances of media culture, the chats were drenched with intimacy and emotion. But it was, as Clifford Geertz suggests of the Balinese cockfight, emotion put in the service of cognitive ends.[99] Just as the Balinese used sentimental performances to learn what it meant to be individuals living in their particular community, so Americans used the fireside chats to feel and to see themselves as part of a common political culture. Progressive presidents, of course, had sought the rhetorical keys to this transformation for two decades prior to FDR's ascension to the presidency. But while the intellectual sweep of their rhetoric was wide, its emotional register was narrow. Progressive presidential communication was rooted in the identities, values and worldview of the white, protestant, middle classes. As such, it was issued with a moral certitude that grated against modern sensibilities, and it romanticized leadership (in the guise of "character") rather than ordinary people. Progressive presidential rhetoric proved capable of inflaming the public, but it died out just as quickly, its staying power limited by its inability to resonate deeply with a heterogeneous mass public.

As instances of media culture, the chats proved more flexible. FDR addressed "you," and listeners had multiple vantage points from which to grasp FDR's image. These qualities opened the narrative structure of the chats to many different interpretations. Listeners as different as urban middle-class white women and rural African American male farmers could bring their own dispositions to the chats. Like the Balinese, listeners might have been stratified socially and economically, but they found in the chats a common feeling, a feeling of recognition, of being recognized and recognizing oneself as part of public life. FDR not only allowed this feeling to arise among his listeners, he praised it as the central source of recovery from the nation's problems. Those who gave themselves over to the feeling of collective bonding were transformed into the heroic protagonists of the president's romantic rendition of the Depression. The invitation proved irresistible to millions of Americans. Its appeal resonated with them precisely because it allowed them to fill out this feeling with assumptions and dispositions rooted in their own social experience. This is to say, it allowed them to "author" themselves in public life, but to do so on terms with which they were familiar and comfortable.

FDR's accomplishment has rightly won him great praise. Echoing many others, Bruce Miroff describes FDR as the most "democratic" of modern presidents, a man who provided an "inspiriting political education ... to teach new lessons in interdependence and national community."[100] Even his critics begrudgingly allow that FDR made a connection to the American public that has not been duplicated by subsequent presidents. This is not for want of trying. In every presidential archive from Truman to Bush, there no doubt exist memos from presidential aides exhorting their president to establish an intimate relationship with the public—like FDR achieved with the fireside chats.[101] Most presidents of the past half-century have tried some version of the chats, but none—not even the "Great Communicator" Ronald Reagan—have met with FDR's success. His chats have been much imitated, but never equaled.

We might ask, however, whether all this effort has not been misguided. The simple fact is that American public life in the interwar period was uniquely configured. Media culture had a public legitimacy it would lose in the post–World War II period. Its posture of romantic realism would change as new marketing and demographic techniques were innovated. For his part, FDR had a rhetorical freedom available only to presidents who occupy the office between the evaporation of one political regime and the constitution of another. In short, FDR makes for a poor barometer of modern presidential communication because the context of presidential communication changed considerably in the post–World War II period. Therefore, it is little use to fault modern presidents for failing to use media culture in the "democratic" manner of FDR. We will do better to ask how these presidents responded to the institutional environment they faced, and how they used the symbolic resources at their disposal. In other words, we would do better to understand the meaning of postwar presidential communication in its context.

Chapter Three

"It's a Technical Problem": Presidential Communication in a Culture of Expertise

WHEN CONSIDERING post-World War II presidential communication, it is worth beginning with the observation that the idea of the rhetorical presidency only gained currency in the 1980s.[1] Why is this useful? Because it gives us some sense of the concerns and conditions out of which the idea sprouted. The simple fact is that Ronald Reagan's ascension to the presidency prompted much of this work. The centrality of President Reagan's rhetoric to his political practice led scholars to seek out its larger meaning for the presidency. What could it mean that a president organized his entire presidency around his communication practices? As they sought answers, scholars quite naturally worked backward. Beginning from the premise that the rhetorical presidency culminated in Reagan's practices, they traced its origins to earlier periods and presidencies. With Hayden White, we might say that, modeled on Reagan's presidency, the idea of the rhetorical presidency came to serve as an important historical trope for the field.[2]

Such tropes do important work. As White observes, it is through such tropes that scholars organize historical events into a meaningful order. Where before presidencies might have seemed utterly distinctive, the rhetorical presidency links them together into a broader evolutionary process. We can now speak of progressive and modern presidents in the same breath. But such clarity and reach is bought at a price. Tropes like the rhetorical presidency push scholars toward some questions and issues—and not others. Ambiguities and differences within and across administrations risk becoming bleached by the light they shed. Tropes like these also tend to wrap history in a gauze of inevitability. President Reagan's practices, for instance, come to seem like the natural culmination of a long-term process in presidential communication. Given what came before, the rhetorical presidency can be made to seem inevitable.

Part of what I wish to do in this chapter is to struggle against this inclination. Modern presidential communication, of which Ronald Reagan's rhetorical practices were the preeminent exemplar, was neither natural nor inevitable. Rather, it arose out of a particular historical configuration, part and parcel of an institutional shift in American politics peculiar to the post–World War II years.[3] At this time, national politics became centered on a presidency-led administrative state ringed by a burgeoning array of interest groups, new kinds of political and media consulting organizations, and professional news organizations. Precursors of all of these developments can be found as far back as the late nineteenth century. But it was only in the postwar years that they came together to form a new institutional context for political life. And this context lent presidential rhetoric a distinctive meaning. As a culture of expertise grew within and around these institutions, presidential communication came to be understood in professional and rational (in the Weberian sense) terms.

Put another way, presidential communication came to be understood as a kind of crafted talk.[4] By crafted talk I mean to refer to a mode of communication preferred by the coterie of professional communicators— media and political consultants, pollsters, policy experts, and the like—who increasingly guided presidential communication in the postwar years. Heavily indebted to the new "science of communication" that emerged in American colleges and universities, crafted talk flowed from a specialized body of knowledge and practices. It contained, for instance, a new vocabulary for understanding the possibilities and purposes of presidential rhetoric. It ushered new techniques of persuasion, and new demographic technologies, into the practice of presidential communication. And, as it did these things, it conjured a new meaning for presidential rhetoric. No longer seen as an effort to model public opinion, or to cultivate a mass public in a flexible, mass mediated mode of address, modern presidential communication came to be understood as a form of opinion management. This sense of what it meant to "go public" had some similarities to the activities of earlier presidents. But its differences from prior notions of the rhetorical presidency were profound, and worthy of our attention.

In this chapter then, I describe and interpret the modern conception of presidential communication. I do so in the context of three case studies involving Presidents Eisenhower, Kennedy (JFK), and Reagan. In a comparison of Eisenhower's nationwide broadcasts to those of FDR, I demonstrate how very differently the two presidents imagined presidential rhetoric. I pay particular attention to the role of the Cold War in naturalizing the new, more managerial style of presidential communication. In an examination of President Kennedy's televised press conferences, I untangle the inner structure of crafted talk, and the role of modern news media in its dissemination. Close inspection of President Reagan's efforts on behalf of his 1986 Tax Reform proposal shows how crafted talk evolved as the institutional conditions of Washington politics began to change in the 1980s. As with the previous chapters, I begin with a brief review of the institutional context in which postwar presidential communication took shape.

Presidential Communication as Crafted Talk

Crafted talk, Lawrence Jacobs and Robert Shapiro tell us, is an effort to "use research on public opinion to pinpoint the most alluring words, symbols, and arguments in an attempt to move public opinion to support ... desired policies."[5] In the jargon of communication science, it is an effort to "frame" political issues in ways that "prime" others to support one's preferences. As Robert Entman has defined it, framing is the process of "select[ing] some aspects of a perceived reality and mak[ing] them more salient in a communicating text."[6] Seeking to control the policymaking process, presidents select attributes of issues that put their views in the best light. Their success does not depend upon changing the policy preferences of others. Rather, it hinges on their capacity to set the political agenda—to determine which issues are discussed and in what way. Ordinary citizens, for instance, may have many feelings or ideas about a particular issue. A frame works by activating, or priming, some of these ideas, feelings, and values rather than others.[7] Using syntax, themes, metaphors, scripts, and other building blocks of images and talk, modern presidents craft messages intended to control the policymaking agenda. This activity is the essence of modern presidential communication.

Described in this way, it is tempting to view crafted talk as a generic activity, one that is characteristic of all presidential communication—perhaps even all political communication. After all, in some sense, doesn't every president try to frame, prime, and set agendas? Isn't this what Theodore Roosevelt was up to in his swing the circle trips? Isn't this what FDR tried to accomplish in his fireside chats? Yes and no. While it is true that all presidential communication has a strategic dimension, its form and meaning, and thus its consequences, can vary considerably. The very fact that today professional observers talk about presidential communication in terms of "frames" and "agenda-setting," rather than, say, character and morality, sets it apart as a distinctive cultural activity. As a unique cultural construction, modern conceptions of "going public" have their roots in an institutional configuration peculiar to the post–World War II years. This configuration has been exhaustively described elsewhere, but it is worthwhile to set out its basic features here.

Perhaps the most important institutional change of the postwar years was that presidents became singularly powerful political figures. The presidency accrued some of this power informally: observers simply began to assume that the president *ought to* lead.[8] But much of it came as a consequence of legislative actions. Acting in response to recommendations by the Brownlow (1939) and Hoover (1947) Commissions, Congress extended the scope and reach of presidential power by giving presidents more influence over government departments and formerly independent regulatory agencies. After World War II, Congress created the Atomic Energy Commission and the National Security Council, putting both under the umbrella of the Executive Office of the President (EOP). The 1946 National Employment Act made the federal government, and the presidency in particular, responsible for the nation's economic growth. As Richard Neustadt and others have observed, the result of these actions was to change expectations for presidential activity. Henceforward, anyone occupying this office was expected to dominate the policy process. Modern presidents became responsible for, among other things, proposing yearly budgets, devising foreign policies, setting defense priorities, and creating domestic programs.

But to accomplish their goals, modern presidents had to navigate a denser and more complex Washington Community than existed before the war. Numbers give some sense of its new scale. From its relatively small size in 1932, the federal government grew by 1961 to consist of nine major departments, 104 bureaus, twelve sections, 108 services, fifty-one branches, 631 divisions, nineteen administrations, six agencies, four boards, six commands, twenty commissions, nineteen corps, and 2.5 million employees.[9] The numbers of political appointees in the top echelons of federal bureaucracies grew to between 500 and 600 positions by the mid-1970s.[10] The layers of job titles in the federal bureaucracies grew from seventeen in 1960 to thirty-three in 1992, an 88 percent increase.[11] The White House Office (WHO) itself saw a similar growth. WHO staff grew from a handful to 423 aides, and to 871 by 1993. Nearly every Washington political institution grew in parallel fashion. By 1992 there were over 7,000 lobbyists registered with the Senate, a jump of over 4,000 in fifteen years.[12] Numbers of Congressional staff grew as well. The greatest explosion occurred in the number of House members' staff, which jumped from 2,441 in 1957 to 6,114 in 1975. But Congressional staff increased across the board. For instance, Senate committee and subcommittee staff grew from 472 in 1962 to 1,120 in 1975, and the Congressional Research Service staff grew from 180 in 1960 to 703 in 1975.[13] The number of think tanks grew in Washington, D.C., from only a handful in 1970 to roughly 100 by the early 1990s.[14]

It was only in the 1940s that the modern, professional news media emerged as well. Professionalism meant more independence for journalists.[15] It meant that by and large they were better educated and better paid. But it also meant that they produced the news in a more consistent, cohesive, institutionalized manner. Released from the control of their editors and publishers, modern reporters nonetheless were immersed in a newsroom culture that rewarded those who hewed closely to its norms, practices, and routines. One of the most important of these norms was the use of sources. Journalists gained independence in large part by confining themselves to following the lead of institutional, especially government, officials.[16] During the 1970s, one scholar found that officials of the federal government composed just under half of the sources for front-page stories of the *New York Times* and *Washington Post*.[17] Among Washington sources, none were more important than the president.[18] This was especially true for network television reporters.[19] One content analysis of CBS News, for instance, has found that the network broadcast between two and three presidential stories a night through the 1960s and 1970s, reaching a peak of 4.5 stories per night during the Nixon administration.[20]

The picture painted by this brief description is of a managerial, news-mediated form of presidential communication. Policymaking became the preserve of highly educated experts, who as a group tended to see politics through a technocratic lens. As President Kennedy once put it, "Most of the [political] problems ... that we now face are technical problems, administrative problems. They are very sophisticated judgments which do not lend themselves to the great sort of 'passionate movements' which have stirred this country so often in the past."[21] This professional lens shaped how presidents came to view their rhetoric. As they entered office, modern presidents looked to implement their policy agenda. The principal problem they faced was managing the bureaucratic morass that politics had become. Truman and Eisenhower attempted to solve this problem by creating advisory committees and new public liaison staff members in the WHO.[22] But the agendas of interest groups and federal bureaucracies often varied greatly from that of the president, and attempts to exert more presidential control were as likely to fail as not. Moreover, even in the late 1950s and early 1960s the political system was moving toward Samuel Kernell's "individualized pluralism," meaning that leaders in institutions like Congress were beginning to lose their grip on the rails of power.[23]

In this environment, presidents preferred "going public" to achieve policy goals. Described in this way, one of the key distinctions of modern presidential communication becomes visible: *going public had little to do with the actual concerns and experiences of ordinary Americans*. Indeed, the new class of professional communicators who devised presidential rhetorical strategies held the average American in very low esteem. The first large-scale polls taken in the 1940s and 1950s seemed to confirm what intellectuals had suspected for some time: the public was at best severely uninformed and at worst irrational.[24] Pollsters found that citizens had little understanding of the issues, or the candidates' stands on them, and that they projected their own views onto their representatives.[25] Scholars like Joseph Schumpeter appropriated Walter Lippmann's argument that, given the public's irrationality, politics was best conducted by professional politicians and bureaucratic experts.[26] Pluralists like David Truman and Robert Dahl argued that politics should be conceived not as a rational discussion of issues by individual citizens, but as a system of bargaining between motivated interest groups.[27] Because individuals belonged to a variety of groups, and not every issue was important to every group, individual participation in the political process was necessarily sporadic and limited. On this view, the lack of citizen participation was a natural result of the nature of politics and of group behavior. In the political imagination of the postwar administrative state, the public played a subordinate role.[28] One can debate whether or not the public had ever been truly sovereign in American politics. It is clear though, that in the postwar period, it was, at best, "semi-sovereign."[29]

Increasingly then, to frame their rhetoric, presidents found themselves turning to cultural resources that *were* highly valued in this environment, namely, expertise, professionalism, and management. Of course, professionalism had been an element of American politics since the 1830s. FDR had a stable of such people working in his administration from its beginning. But it was only in the postwar era that professionalism became the *sine qua non* of presidential politics. From Eisenhower forward, one sees a gradual, but seemingly inexorable movement of political and media consultants, speechwriters and pollsters, public relations and advertising experts into the field of presidential communication.[30] Compared to the progressives, this group has little faith in the power of morality to solve public issues. If asked, they would likely view the organic vision of the nation held by TR and Wilson as little more than superstition. They might praise FDR's public appeals, but more for its result than its form. And they certainly would loathe the relative inefficiency of his operations, and the lack of control he and his aides exercised over the communication process. In their hands, presidential communication became the output of one set of very highly trained professionals worrying about, engaging with, and speaking to other highly trained professionals. It became, in other words, a form of crafted talk.[31]

To set crafted talk apart as a distinctive form, it is useful to briefly compare it to progressive presidential communication. In this regard, the most obvious difference is that crafted talk is thoroughly professional. This quality distinguishes modern presidential talk in several ways. For example, crafted talk is produced by many individuals (speechwriters, consultants, political aides, policy experts) within bureaucratic organizations. Of course, presidents have used speechwriters since the founding.[32] But before the presidency of FDR, presidential speechwriting tended to be idiosyncratic. Theodore Roosevelt "rolled his own," as he sometimes put it. He spent the summer of 1907 writing the six speeches that he would deliver during his Fall "swing-the-circle" down the Mississippi River. Similarly, Woodrow Wilson kept a typewriter in the Oval Office and personally typed all of his speeches, even the comments he made during his press conferences. Once FDR broke the taboo against openly using speechwriters, presidential talk increasingly became more bureaucratized, and thus more uniform. That is, it became less characteristic of the person and more of the Office.[33] It also became a specialized body of knowledge in itself. Practices and techniques of presidential communication began to be codified, genres, guidelines, and rules to be imprinted. They were combined with practices and insights of a science of communication that had emerged in the academy during the postwar years.[34] Professional communicators, for instance, learned of the value of simplicity and repetition in presidential appeals. They learned more about how individuals process political messages, and thus, how to use words and phrases to activate particular responses. They learned more about demographic groupings; using focus groups and other devices, they learned how words, phrases and themes might "play" across these groups. Politicians in every era have some sense of the importance of these principles. But, in the postwar period they became systematized into a body of knowledge held and used by a class of professional communicators.[35] As new presidents assumed office, this body of knowledge itself began to shape expectations for how presidents ought to speak. Finally, professionalism meant that presidential speech became more impersonal. TR and Wilson saw the bully pulpit as an opportunity to display personal character. And they took journalistic efforts to portray them in sensational or entertaining ways as a personal affront. Today, such personal reactions are relatively more rare. Though they often smart at press treatment, at some level presidents now accept that journalists are only "doing their job," just as reporters view presidential speech in the same light.

Crafted talk is also a more situational form of rhetoric. Imbued with a sense of the nation as an organic entity, progressive presidents sought to identify universal values and themes. For instance, whatever the initiative, TR always framed his policies in terms of a bedrock set of moral verities: character, efficiency, duty. He saw such qualities as intrinsically American, as the "heart" of the nation. Any "good" policy, on this view, must necessarily conform to these fundamental truths. Modern crafted talk has lost this holistic, organic image of the nation. It is true that a president like Reagan appeals to similar moral verities. But even with Reagan audiences were seen not as part of a collective whole. Excepting the occasional national address, most of Reagan's speeches were targeted to demographic groups with discrete, often competing interests. In such a context, Reagan was more apt to shape moral verities to the requirements of a particular piece of legislation or audience. Using polls, focus groups, and other research instruments, modern presidents search for the themes, symbols, and words that will resonate with particular demographic groups. Crafted talk is thus a more psychological rhetorical form than progressive presidential communication.[36]

In all of these ways, both institutional and cultural, crafted talk lends the rhetorical presidency a distinctive meaning. "We expect," famous PR man Edward Bernays stated confidently in 1947, "our elected government officials to try to engineer our consent...."[37] Bernays was perhaps one of the more hyperbolic proponents of the new view, but his language struck a cultural nerve peculiar to the postwar context.

"Fulfilling the Needs of a Great Industrial Organization": *Eisenhower's Fireside Chats*

Given this description of crafted talk, one is tempted to ask: how did it ever gain public legitimacy? After all, historically the United States has been steeped in democratic—even populist—sentiments. How did a form of rhetoric with such contrasting implications for public life ever become accepted? The answer, I think, lies with the Cold War. Managerial forms of mass communication had been increasingly common in American politics since the turn of the century. But they never seemed as neutral, as ordinary, or as inevitable as they became during the Cold War. Certainly, a few commentators worried about the new presidential penchant for managing public opinion. But as a pervasive presence in American culture, the Cold War bestowed an authority and legitimacy on crafted talk it would not otherwise have obtained.[38]

Dwight D. Eisenhower worried less than many others—he was a dedicated cold warrior with an interest in public relations—but he was not the most ardent advocate of the new vernacular.[39] Not only did he dislike the extremism of anticommunist conservatives like Joseph McCarthy, he was suspicious of militarization and worried about the Cold War's effect on the nation's core democratic principles. He sought, as he put it during the 1952 presidential campaign, a "middle way." As a moderate in extreme times, Eisenhower's experience is instructive. Most importantly, it shows just how far the Cold War moved the middle (the average or ordinary) of presidential communication. Eisenhower was no extremist, but he often found himself adopting extreme views, if only to counter his critics. He worried about public hysteria, yet fanned its fears when it suited his purposes. He hailed the resourcefulness of ordinary Americans, but approached his communication with a determination to engineer public consent for his policies. His nationwide speeches were commonly labeled "fireside chats," yet they assumed a very different stance toward the public from Roosevelt's original renditions.[40]

Ironically, for someone so instrumental in ushering in new forms of presidential communication, Eisenhower personally shied away from the spotlight. He had to be convinced by aides to hold regular press conferences.[41] He disliked television, insisting that he didn't "like to do this sort of thing. I can think of nothing more boring for the American public than to have to sit in their living rooms for a whole half hour looking at my face on their television screens."[42] And he generally believed that communicating with the public was less important than negotiating with legislators. "I think it is fair to say," he once wrote to a friend, "that in this situation, only a leadership that is based on honesty of purpose, calmness and inexhaustible patience in conference and persuasion, and refusal to be diverted from basic principles can, in the long run, win out."[43]

But he held a longstanding fascination with the uses of propaganda and public relations in foreign affairs. "I don't know much about psychological warfare," he said during the war, "but I want to give it every chance."[44] In office, he placed psychological warfare at the heart of his Cold War strategy.[45] He replaced Truman's Psychological Warfare Board with an Operations Coordinating Board (OCB), making it an arm of the National Security Council, created the United States Information Agency, and in National Security Council Memorandum 5412/1-2, mandated "covert operations ... propaganda, political actions ... deception plans and operations" by the CIA.[46]

Occasionally, these propaganda operations bled directly into domestic politics, as when Eisenhower delivered his famous "Chance for Peace" and "Atoms For Peace" speeches.[47] More generally, their tenor suffused the president's domestic initiatives. Just as he relied upon media professionals like C. D. Jackson to wage psychological warfare abroad, Eisenhower relied upon media professionals like William E. Robinson and Siguard Larmon to advise him on domestic political communications. These men advised Eisenhower to approach domestic political communication with, as Larmon once put it, "the same careful planning and strategy as you and your staff employed in setting up the invasion of Normandy."[48] Throughout his presidency, Eisenhower turned to media professionals to create media "invasions" in response to domestic crises: from his battles with Congress over the Bricker Amendment to desegregation.[49] He even toyed with the idea of creating a "Board of Strategy"—a domestic version of the Psychological Strategy Board—asking, among others, William Paley (president of CBS), Raymond Rubicam (president of the PR firm, Young & Rubicam), and Larmon to serve as its head.[50]

Most of these activities were kept secret, indicating that, as with any invasion, deception was central to their success. And many did not involve Eisenhower's direct participation. But, Eisenhower's aides knew that his public popularity was a critical weapon in the administration's policy battles, and they constantly searched for forums and formats in which he might address the nation. Almost inevitably then, Eisenhower found himself drawn into his administration's public relations campaigns. Televised addresses to the nation came to be his staple forum.[51] The precedent, of course, was Franklin Roosevelt's fireside chats. Having watched Roosevelt use the chats to his political advantage, Eisenhower's aides immediately grasped the potential of television. As Henry Cabot Lodge put it, Eisenhower was to become "our first television President, just as Roosevelt was our first radio

President...."[52] But Eisenhower brought to television a very different sensibility than Roosevelt brought to radio. Exploring these differences reveals the nature and significance of the transition to modern presidential communication.[53]

Eisenhower's performative skills were something less than FDR's, and his success in mimicking the original chats was uneven. Characteristically, he hired actor Robert Montgomery as a television consultant in late 1953 when it became apparent that his early efforts were less than stellar. Still, there was much in Eisenhower's addresses that resonated with FDR's original chats. Like FDR, Eisenhower sometimes spoke in personal pronouns, referring to himself as "I" and "me," and addressing the public as "you" and "we." He often used anecdotes and homely examples to demonstrate a complicated point. "The whole matter," he once said of the federal budget, "is rather like buying C.O.D."[54] He sought to project a kind of persuasive intimacy, casting his critics as unreasonable just as he spoke to his viewers in personal tones. "You will hear people talking [about unemployment]," he said on one such occasion, "But these people who look on ... so gloomily never say to you that there are more than 60 million people today gainfully employed in the United States...."[55] If his addresses rarely reached the performative heights of the original fireside chats, one can at least see a family resemblance. Indeed, the resemblance was close enough that most commentators simply accepted that Eisenhower's addresses were something like FDR's appeals.

However, examined more closely, these similarities pale in comparison to the significant differences between the broadcasts. The most dramatic difference lay in the narrative structure of Eisenhower's speeches. Recall that in his chats FDR conjured a romantic narrative in which a heroic public—in concert with its president—waged battle against corrupt politicians and businessmen. The Cold War narrative imagined by Eisenhower's speeches was no less romantic. If anything, good and evil were drawn even more starkly in his addresses. "We live," Eisenhower told his viewers, "in an age of peril." Nothing less was at stake than "the preservation of freedom" itself. The United States found itself under attack by "an aggressive communism, an atheistic doctrine that believes in statism as against our conception of the dignity of man, his equality...." It was, Eisenhower concluded, a "struggle of the ages."[56]

But the characters involved in Eisenhower's romantic Cold War tale were decidedly different. Eisenhower wove a story in which heroic *institutional* figures—scientists, military personnel, policymakers—waged battle, in concert with their president, against the forces of evil. Eisenhower argued that the nation's security was ensured by his "associates," men and women who had given "national planning careful, personal study and analysis," and come to "the best composite judgment available for the fulfillment of our security needs." He suggested that a "stronger and better America" was to be created by "public servants," whom he cast as people of "unimpeachable honesty and decency and dignity."[57] Unlike in Roosevelt's chats, in which the public was the main protagonist, institutional actors claimed center stage in Eisenhower's addresses. "My friends," Eisenhower reassured his viewers, "we have ... a Government that is ready to act whenever necessary...." Where FDR identified the confidence of the American people as the wellspring of progress, Eisenhower told his viewers that "One of the most important things ... is the attitude of your Government."[58]

The president sat at the center of the institutional world conjured by Eisenhower's addresses. "To this office," Eisenhower told his audience, "there comes every day from all parts of the land ... a steady flow of dispatches, reports and visitors.... On the basis of this information, decisions, affecting all of us, have to be made every day.... Your President ... must make [these] decisions...." Like his expert aides, Eisenhower made these decisions by "stud[ying] every detail" of bills written by government experts; weighing the "facts," consulting with authorities, and making considered judgments. "In this overall conviction," he stated to his viewers on one occasion, "I am supported by the mass of the best military opinion I can mobilize, and by scientific and every other kind of talent that is giving its attention to a problem to which I personally have devoted a lifetime." Sometimes, he opposed proposals because they contradicted the national interest. Other times, he was disappointed in the progress of government programs, but not for himself: "when I am disappointed, I mean I am disappointed for all of us—160 million people."[59]

The public played a limited role in Eisenhower's imagined world. It remained "alert and informed." It was "vigilant" and "diligent," expressed "patience," "dedication," "self-restraint," and "self-discipline." It considered government as a provider of services and weighed policy proposals with a concern for its self-interest. Most often, the public worried; it expressed frustration and panic at Soviet threats to its security. Its feelings occasionally veered toward hysteria, leading Eisenhower to counsel self-discipline and restraint.[60] At times, it appeared as if the public was little more than a stumbling block to government objectives. At others, it served as a Greek

Chorus, providing background noise and commentary, and at still others it stood as a passive audience to the main action, responding to but not fundamentally altering the events.

At no time did Eisenhower open his speeches to the social experience of his viewers. Rather than engage his viewers by inviting them into his imagined world, he used language in a way that distanced them from the political process. This is evident in a number of ways. For instance, Eisenhower tended to use a language of rationality.[61] If the most common word in FDR's speeches was "you," in Eisenhower's addresses it was "facts." Eisenhower was always concerned to "state the facts," to "give you a few more facts," and to "face the facts." It is with facts that policymakers "plan," "study," "calculate coldly," and reach "judgments." And it is only as these professionals are armed with the facts that they "watch vigilantly," "oppose unsound proposals," and generally serve as a "great bulwark" for democracy.[62] In contrast to the ability of experts to understand and coordinate government policy, Eisenhower routinely implied that government was too complex for average individuals to understand. "I can talk only about a few essential facts in this [tax] program," Eisenhower told his audience, "because ... this 900 page book is the new tax program, and this 500-page book is the explanation made by the Ways and Means Committee of the House of Representatives...." On another occasion, he alerted his viewers that he would talk about the federal budget only from an "overall viewpoint ... [because] the budget now before Congress is huge."[63] Finally, Eisenhower sought to distill his messages in simple, repetitive slogans. As members of Siguard Larmon's staff put it to the president at one meeting, "the techniques of the [advertising] trade of simplification—and repeating and repeating—[were] necessary...." Or, as Larmon counseled the president on another occasion, the president needed to distill his policies into "a symbol, theme or slogan ... [one] that should be easily defined and easy to remember...." Larmon suggested the theme of "strength."[64] This never became the administration's official slogan. But Eisenhower nonetheless tried it out in at least one speech: "The administration took over ... determined [to implement] a very broad program for strengthening America, strengthening it at home ... and making certain that it would be stronger internationally...." On another occasion he organized his speech in support of a labor bill around the catch phrase, "I want that sort of thing stopped. So does America."[65]

This language tended to make Eisenhower's addresses much less fluid and flexible than FDR's chats. For instance, Eisenhower usually referred to viewers not as an ambiguous "you," but as the "good American." He described the "good American" in some detail. This "American" did not "ask for favored position or treatment ..." and was "proud to carry his share of [the] national burden." He displayed a "spiritual strength" and "values" that linked him with every other American, "surmount[ing] any division [among Americans] of whatever kind...." By lauding the positive attributes of the good American, Eisenhower evidently hoped that his viewers would identify with this construct. Inhabiting this role, Eisenhower told his viewers, was to become part of "the greatest force that God has ever allowed to exist on His footstool."[66] It was also, not surprisingly, to practice the patience, discipline, and restraint preferred by the Eisenhower administration.

To reinforce his message of discipline, Eisenhower cloaked himself in the majesty of his office. "Tonight," he began a speech on events in the Middle East, "I report to you as your President." As the "President," Eisenhower talked on behalf of the "government" and his "administration," which together composed the national "viewpoint." As the government's representative, Eisenhower communicated its "convictions" and "principles," its "policy," and "positions." Eisenhower wanted his audience to recognize him not as an individual, but as the institutional voice of the federal government, a position that lent power and authority to his words. "To make this talk," he told his audience at the outset of his speech on Little Rock, "I have come to the president's office in the White House. I could have spoken from Rhode Island, where I have been staying recently, but I felt that, in speaking from the House of Lincoln, of Jackson, and of Wilson, my words would better convey ... the firmness with which I intend to pursue [my] course...."[67] If viewers were reluctant to practice self-restraint and discipline of their own accord, perhaps they would do so at the behest of the most powerful individual in the country—the president.

Taken together, Eisenhower's speeches worked to manage rather than to engage public opinion. They reassured and placated: your government, Eisenhower repeated time and again, is in control. And they legitimized: my policies, Eisenhower implied, are based on facts and cold calculations. But, in doing these things they tended to refract rather than reflect public opinion. Rational language and repetitive phrases deflected viewers' attention on to the alternately genial and authoritative personality of the president. In some sense, FDR achieved something similar in the fireside chats. But FDR also opened his chats to the social experience of his listeners in a way that linked them to a shared imagined public life. Concerned more with management than engagement, Eisenhower's addresses did not take this crucial step. The result was a political process symbolically sealed off from the collective imagination of average Americans.

Nothing in this narrative structure—the flattery of institutional representatives, especially the president; the concern for facts and administration; the diminution of the public in national affairs—is especially surprising. It conforms to social trends stretching back at least a hundred years to the rise of the organizational society and the emergence of the presidency as a primary institution in national politics. If it refuses the progressive stress on organicism, it at least partially fulfills the progressive dream of placing public life in the hands of professional experts. Being the first "organization president," it was natural that Eisenhower framed national life in ways that emphasized the role of professional managers like himself. For instance, he often talked of establishing "an effective public relations position," that involved "a task not unlike the advertising and sales activity of a great industrial organization. It is first necessary to have a good product to sell; next it is necessary to have an effective and persuasive way of informing the public of the excellence of that product."[68] This language seems perfectly compatible with the "organization man" of whom Eisenhower was an exemplar. As a political scientist remarked at the time, Eisenhower's style of leadership was a "trend of the times—the Organization Man in control; the spirit of teamsmanship, cooperation, and coordination ... the attitude of the professional administrative manager...."[69]

All the same, the implications of crafted talk for American democracy were so profound, one might have expected more protest—or at least more worrying—among commentators and critics. During the first half of the twentieth century, manipulative styles of presidential communication sometimes emerged—especially during the world wars—but they were accompanied by a steady stream of criticism. This criticism did not necessarily stem the tide of presidential propaganda, but it did make room for alternative rhetorical forms. By the 1950s, this criticism was severely muted, making presidential communication more uniform and homogeneous. It is true that a few commentators worried about the rise of a "power elite" in American politics.[70] Others noted that Eisenhower's use of public relations transformed public policy into a kind of salesmanship.[71] But these were relatively few in number.

Their relative paucity indicates how strongly the Cold War defined the meaning of modern presidential communication, setting new boundaries of appropriateness and legitimacy. A column by James Reston of *The New York Times* illustrates how the Cold War shaped mainstream response to

Eisenhower's addresses.[72] Reston was a constant thorn in Eisenhower's side throughout his eight years in office. In May, 1956, Reston wrote a column that alluded to events just before the Soviets launched *Sputnik*, but after *Brown v. Board of Education*. Reston described the setting in the terms of Cold War assumptions. On the international front, he saw an entire corpus of issues linked to the Cold War: "disarmament, the problem of foreign aid, the rising clamor in Asia for American assistance, the decline in the North Atlantic Treaty, uprisings in Africa...." Reston worried that "Extremists ... have tended to dominate the news and [threaten to] overwhelm ... moderates." Presidential leadership, Reston argued, was of paramount importance. In particular, the president ought to communicate with the public. "At no time," Reston wrote, "since the end of the last war has there been a greater need now for a presidential explanation of the terrible dilemmas facing the people and their Government." In line with the cultural sensibility of the time, Reston viewed communication as a crucial weapon in the current "war of images." But not just any form of communication. Press conferences were the "wrong forum" because they could not be controlled. Instead, Reston urged the president to conduct "fireside chats" with the public. These televised addresses were preferable to news conferences because they could be "carefully prepared ... controlled and directed to the mood of the time...." This is to say, they could be crafted with all the precision of strategic models of communication, and in their precision they might allow the president to manage the terrible dilemmas facing the country.

In Reston's column, one finds a basic Cold War view used as justification for more—not less—presidential crafted talk. The United States was engaged in an international struggle for freedom. The stakes of this struggle were so high, Reston assumed, that Eisenhower ought to use every weapon at his disposal to wage it. That is, Reston argues that Eisenhower ought to employ more crafted talk—not less—*because* the Cold War demands it.[73] In Reston's view, the problem with Eisenhower's communication was not its deviation from a classical democratic vision of American politics, but that it *was not doing enough* to manage public opinion. In the context of the Cold War, Eisenhower's "middle way" of opinion management seemed inadequate to his critics because it did not do enough to harness the public more tightly to the government's purposes. Both conservatives and liberals were unanimous in this indictment. It began early in 1953 and continued throughout Eisenhower's eight years in office. Conservatives indicted Eisenhower for not attacking the New Deal just as liberals called him "Mr. Get-Along" for failing to expand it.[74] After only six months in office, *The Nation* accused the president of "vanishing" because "he has had less and less to say and what he has said has been less and less interesting."[75] Just weeks later *The New Republic* claimed that Eisenhower "had reached his point of no return. Either he takes leadership now or loses it for good."[76] Criticisms only got worse as events unfolded. On McCarthy, the president was tarred from the Left for not speaking out against him and derided on the Right for not supporting him.[77] When the Soviets launched *Sputnik*, elites of every political stripe issued a collective protest at the president's inability to "stand up" to the Communists. And when the Arkansas Governor refused a Federal judicial order to desegregate public schools, Eisenhower was lambasted for not leading public opinion more strongly on issues of race.[78] "He has never sought to influence," one columnist said of Eisenhower, "He has never brought his prestige to bear on … Congressional leaders…. He has refused to act as a politician or as a statesman or as a spokesman for the national conscience."[79] To his critics, Eisenhower failed not because his methods were undemocratic, but because they were weak.

These criticisms register a complicated cultural terrain. Critics clearly accepted that the "age of peril" required presidential use of crafted talk. Most, after all, were the very type of expert that Eisenhower's speeches flattered. This led them to ignore the antidemocratic implications of the president's rationalistic, institutional rhetoric. At the same time, his critics wanted the president to be more vocal, to engineer consent in a more strenuous manner. Worried by the success of extremists, they counseled the president to become an extremist in favor of moderation—to use extreme techniques on behalf of moderate principles. A third vaguely articulated sensibility swirled around these others: that presidential decisions ought to be more visible. This notion was a faint echo of the classical democratic vision: if the public was no longer required to participate in political decision making, those decisions, Eisenhower's critics maintained, ought at least to be publicly visible. It was particularly embraced by journalists, who disliked Eisenhower's inclination to ignore them. Taken together, these criticisms confronted Eisenhower with a complicated equation. He was being counseled to be restrained, disciplined, and professional, but also to be vigorous and energetic—and to reach this balance in full public view.

Given this complicated amalgam, the frustration Eisenhower expressed about reactions to his communication practices seems understandable. "I know how good I could make myself look," he told his advisers, "everyone who's yapping now would be cheering ... if only I would do my 'leading' in public—where they could see me.... [W]ell, I can't do that...." To a friend, he lashed out at the "table-pounding, name-calling methods that columnists so much love," because in his mind they were "normally futile."[80] On his view, he and his aides ought to be left alone to do their jobs. One practiced moderation by being moderate—not by adopting extreme measures on behalf of moderation. And the danger of the times demanded secrecy. The more he invited the public into his decision-making process, he believed, the more he revealed to the enemy.

This bickering ensued throughout Eisenhower's eight years in office. It throws into relief the meaning of presidential communication conjured by the assumptions and expectations of crafted talk. Despite their disagreements, Eisenhower and his critics shared a set of basic assumptions. They agreed, for instance, that communication was important to the policymaking process, and that institutional actors ought to wage a "war of words"; they agreed that engineering public consent was crucial to political success; and they agreed that public participation in the policymaking process was unnecessary. Moreover, in sharing these assumptions they reached consensus on one other: even if the means at their disposal were not strictly democratic, the ends—preserving democracy in the United States and the rest of the world—justified their use. These were widely shared "facts" that defined the meaning of "going public" throughout the modern period.

Eruptions of disagreement between this and prior understandings of presidential communication, especially progressive interpretations, were generally muted. Progressive critics were labeled unscientific, idealist, and lacking in intellectual rigor. Disagreements within the new Cold War common sense were more public and sustained. Were there limits to the means that could be justified by Cold War ends? How was one to respond to the extremism of the Cold War within its terms? What did it mean to be responsive to the public in an imagined world dominated by professional political elites? How could the president discharge his obligations, yet do so in a way that remained publicly visible? Eisenhower and his critics did battle within the boundaries of this Cold War frame.[81]

To contemporary eyes, a president who launched waves of international and domestic public relations campaigns and who pioneered nearly every television format used in politics today hardly seems passive. But to Eisenhower's critics, the president's restraint could look like passivity when viewed against a background of an "age of peril." Indeed, compared to the histrionics of the extremists, Eisenhower seemed like a wallflower. Thus, it is against the backdrop of the Cold War that we can understand how crafted talk gained legitimacy. In an age of peril, political elites accepted crafted talk as necessary and even ordinary. Compared to all-out nuclear war, a little propaganda and public opinion management could be seen as correct, even responsible, policies. At the same time, the professional style of crafted talk made Cold War extremism more objective and neutral. The Cold War did not cause the rise of crafted talk. That distinction lies with a broader organizational shift in American politics. It did, however, lend crafted talk legitimacy.

The Dramatic Theater of JFK's Televised Press Conferences

Sitting in his assigned seat (second row center) on January 25, 1961, waiting for President Kennedy's first televised presidential press conference to begin, Chalmers Roberts recalls thinking what must have been on the minds of many reporters in the room: that "a new era of political communication" had begun.[82] Roberts' observation was something of an exaggeration. In a strict sense, JFK's live televised press conferences were merely an extension of Eisenhower's format for meeting reporters.[83] Eisenhower went so far as to televise his press conferences on a tape-delayed basis. JFK took the next step and made them live broadcasts. At the same time, there *did* seem to be something different about JFK's news meetings. The physical space in which JFK held his press conferences, a newly constructed State Department Annex, gives some sense of the transformation. Eisenhower conducted his news meetings with little regard for the television cameras. Usually, he stood before a desk in the Indian Treaty Room at the White House. In contrast, JFK stood on a platform six feet above the floor in an auditorium-sized room specifically designed for television. Where Eisenhower often relaxed by leaning against the desk with arms folded, JFK never strayed from behind a lectern adorned with the presidential seal. Eisenhower stood very close to reporters who sat in a disorganized pattern of wooden chairs. JFK looked down on reporters who sat in eight hundred plush, reclining chairs, the first few rows of which were assigned to the elite press. Cameras were positioned at odd angles in the back and sides of the Indian Treaty Room. In the State Department Annex, a special area was carved out of the middle rows for two cameras, and two other cameras were positioned at either end of these rows. During JFK's meetings, huge boom mics loomed over the seats to capture reporters' questions. Diffused television lighting lit the chairs in a subdued glow, while more harsh lights were directed at the podium standing center stage on the platform. Network executives overlooked the scene in special, glass-encased rooms above the back of the auditorium.

Another way of saying this is that JFK's news meetings were made for television. Unlike Eisenhower's news meetings, JFK's were organized for the cameras, not for reporters in attendance. This gave the meetings the feel of a Hollywood production more than a presidential press conference. *Time* magazine called them "show-biz conferences," and *The Nation*'s media critic Ted Lewis suggested that they were more about the projection of JFK's image than about informing the public. Russell Baker wrote that in his news meetings Kennedy seemed a "new star with tremendous national appeal and the skill of the consummate showman."[84] In his weekly radio broadcast, Alistair Cooke described Kennedy's first press conference as "dramatic theater" with a "disturbing hint of Hollywood about it."[85]

Understandably, reporters were unenthusiastic about the new format. Many agreed with James Reston that they were the "goofiest idea since the hula hoop."[86] Much of their consternation stemmed from longstanding expectations they held about their meetings with the president. Reporters imagined these meetings as a singular opportunity to query the president, the preeminent source of Washington news. "For one intense moment," Robert Pierpoint recalls thinking that the presidential press conferences allowed "the reporter and the President to spar one-on-one."[87] By speaking more to the camera than to reporters, Kennedy threatened this institution. Reporters sometimes blamed themselves for allowing the president to get away with this breach of tradition. In a memoir, Tom Wicker confesses that the press did not put Kennedy "under as close and searching scrutiny as it should have." Chalmers Roberts submits that he, like other newsmen, "was too readily captivated by the Kennedy charm." Almost defensively, Helen Thomas suggests that reporters did not press Kennedy because "he was one of us; that is, one of our generation—the first president born in the twentieth-century."[88] More often, however, they blamed Kennedy and his aides for turning their cherished institution in to a staged drama. "Reporters became spear carriers," Peter Lisagor recalls of JFK's news meetings, "in a great televised opera. We were props in a show, in a performance.... We were simply there as props."[89] With Lisagor, many reporters felt powerless to prevent the president from using television to bypass them and speak directly to the public. Feeling so powerless, many stopped asking questions or taking notes at the news meetings; eventually, they stopped attending altogether.

There is something to the reporters' complaints. JFK lost few opportunities to use TV to enhance his personal image as a glamorous, can-do manager of the public's business.[90] At the same time, this view substantially distorts the meaning of these news meetings. Put simply, TV did not give JFK—or subsequent presidents—unmediated access to the American public. Indeed, examined closely, it is apparent that much of JFK's talk in these news meetings was not even intended for the home audience.[91] The president's press conferences were made for TV, but, as it entered into American politics, the medium was enveloped in the assumptions and expectations of a wider practice of crafted talk. Even on TV, JFK's talk was still pitched to specific constituencies, which, if they weren't overseas, were generally located in Washington, D.C. In line with the rational nature of crafted talk, the president usually stuck to a carefully developed script that stressed key facts, details or terms, not the expression of personal charisma. Reporters played a crucial role as mediators of the president's talk, giving over their news columns to parsing and disseminating his words. And all of this activity went on between JFK, reporters, and other political actors—not between the president and the public. JFK's press conferences then, may have been "dramatic theater"; but they were dramas played out by a political class in Washington, D.C., not Hollywood.

Consider, for instance, that Kennedy's news meetings received more coverage than that of any prior presidential press conference.[92] Despite the fact that he conducted only about one-third the number of press conferences as Franklin Roosevelt, JFK's news meetings garnered nearly the same total number of front-page column inches.[93] In my sample, Kennedy's press conferences drew an average of three stories per conference. (see Table 3.1)[94] More strikingly, these news meetings captured the right hand lead (RHL), traditionally the most important news story of the day, in 101 of the 160 front pages (or just under two-thirds of the total). At one level, these numbers demonstrate the extent to which reporters followed their journalistic routines in determining newsworthy topics. By this time, the presidency had come to dominate national politics.[95] Televised or not, journalistic routines guaranteed that by virtue of his centrality to the political system, the president's words were newsworthy. But they also indicate that, regardless of their high production values, Kennedy's news conferences generated an enormous variety of newsworthy material.

Moreover, very little of this coverage focused on Kennedy's personal image. In my sample, the coverage is remarkable for the lack of such reporting. Though they often asked the president for his views on issues,

reporters' stories tended to stress the issues themselves, not Kennedy's
opinions. This is a finding similar to that of Elizabeth Keyes, who in a study

Table 3.1: Amount of News Coverage, JFK Press Conferences (n = 20)

	Total Stories	RHL Stories
The New York Times		
Number	104	11
Average/Percentage	5.05	55.0%
New York Herald-Tribune		
Number	55	17
Average/Percentage	2.84	85.0%
The Washington Post		
Number	83	18
Average/Percentage	4.15	90.0%
The Washington Evening-Star		
Number	61	8
Average/Percentage	3.05	40.0%
Chicago Tribune		
Number	32	11
Average/Percentage	1.6	55.0%
Kansas City Star		
Number	30	8
Average/Percentage	1.16	40.0%
Los Angeles Times		
Number	77	18
Average/Percentage	3.8	90.0%
The San Diego Union		
Number	47	10
Average/Percentage	2.35	50.0%
Total		
Number	489	101
Average/Percentage	3.0	63.0%

of newspaper coverage of Kennedy's press conferences found "no evidence
… that the conferences served in any way to enhance the personal image of
the President via the press."[96] More broadly, these results confirm the pattern
of twentieth-century presidential personal news coverage found by Rodger
Streitmatter.[97] Analyzing the front pages of several newspapers for the fifteen
twentieth-century presidents (through Reagan), Streitmatter discovered that
personal news coverage declined over time rather than increased, with
Theodore Roosevelt receiving the most such coverage, Richard Nixon the
least, and Kennedy somewhere in the middle. This coverage demonstrates
that, whatever their capacity to foster Kennedy's personal image, the
president's news meetings had other purposes as well.

Given the level of preparation by Kennedy and his aides, it is obvious
that they took very seriously these meetings with reporters.[98] For every press

conference, policy positions were funneled through the Executive departments while press secretary staff monitored issues of interest to reporters. Often, press conferences were timed with other actions, like an executive order, an important conference, or a bill sent to Congress. Their goal was to reach specific constituencies by crafting opening statements and answers to reporters' questions that used particular syntax, themes and metaphors. For example, at his February 15, 1961, news meeting, the president issued a stern warning to the Soviet Union over its activities in the Congo. In his opening statement, he declared that he was "seriously concerned" about the "threat of unilateral intervention in the internal affairs of the Republic of Congo," and that the United States "will continue to support the United Nations presence in the Congo" and "defend" its charter.

The next day's news coverage demonstrates the power of this kind of framing. The headline in all eight newspapers in my sample conveyed the president's warning to the Soviet Union.[99] They reported that, as it was put in *The New York Times*: "The President declared he was 'seriously concerned' at what appears to be a threat of unilateral intervention...." Two of the eight, *The Washington Post* and the *Los Angeles Times*, used this expression to open their stories. Other phrases taken from Kennedy's statement describing these activities as a "risk of war," and "dangerous and irresponsible," also appear in all eight newspapers. Kennedy routinely used the news in this manner. Consider, for instance, the power of his opening statements to shape the next day's news. The president began eighteen of the twenty news conferences in my sample with opening statements. These statements generated ninety-two total RHL stories. In other words, five of the eight newspapers on average led with a RHL story on Kennedy's press conferences. Moreover, fifty-eight of these stories, or 63 percent of the total, were taken directly from Kennedy's opening statement. This kind of journalistic attention gave the president an extraordinary opportunity to dominate the news with issues, themes, symbols and words carefully chosen by his communication advisors.

However, even though reporters focused a great deal of attention on the president, they did not treat him in an especially deferential manner.[100] Indeed, journalists rarely addressed Kennedy as anything other than a politician—and one politician among others at that. Most of their questions (by my count, over 80 percent) asked the president to comment on the opinions or statements of other politicians, or to justify actions he had taken on particular issues. These questions sometimes took the form of a request for a personal response to an issue, as in "What do you think?" "Do you feel

...?" or "Would you comment on ...?" Other times they asked for a comment or justification on specific actions taken by the president or the administration, as in, "What are you doing about ...?" or "Why did you take this action?" These question types carried with them the assumption that Kennedy was a political actor whose views and actions were properly situated in relation to those of other political actors. In contrast, very few (9 percent) of reporters' questions approached Kennedy as a preeminent political actor, that is, as the representative of the United States, or even of his own administration. These questions explicitly addressed Kennedy in more distant and respectful tones, as in, "What is the United States' position on ...?" but they rarely appeared in the transcripts.[101]

The best register of how reporters approached Kennedy lies in their use of question-prefaces. For instance, on January 31, 1962, a reporter began his question with this comment:

> Mr. President, some of the critics of your urban affairs plan charge that it's an invasion of States' and local rights. Would you comment on that, and would you also comment on it in a larger frame? For instance, what do you think of the argument that big government, so called, might not need to be so big if State and local governments were more efficient in fulfilling their duties?[102]

Here, the reporter constructs two potential conflicts, one over the question of State's rights and another over the question of state government efficiency, and asks Kennedy to respond in terms of this frame. Such prefaces are common in the press conference transcripts, and demonstrate that reporters approached the president first as a political actor and only secondarily as the "President." Moreover, reporters proved unwilling to allow Kennedy to set the terms of their questions with his opening statements: only 20 percent of their questions referred to a topic addressed in these statements. In fact, an average of fifteen topics were covered per press conference which meant that in a thirty-minute meeting topics were changing at least once every two minutes.[103]

These numbers suggest that while live television lent Kennedy more control over the production of the press conferences, it did not alter the basic structure of the questions put to the president. As they had with every president since Wilson, reporters questioned Kennedy aggressively. Kennedy might refuse to convene a press conference, or offer perfunctory answers, but these tactics did not dissuade reporters from taking control of the interactions within these news meetings. Once he delivered his opening statement, Kennedy relinquished control of the press conference agenda to the reporters.

Far from "stage props," then, reporters exercised great control over the flow of interactions in the televised press conferences.

Their power obviously presented Kennedy with a challenge. If he wanted to stress some issues rather than others, and do so in a way that put his views in the best light, his opening statements would not be enough. To increase his control over the conferences, he might hold background briefings with reporters or plant questions, practices which sometimes worked to steer questions in one direction or another. But even then he would still be faced with many questions on issues that he either did not want to discuss, or which were framed in a manner he did not want to accept. In my reading, I have discerned five strategies Kennedy routinely used to deal with these kinds of questions. (see Table 3.2) First, Kennedy might skirt questions by claiming that the issue raised was too complex, or that he did not have enough information to form a proper response. Second, he often asserted that more study was needed on an issue, and that he would answer the question when such study had been completed. Third, he sometimes stated a preexisting government position on an issue, or, fourth, offered his own personal view. Finally, he framed the question in terms different than that offered by the reporter, and proceeded to answer this reframed question.

Table 3.2: Types of JFK Answers to Reporters' Questions (n = 502)

Type	Number	Percentage
Too Complex/Not Enough Information	31	7.0
More Study is Needed	58	12.0
Government Position	53	11.0
Individual Position	107	21.0
Reframe the Question	205	41.0
Miscellaneous	48	8.0

The distribution of these answer types reveals much about the nature and significance of crafted talk. For instance, confronted with a difficult or complex question, a natural inclination is to admit that one simply does not know the answer, or that more study is needed before an answer can be given. Fifty years before, Wilson felt perfectly comfortable acknowledging as much in his press conferences, as evidenced by the many occasions on which he simply could not, or would not, answer reporters' questions. It is telling that Kennedy rarely resorted to these kinds of responses. Of the 502 questions asked of him in my sample, he refused to answer only six.[104] On nine other occasions, Kennedy indicated that he did not wish to respond to a question, but found himself answering anyway. For example, when asked during his August 30, 1961, news meeting if he had any comment on Richard Nixon's criticisms of his handling of the Berlin crisis, Kennedy at first replied, "No, I don't." Then added:

> We are in a situation in Germany which is fraught with peril and I think that anyone who is aware of the nature of the destructive power that's available to both sides should, I would think, be careful in attempting to take any political advantage out of our present difficulties.[105]

Two paragraphs later, he ended his "no-comment." This reluctance to admit ignorance indicates the changed role of the president in the political system. In the professional environment of postwar politics, presidents were expected to demonstrate the competence of any good manager. Part of that competence included a command of information on activities across the federal government.

This managerial role also precluded reliance on two other kinds of responses: stating the government's position or his personal view on issues. As a manager, the president played a vital professional role. Indeed, this role so dwarfed his personal life that, for all intents and purposes, a president had no other role—personal or otherwise—than being the president. For this reason, uttering personal opinions was useless: such opinions would always be interpreted in terms of his official position. Moreover, presidents managed a government that had, by the 1960s, become enormous. It was so big that it comprised a mini-political universe of its own, complete with interest groups and factions. For a president to state a unitary government position in the midst of this fractured bureaucracy risked aligning himself with one group against another—a dangerous move not be taken lightly—or often—if a president was to maintain room for political maneuvering.

In this institutional context, it is not surprising that Kennedy chose to reframe reporters' questions in over 40 percent of his responses. This kind of response allowed him to respond to expectations, and at the same time to push forward a legislative agenda. An example gives some sense of this process. During his March 21, 1963, press conference, Kennedy was asked this question:

> Mr. President, you have been warning with repeated frequency lately about the possible dangers of a recession. Some of your supporters, in and out of the administration, are expressing concern that your main thrust against it, namely, a larger tax cut, may not get through this session. If that should happen to be the case or if you got an inadequate tax cut, do you have another alternative against recession?[106]

"What-if" questions are often the most dangerous type for a president because they invite him to consider hypothetical situations, his answers to which might have real consequences. In this case, anything he says about what he will do if the Congress does not pass his tax cut might be used against him in the real negotiations over the issue. This particular question is especially difficult because Kennedy's own prior utterances are used to construct the hypothetical situation. What will you do, the reporter asks, if your only initiative, a tax cut, is not available to stem the recession which you yourself have stated is likely to occur in the near future?

Kennedy's response is a classic effort to reframe the question. "Well," he starts, "in the first place we don't believe that there will be a recession this year." Notice that he adopts the institutional role ("we") of speaking for the administration. And notice also that the statement undercuts the premise of the question. After giving some evidence for this assertion, Kennedy frames a new question: "If you are suggesting that I would look with equanimity upon the failure of Congress to act this year on a tax cut, that would be wholly wrong." Here, Kennedy suggests that the question is not how he would respond to a hypothetical recession without his tax cut, but how he would respond to the defeat of his tax cut. This opens the way for him to frame his tax plan as a "prudent" response that is all the more important given that "the prospects look good in 1963." That is, the tax cut is less a political action than one of common sense, which the Congress should "naturally" support. Thus, Kennedy framed the question in a way that allowed him to make an explicit appeal for passage of his legislation.[107]

It is, perhaps, natural that Kennedy would seek to reframe questions whose premises threatened to embroil him in difficult political conflicts. But the appeal of this device was so strong that even when he accepted the premises of a question, Kennedy often used this answerform. For example, during his April 21, 1961, press conference, he was asked whether he thought his educational program would be "persuasive" in the current Congressional session:

> I hope so because I really believe that the tax credit program, in fact the whole tax bill, was carefully considered by people in the Treasury as well as the Council of Economic Advisers. It had the strong support of Mr. Dillon and others who have given this matter great consideration.... But it is a technical matter, it involves important interests. And I think it will ... be very soberly considered.[108]

The premise of the question centered on Congressional reluctance to pass Kennedy's tax credit program and stressed the conflict between Kennedy and the Congress. While accepting its basic premise—the reluctance of Congress to pass his program—Kennedy framed Congress' reluctance not in terms of conflict, but in terms of the issue's technical complexity. At bottom, he states, it is a "technical" matter that requires "sober consideration." But it is a technical matter that has the strong support of key bureaucratic experts at the Treasury Department and the Council of Economic Advisers.

As these examples suggest, Kennedy's news meetings may have been dramatic theater, but they dramatized talk itself as much as the president's persona. Kennedy's aides devoted considerable energy to the way the president looked during these press conferences. But they devoted as much, if not more, time to framing Kennedy's answers in ways that put his position in the best light. As Theodore Sorensen put it, the press conference was Kennedy's vehicle both for "inform[ing]" and "impress[ing] the public."[109] Or, as James Reston described his performance, Kennedy "overwhelm[ed] you with decimal points [and] disarm[ed] you with a smile and a wisecrack."[110] The two—Kennedy's appearance and his talk—cannot be separated.

But of the two, Kennedy's talk worked more as an "interpretive guide" for reporters and viewers. Indeed, one of the main criticisms leveled at Kennedy throughout his three years in office was precisely that he talked too much and emoted too little. Already on October 31, 1961, James Reston wrote in his *New York Times* column that Kennedy "simply will not grapple with the philosophic and educational responsibilities of the presidency.... It is an administration of intelligent educators who will not educate...." Kennedy apparently was aware of his dilemma. In a polling report written by Louis Harris, dated March 22, 1961, Harris told the new president that though his press conferences were "widely acclaimed" as "feats of incredible personal accomplishment," they did not register "the genuine human feeling in day-to-day terms." Only 6 percent of the people responded that Kennedy "really cares about people."[111] But that was precisely their appeal for the president. They allowed him to frame issues for a wide variety of constituencies.

Of course, even if many of his statements were targeted to specific constituencies, Kennedy still would have liked his press conferences to attract the widest possible audience. This meant broadcasting during primetime hours. However, these hours were highly lucrative for the networks and their affiliate stations, a time slot they were reluctant to relinquish to Kennedy on a consistent basis.[112] Kennedy's only recourse was to schedule the conferences at 4:00 p.m. EST at the latest (and 10:00 a.m. at the earliest) in time for the fifteen-minute network news shows and for local rebroadcast later that evening. This system worked fine for the network news. But many affiliate stations were reluctant to broadcast the conferences. In a letter to Salinger dated February 5, 1962, Leonard Reinsch (a Kennedy media advisor) warned Salinger that "the number of clearances for the televised presidential news conferences has dropped drastically." Due to viewer complaints, many stations would not preempt the usual children's programming that started at 5:00 p.m. to carry the president's news conference. Though one station might broadcast the conference, the others in the local area did not. "Consequently," Reinsch writes, "the audience turns away from the news conference [broadcast on one station] to the other ... stations."[113] Moreover, the networks would not provide their taped versions of the press conferences to non-affiliate stations. On their view, these edited versions of the news meetings were "network produced" programming that should not be given freely to independent stations.[114]

This kind of negotiation permeates these events. As I have suggested, reporters held a great deal of power in these meetings. They chose which issues to highlight and which of the president's words to emphasize. They set the issues within particular narrative frames. And they indexed the president's responses along with the voices of other Washington officials. These choices were merely part of the routine by which reporters transformed events into news stories. But the power of the elite press lent them added significance. Choices made by *The New York Times*, the *New York Herald-Tribune*, *The Washington Post*, the *Los Angeles Times*, the wire services, and perhaps the major news magazines, did much to shape the climate of elite opinion in Washington, D.C. To the extent that they embraced the routines of their print brethren, early television journalists also relied on these choices to make decisions of their own as to which issues to focus upon and how to turn them into news stories.[115] Reporters, therefore, acted as gatekeepers for the president's words.

Consider, for instance, coverage of Kennedy's announcement during his January 31, 1962, press conference of a government investigation into excessive stockpiling of strategic materials. Reporters from four newspapers focused on the fact that Kennedy termed his announcement an "important" one.[116] *The New York Herald-Tribune* interpreted this expression to mean that the "investigation would be undertaken with full Administration cooperation...." The *Los Angeles Times* took the president's pronouncement of his "astonishment" at the sheer size of the stockpile, as an indication that he "clearly [wanted to involve] the Eisenhower administration in what he called excessive stockpiling." *The New York Times* took the same quotes to "reinforce the belief that Mr. Kennedy sought disclosure of past events and policies rather than anything that might touch his own administration." Here, reporters have done more than report the president's statement. They have stressed particular words, and put those words in a larger narrative frame, one involving partisan conflict (Republican versus Democratic administrations), and an effort by the Kennedy administration to deny responsibility for the stockpiling program.

Reporters often relied on their own political expertise to put the president's words and actions in contexts of their own choosing. For instance, Warren Unna of *The Washington Post* connected Kennedy's policy of accepting Chinese refugees from Hong Kong to an earlier solution he had advocated, concluding that the president had "noticeably backed away from offering any solution for helping" refugees who had recently left Communist China.[117] On the president's farm policy, David Broder of the *Washington Evening-Star* discounted the effort of "administration officials" to deny that Kennedy wished to limit Congressional power over farm policy, concluding that "the effects of the plan apparently would be to make Congress, in the farm field ... a board of final review."[118] Rowland Evans of *The New York Herald-Tribune* wrote a page-one story on Kennedy's difficulty in getting his legislative agenda passed from a single question during one of his news meetings. Reporting that the president "lamented the fate of his beleaguered program," Evans went on to index Kennedy's response in relation to the "Republican mood" toward the program, including a quote from Representative Mason, the senior Republican on the House Ways and Means Committee, to the effect that Kennedy would not get any controversial legislation through the Congress.

News coverage of the press conferences is littered with this kind of reporting. It shows that the very routines that marked reporters as disinterested professionals made them important players in the process of presidential issue framing. The organization of their beats ensured that they never strayed far from the insular world of Washington politics. While they acted as conduits for official Washington—as evidenced by the amount of coverage Kennedy's news meetings received—they also participated in the process of framing political issues. They tended to look for political conflict, often pitting one source against another. They chose words and phrases that lent narrative continuity and drama to their stories. And they relied on their own political knowledge, gained from years of observation, to put actions and words in wider contexts. Their negotiations with the president and other Washington political actors constituted the basic process of presidential crafted talk.

Spin Control: Ronald Reagan's Campaign for Tax Reform

Kennedy's mastery of crafted talk set a blueprint for presidential communication throughout the 1960s and 1970s. However, by the early 1980s presidential scholars had become worried that the "imperial presidency" underpinned by such practices had become "imperiled."[119] At the heart of these fears lay a worry that presidential crafted talk no longer worked. In the hands of a strong president like Richard Nixon, it threatened to become sheer demagoguery. In the hands of a weaker president like Jimmy Carter, it seemed incapable of harnessing a political system that had become extraordinarily large and unwieldy. During the 1970s, Congress fragmented into hundreds of mini-political enterprises; interest groups clogged the system; and journalism seemed to be losing its professional bearings.[120] In this environment of "spin"—a frenetic effort to frame issues undertaken by many groups—pushing through policy initiatives was tantamount to herding cats. If the president could not do it, observers worried, then the system had become effectively ungovernable, because no other political actor had as much visibility or power.

Ronald Reagan showed these fears to be unwarranted. In his 1981 campaign for tax cuts, and again in his 1986 campaign for tax reform, Reagan demonstrated the kind of rhetorical leadership that many thought was impossible in the more decentralized political environment of the 1980s. By "going public"—traveling across the country to give countless speeches, addresses, comments, and interviews—Reagan harnessed the political process to his legislative goals. His success led commentators to reach for new superlatives. Reagan was the "Great Communicator," the "prime-time president," a man whose intimate relationship with the public formed a "teflon" exterior that rendered him immune to Washington criticism.[121] His former life as a Hollywood actor seemed of a piece with this interpretation. In his staged-managed rhetorical performances, observers saw the culmination of a trend that stretched back to the first Roosevelt—the transformation of presidential communication into a politics of pictures.[122]

While there may be much to laud in Reagan's accomplishments, too much praise risks exaggerating the uniqueness of his rhetoric. It is true that the president faced a more fragmented, entrepreneurial political environment than, say, Presidents Eisenhower or Kennedy faced. And it is true that he spoke more often in more and smaller venues than these latter presidents.[123] Fundamentally, however, President Reagan operated on the same institutional field as these other presidents. There may have been more bureaucrats, technocrats, academics, consultants, and policy "wonks" surrounding the political process, but, as in the 1950s and 1960s, these were still professional political actors. Like professionals in and around prior postwar administrations, they viewed presidential communication through the same cultural lens. Indeed, one can trace a clear genealogical line of these professionals from Kennedy to Reagan. Many of Richard Nixon's aides absorbed important lessons of presidential communication from their work against Kennedy in the 1960s presidential campaign. They took these lessons to heart in the 1968 presidential campaign, and brought them to the center of Nixon's White House in the guise of the White House Office of Communication (WHOC).[124] Many of Reagan's aides (e.g., David Gergen and Patrick Buchanan) were veterans of this Office, and carried forward their experience into the Reagan administration. Differences between the rhetoric of Reagan and prior presidents of the postwar years, then, were more a matter of degree than of kind. The pace and scale of Reagan's rhetoric was more aggressive—hence the introduction of a new term, "spinning," to describe presidential communication—but the way it defined the aims and purposes of presidential rhetoric remained of a piece with postwar presidential communication.

Reagan's 1986 campaign for tax reform demonstrates this continuity. Tax reform seemed an unlikely issue to be embraced by the president during his second term.[125] Ideas for reforming the tax system had percolated in Washington for over thirty years, but a great number of groups with a vested interest in the current system prevented these notions from gaining much traction. In fact, the Reagan administration would not have embraced the issue at all if it had not been for a strategic calculation by his handlers. Fearing that Walter Mondale might use it during the 1984 presidential campaign, they added tax reform to the Republican platform and included it in Reagan's 1984 State of the Union message. After Reagan's landslide victory, the White House saw tax reform as an opportunity to increase the base of the Republican party and appeal to conservative Republicans (like Jack Kemp) who were also attracted to the idea.

Still, it was not a surprise that when President Reagan announced his tax reform proposal (sometimes called "Treasury II") on May 28, 1985, in a

nationwide televised address, he faced a highly motivated, and mobilized
Washington Community. Minutes after the president concluded his speech,
Dan Rostenkowski, Chairman of the House Ways and Means Committee,
followed with a short Democratic response to the president's message. He
not only shared the same stage as the president, he used some of the same
props. At the end of his remarks he asked citizens to "sit down and write a
letter to Washington. Even if you can't spell Rostenkowski, put down what
they used to call my father and grandfather, Rosty. Just address it to Rosty,
Washington D.C." So many people in the Washington Community wore
"Write Rosty" pins in the days after the speech that columnist Mary
McGrory was prompted to ask, "has a star been born?"[126]

The Washington Community did more than just wear pins. A *New York
Times* reporter observed that two weeks before the announcement "lobbyists,
law firms, think tanks, accounting firms, newsletter mills, consultants, public
relations concerns, [and] journalists [were] monitoring and attempting to
influence the shifts in the Government's taxing and spending."[127] The
American Enterprise Institute assured reporters that three of its top scholars,
Barber B. Conable, Jr., a former Representative and Ways and Means
Committee member, John H. Makin, an economist, and Norman J. Ornstein,
a political scientist, would be manning the phones to answer questions. Two
days after Reagan's speech, a line of lobbyists "reach[ed] 130 yards down
the corridor" of the Longworth House Office Building, all of them anxious to
witness the first day of hearings on the subject by the House Ways and
Means Committee.[128] During Reagan's five-week publicity campaign,
interest groups paid lobbyists millions of dollars to coordinate print and
television advertising campaigns with more direct efforts to influence
members of Congress.[129] They hired tax experts to conduct studies showing
how the tax plan would affect their businesses—and publicized the results in
a blizzard of press conferences and publicity releases. They hired still other
experts and former politicians to write opinion columns in influential
newspapers and magazines, and to appear on news shows to argue their case.
They tested slogans and arguments in public opinion polls, held meetings
and conferences to attract media attention, and planted stories with favored
journalists that warned of the proposal's impact on their industries.

News coverage represents another measure of this activity. From May 1st
to June 30th, *The New York Times*, *Washington Post*, and *Los Angeles Times*
published 225 stories on tax reform. These stories included 254 quotes from
members of Congress, 252 from special and public interest groups, 161 from
think tank and academic experts, and 33 from political experts, or 700 total

quotes (or just over 3 per story) from various Washington Community players (see Table 3.3).[130] They also included references to 34 separate studies conducted or commissioned by interest groups and think tanks, as well as 17 studies done by various Congressional agencies and offices.

Table 3.3: Sources of Tax Reform Coverage in NYT, WP, & LAT (May 1st-June 30th, 1985, n = 252 stories)

Source	Number
Congress (including legislative aides)	254
Special/Public Interest Groups	252
Think Tanks/Academic Experts	161
Political Experts	33
Total:	700

The extent of this cacophony was unusual—few issues affected as many interests as tax reform—but the nature of the noise itself was not. By the 1980s, crafted talk had diffused through a more porous institutional environment, making an unruly, noisy political process the rule rather than the exception.

Reagan's team of communication experts were charged with taming this unruliness. Led by Patrick Buchanan, director of WHOC, the president's aides relied on a strategic blueprint made famous during the 1981 tax cut debates: weekly long-term strategy sessions for policy officers and press handlers; daily meetings of the White House communication group to coordinate the White House theme for the day; coordination of executive branch officers so that this theme was repeated throughout the administration; constant efforts to work the press; seminars to educate spokespeople of the federal bureaucracies; polling and marketing research to calibrate the message.[131] A core group of communication and policy strategists met each morning to discuss the ongoing effort to sell tax reform. They devised daily themes that were used to stage each presidential appearance. White House officials were counseled to repeat the theme in their own public comments.[132] On days when the president did not speak, other officials and spokespeople were briefed and sent to speak to citizens' groups, conferences, meetings, conventions, and local and national news media. The effect was to saturate Washington, but most importantly the Washington news media, with calls for tax reform.

Reagan's participation in this campaign began with his national address, and continued in a series of addresses and speeches designed to capture and retain the news media's attention. From the end of May to the end of June, the president gave the usual nationally televised address and two radio addresses to the nation—forms of communication innovated by prior presidents. But, in a move distinctive of the age of spin, Reagan also traveled to 12 different cities to speak to 14 different groups about tax reform, met with another 3 groups in the White House, and held one news conference.[133] En total, Reagan talked about tax reform to one group or another on 21 occasions over these 35 days.[134] (see Table 3.4)

Table 3.4: Reagan's Early Campaign for Tax Reform May 16-June 28, 1985[135]

Date	Occasion
May 16	Speech at Annual Republican Senate/House Fundraising dinner
May 24	Remarks at Annual Meeting of the National Association of Manufacturers
May 25	Radio Address on Tax Reform
May 27	Speech at Walt Disney's EPCOT Center
May 28	Televised Address to Nation on Tax Reform
May 29	Remarks on Tax Reform to Concerned Citizens
May 30	Remarks to Citizens of Williamsburg, VA
May 30	Remarks to Citizens of Oshkosh, WI
May 31	Remarks at Greater Valley Corporate Center in Malvern, PA
June 1	Radio Address on Tax Reform
June 4	Remarks on Tax Reform at a Meeting with Corporate Leaders
June 5	Remarks at AT&T Technology Plant in Oklahoma City, OK
June 6	Remarks at Northside High School, Atlanta, GA
June 7	Remarks & Q&A Session with Economic Editors during White House Briefing on Tax Reform
June 13	Remarks to Citizens of Bloomfield, NJ
June 18	News Conference
June 19	Remarks & Q&A Session with Members of Chamber of Commerce, Mooresville, IN
June 19	Remarks at Annual Convention of U.S. Jaycees in Indianapolis, IN
June 21	Remarks at Annual Convention of Lions Club International in Dallas, TX
June 27	Remarks to State & Local Officials during White House Briefing on Tax Reform
June 28	Remarks at Luncheon w/Community Leaders in Chicago Heights, IL
June 28	Remarks to Citizens in Chicago Heights, IL

To the extent that this series of public comments kept the news media's attention focused on tax reform, and more specifically, on the president's plan, they focused the attention of other political actors as well. But it was not enough for the president simply to get others to talk about tax reform. Success required that he get them to talk about the issue in particular ways.

That is, he needed to provide a frame for the issue. That frame became apparent in his first radio address, in which Reagan argued that his proposal "recogniz[ed] the central role of the American family in preserving … our nation's values." Borrowing a frame from the Democrats (particularly Senator Bill Bradley's version of tax reform, the "Fair Tax Bill"), he contended that the proposal was "fair" because it prevented the rich and powerful from "avoiding paying their fair share." He argued that the United States stood "on the threshold of a new technological age," which his proposal would usher in by facilitating economic growth. And he suggested that his proposal created a "sleeker" tax code that would prove simpler and more efficient than the "rickety, jerry-rigged" current system. "Pro-family," "fairer," "pro-growth," and "simpler": these four phrases constituted the president's frame.

Over the five-week campaign, the president repeated these phrases over and over. In his televised address (delivered May 28th), he argued that his tax reform proposal promised a system that was "clear, simple, and fair for all." In brief remarks to corporate leaders (on June 4th) he argued that the present system was "unfair." At the annual convention of United States Jaycees (June 19th), he suggested that the current tax system "with 14 different tax brackets … stifle[d] hard work and success [and] singled out families for cruel and unusual punishment." In contrast, his plan was more "simple," gave families "long-overdue relief," and made "special privileges" pay their "fair share." On nearly every occasion he was sure to mention that his proposal would foster "a new technological age." The singular feature of Reagan's appeals was not their content, but their form: every remark couched in the frame of family, fairness, simplicity and growth. Just as he organized his first radio address on the issue in these terms, so Reagan structured his last set of remarks: "I came to talk," the president said to citizens in Chicago Heights 34 days after his first radio address, "about tax fairness and simplification."

The relentlessness of Reagan's rhetorical discipline paid off to the extent that the Washington Community no longer debated just any aspect of tax reform, but instead discussed his proposal's relative fairness, simplicity, impact on economic growth, and pro-family orientation. Of the four, fairness became a particularly important frame. During the five weeks of media coverage, columnists both for and against the proposal accepted fairness as a benchmark for evaluating the plan. Conflicts between Congressional Democrats and Republicans centered on the bill's relative fairness: was it "unfair" to the middle classes? Fair to the poor? How did it impact the rich?

A congressional aide predicted that members of the Ways and Means committee would review the proposal for "specific examples of unfairness." House Speaker Tip O'Neill warned that he could support the president only if he "presents a fair tax bill." Encapsulating this debate, CBS news anchor Dan Rather led into Reagan's May 28th television address by noting that "Mr. Reagan says his proposals will make federal taxes simpler and fairer. Critics of the plan call it, among other things, basically unfair...." Business leaders who disagreed among themselves on various aspects of the proposal nonetheless agreed with the president that aspects of the current tax system were unfair. Political consultants debated various scenarios in which one party or the other gained control over the fairness question. Even complaints about the proposal were framed in terms of fairness, as when representatives of California and New York cried foul upon hearing that the proposal repealed the state income tax deduction.[136] Reagan's frame exerted a gravitational pull on the Washington Community, inviting it to talk about tax reform, and to talk about it in these terms rather than others.

The news media also played an important role in shaping the cacophony surrounding tax reform. Most obviously, as a gatekeeper of the public sphere, they determined who gained entrance and how much attention these individuals would receive. I have already shown that sources for newspaper coverage typically came from one of three groups: professional representatives of organizations which had a stake in the outcome, experts (usually at think tanks or universities) on the technical issues involved, or members of Congress. Except for twelve quotes from ordinary people in four stories on the "public's" reaction to tax reform, these groups comprised all of the actors who appeared in newspaper coverage. Network news coverage had the same profile. Over the same time span (May 1st–June 30th), 37 network news stories contained 101 sources, all but 16 of which were politicians, representatives of interest groups, or experts. (See Table 3.5)

There are interesting differences between print and network news. The networks, for instance, were more likely to use the president as a source of news than print journalists.[137] On average, they were also more likely to include ordinary people as representatives of the "public" in their stories. Overall, however, professionalism and expertise were as important to gaining access to the airwaves as they were to gaining access to the news hole.

The news media also determined how much attention the debate would receive in the public sphere. Not long before, the news media simply covered whatever official Washington was debating. By the 1980s, however, the news business was more economically competitive and less centralized. In part, this meant that the news media simply preferred other kinds of news—entertainment, consumer, science, human interest—over the "hard" news of Washington politics. It became more difficult to interest news media in any political issue for an extended length of time. But this competitiveness also instilled a certain "pack" mentality among Washington reporters. Many news outlets (from cable to local affiliates) now competed to break stories. No reporter wanted to be left behind, covering the same old news, and every media organization engaged in a constant search for the new in news. The curious result of this competition was that reporters tended to stampede en masse from one story to the next in rapid succession. Once in the glare of media attention, every nook and cranny of a story became visible. Once out of that glare, it almost ceased to exist.

Table 3.5. Network Sources, Tax Reform Coverage (May 28th–29th, 1985, n = 37 stories)

Source	Number	Percentage
White House	23	22%
EOP	3	3%
Congress	24	24%
Special Interest Groups	24	24%
Public	16	16%
Political Experts	5	5%
Think Tank/Academic Experts	6	6%
Total	101	100.0

Something like this process can be seen in coverage of tax reform. For instance, Figures 3.1 and 3.2 show the pattern of coverage in print and television news. Each exhibits the same profile: a relatively low level of attention before and after the president submitted his proposal, and a high level of attention for the four days beginning May 28th. The three newspapers in my sample devoted, on average, about 3.5 stories per day to tax reform during the days prior to May 28th and after May 31st (or a little more than 1 story per day per paper). In contrast, they devoted nearly 17 stories a day to tax reform (or over 5 stories per day per paper) from May 28th–May 31st. Similarly, total network stories broadcast before May 28th and after May 31st averaged about 80 seconds, or about 23 seconds per network. But during the four days between May 28th and May 31st, *each network* devoted about 80 seconds per day to tax reform (or 241 seconds total). The result: a white hot glare of media attention on the days surrounding publication of the president's proposal, and a relatively low level of attention at other times.

Other analysts have found that the networks give contemporary presidents less airtime than in the past.[138] Still, this pattern of coverage clearly gives the president an advantage in setting the terms of public debate. His frame of tax reform received unparalleled attention, while other political actors competed for a much reduced media attention in the days, weeks, and months after.

The news media were also interpretive gatekeepers. During the months of May and June, for instance, our three newspapers devoted 15 stories (or 5 per paper) to explicit analysis of tax reform. Typically, these stories were distinguished by a box with the words "news analysis" next to the column. So many other stories, however, had the feel of analysis that it is sometimes difficult to tell the two apart. For instance, in a front-page news story David Broder offered the opinion that Reagan's proposal "spell[ed] relief for many taxpayers and headaches for others...." Another *Washington Post* reporter began a news story on the first page of the Business section with: "If your nose is beginning to suspect that 'tax reform' bears a certain olfactory resemblance to the aroma of putrefied pork that occasionally wafts downwind from Capitol Hill, let me tell you a story." On the front page of the *Los Angeles Times*, Michael Wines wrote that "even sharp-eyed economists have overlooked it, but tucked deep within the Reagan administration's 460-page tax reform proposal is a multibillion-dollar kicker...."[139] This reporting shares a certain informality and evaluative sensibility. Unlike a conventional news story, it concentrates on the question of why rather than who, what, when, and where. It is interested not in revealing actions but in setting actions in a particular frame. Moreover, the authority for this evaluation seems to rest in the reporters themselves—the expertise and celebrity of "David Broder"—rather than in conventional news routines.

Another indication of reporters' preference for analysis and synthesis was that more stories had no obvious source, no particular "peg"—a quote, a press release, a meeting—to some action out in the world. "Plan Would Reduce Bills for 63%," a headline indicated on page one of the *Los Angeles Times*. How did the reporter, Richard Rosenblatt, know this? Apparently,

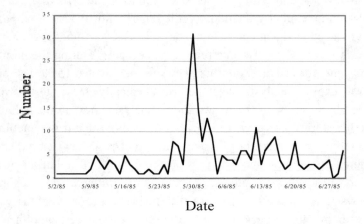

Figure 3.1: #Stories, NYT, WP, LAT, Reagan Tax Reform

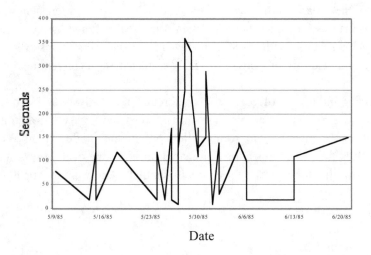

Figure 3.2: #Stories, Network Evening News, Reagan Tax Reform

because he personally had studied the plan closely. He confidently elaborated how the bill would affect different social groups without once citing a source. Thomas Edsall of *The Washington Post* wrote a similar story on the politics of tax reform, arguing that Reagan's proposal promised to create "bizarre alliances" in Congress—again, without citing a single source.[140] In these kinds of stories, reporters took it upon themselves to dissect the tax bill without mentioning a source for their conclusions. Other times, papers generated news themselves by conducting public opinion polls or commissioning studies by experts.[141]

One sees a similar pattern in television news. Television reporters tended to speak over their sources' statements, preferring to interpret what was being said rather than allowing the public to hear it firsthand.[142] And more of their commentary had a critical, cynical edge. For instance, in a May 28th ABC news story on Reagan's proposal, Chairman Dan Rostenkowski is quoted as saying that he hopes the House Ways and Means committee can "improve" the bill. "What this means is that Rostenkowski wants the final bill …" Brit Hume opined, "to bear his or at least the Democrat's stamp, not Mr. Reagan's." After describing the "legions" of lobbyists waiting to "peck away" at the plan, Hume concluded that viewers shouldn't be surprised "if the biggest fight of all is over which party gets the credit if tax reform does pass." On the same evening, CBS news correspondent Bill Plante argued that President Reagan's "ultimate goal" in tax reform was to "win the allegiance of millions of voters and make Republicans the majority party." His colleague Jane Bryant Quinn concluded her piece by saying that, if passed, tax reform would "keep tax payers frustrated and accountants living high for years."

This more synthetic, evaluative style of reporting served various needs. The political process had become more complex and technical, requiring more explanation. But the style also allowed journalists to develop a personal voice, which became increasingly important in the entrepreneurial environment of the contemporary news media. More broadly, the style was also a product of the new economic competition within television journalism. In this environment, reporters could no longer ignore their audiences.[143] Hume, Bryant and others issued their cynical commentary not solely as experts, but as champions of ordinary Americans. Their cynicism served to place them above the ugly world of politics, alongside their viewers, in contemplation of politicians' abject pettiness. In a move reminiscent of 1920s advertisers, reporters increasingly used their cynicism to place themselves at the side of their audiences. Whatever its source, this style placed limits on the ability of other actors—even presidents—to frame initiatives free of reporters' synthesis and evaluation.

Along with President Reagan then, the news media lent shape to the cacophony of crafted talk surrounding tax reform. Reagan foregrounded the issue for the Washington Community, and set important criteria by which it would be discussed and evaluated. The news media acted as gatekeepers into the arena: they sifted out the voices of all but those of professional political actors and experts; they determined how much attention the issue would receive in the public sphere; and they glossed the debate in a layer of synthetic gauze, framing the motivations of other actors and the efficacy of the process generally in their own terms.

The effect of this reporting was to define the issue of tax reform almost wholly in terms of political strategy. Take, for instance, the coverage from May 28th to May 31st—the period in which Reagan's plan received the most sustained media attention. Our three newspapers published 55 reports on tax reform over these four days. All of these stories can be divided neatly into two categories. A first category, comprising 17 of the 55 stories, concerns the technicalities of the president's proposal. With the help of experts, reporters explain the nuts and bolts of the plan: how many tax brackets; which deductions are included and excluded; how the plan would affect various industries and groups; who would pay more and who would pay less. To help them distill the data, they include many sidebar graphs, charts and tables. For example, in its May 29th coverage, *The New York Times* includes one box on its front page ("In Brief: Reagan's Key Points"), another half-page box on page 17 ("Comparing the Proposals with Current Law"), two more boxes on page 20 ("How the Rates Would Change," and "The Tax Proposal's Impact on Families"), and a final half-page box on page 21 ("White House's Summary of Plan"). Taken together, this represents approximately two and a half pages of condensed facts and statistics.

The remaining thirty-eight stories are dedicated to cataloguing the strategic responses of the political actors involved. Readers learn of threats and warnings issued by various interest groups: "New York Leaders Oppose Plan Vehemently"; "Sports Industry Boos Reagan Tax Proposal"; "Overhaul Proposal Draws Fire in High-Tax States"; "Business Fights for Capital Gains." They learn of Reagan's strenuous appeals and Congressional reaction to the proposal: "Reagan Parades Simplification Plan Along 'Main Street America'"; "Tells Sympathy for 'Cult of Cheating'"; "Tax Battles Ahead But Leaders See Reform of System"; "Congressional Reaction Mixed." The political strategies and motivations of the various players are of paramount importance in these stories. Hedrick Smith suggests that the plan represents Reagan's "instrument for carrying forward his long campaign against the progressive income tax." George Skelton proposes that the plan offers the Republican Party an "opportunity to shuck off [its] country club image." Lou Cannon suggests that the plan has more immediate importance for "revitaliz[ing]" the president's second term. And David Broder detects a possible political benefit for Rostenkowski, who might use it as a tool for winning the House speakership after the next election.[144]

If anything, network coverage blended technical aspects of the plan and political strategies into an even more cohesive narrative form. On May 28th, the networks devoted a total of sixteen minutes (over five minutes per network) to tax reform. As with print coverage, all of this time was spent explaining the plan, describing how it treats various social groups (often with the help of tax experts), and detailing likely conflicts and strategies. However, these themes are combined so seamlessly in network coverage that it is difficult to tell where facts end and strategies begin. For instance, in its coverage that night, CBS news reporter Bill Plante's two-minute report presented the following information in order.

> President Reagan unveils his plan to win the allegiance of millions of voters to the Republican Party.
>
> The Plan lowers most people's taxes but increases business taxes.
>
> The President will use a populist strategy to sell the plan as a benefit for the majority of Americans at the expense of the rich.
>
> Comment by political strategist Lee Atwater describing this strategy.
>
> Opposition to the plan will be massive, but Democrats will work with the President.
>
> Mr. Reagan's speech (that night) is the opening shot in his toughest political fight ever.

NBC coverage mirrored that of CBS. Chris Wallace's 90 second report that evening conveyed the following information:

> The President is in for a political fight.
>
> His plan's chances for success are at best 60–40.
>
> Biggest resistance will come from "smokestack industries" which will lose tax breaks.
>
> High tax states like New York will also resist the plan's intention to do away with state and local income tax deductions.
>
> [A]bout 23% of Americans will see their taxes increase.

> President will conduct a three-phase strategy to sell his plan: a series of trips in the
> next few weeks; a summer lull as Congress conducts hearings; and a recharged sales
> pitch in the Fall.

This seamless mixing of facts and strategy leaves the impression that there is
no effective distinction between them. Aspects of the president's proposal
and responses of his critics are both couched as strategic moves in a political
game.

Elements of strategy and tactics, in other words, are so central to crafted
talk that there is little room to consider issues from other angles. Take, for
instance, the issue of fairness. Traditionally, fairness in the tax system had
been construed in terms of progressivity: those who made more money paid
more in taxes. President Reagan argued for his tax plan on different grounds.
He argued not that it was "progressive," but that it "leveled the playing
field." In these terms, fairness came to be defined as equality rather than
progressivity. Reagan himself highlighted this conceptual distinction, and
caused a small stir in the process, while on a trip to Madrid in mid-May,
when he proudly stated that his plan would promote economic growth
because it was less progressive than the current system.[145]

A few observers—notably, Democratic lawmakers—noted the difference
and its possible consequences.[146] It opened an opportunity to consider a basic
value choice embedded within the issue of tax reform: do we as a nation
value equality in our tax structure more than progressivity? For the most part,
however, this public debate never took place. Instead, politicians, experts,
and journalists preferred to speak about fairness through the vernacular of
crafted talk. Fairness in these terms came to be defined as a political "issue,"
one that Democrats once controlled but with Reagan's proposal was now up
for grabs. Certain kinds of questions were naturally raised by this focus: what
was Reagan's "strategy" for wresting control of the issue away from the
Democrats? How would the Democrats respond? Most importantly, who
would win? The coverage shifted demonstrably toward these sorts of
questions. On May 7th, *New York Times* columnist Tom Wicker noted that
the Democrats may "have lost one of the most important issues of the
future…." On May 13th, Robert Shogan of *The Washington Post* wrote that
tax reform represented an opportunity for Republicans "to shed once and for
all their image as a rich man's party," while Democrats hoped to dispel their
party's stigma as a champion of special-interest groups." On May 17th,
Bernard Weintraub continued this theme in an interview with Patrick
Buchanan, who argued that, "This will reach working-class Americans,
Hispanics, blacks, Catholics…. This is a reach for the conservative

movement to bring these people into the Republican party."[147] A few days later Hedrick Smith outlined the Democratic counterattack, which consisted of getting a version of Reagan's tax reform plan through the Democratically controlled House and hoping (because of its unprogressive profile) that it languished in the Republican-controlled Senate. They would then have the best of both worlds: a defeat of Reagan's plan and an argument in the next election that Republicans had stifled a popular issue. Over the next several weeks, all of the participants—politicians, experts, and the news media— continued to focus on this theme: Republicans arguing that the plan was "fair" because it lowered tax rates for most people; Democrats arguing that it was "unfair" to the middle classes; tax experts using facts and figures to buttress the arguments of one side or the other; columnists picking winners; and reporters dutifully analyzing the spectacle.[148]

Democracy without Citizens

Writing at the end of the 1980s, Robert Entman found that the political process had become a "vicious cycle."[149] While competition in the political market forced elites to "manage publicity rather than illuminate the truth," competition in the economic market forced reporters to "depend upon elites and make news attractive to the largest number of consumers."[150] The result of this cycle, he concluded, was a curious phenomenon: democracy without citizens. Modern politics involved more players, was more fragmented, more open to a greater diversity of groups and interests. At the same time, it had become more insulated from the participation of ordinary Americans. Fewer Americans participated in public life, or even voted. And a general sense of cynicism and mistrust had come to pervade relationships between citizens and officials.[151]

This notion—democracy without citizens—encapsulates a good deal of the conventional wisdom about modern presidential communication. Looking for causes of this condition, some blame television; others, like Entman, look to the news media for answers. Still others focus on the rise of professional polling, the fragmentation of Congress, the demise of political parties, or the incredible abundance of interest groups in the political system. Listed in this way, we can see that all of these processes have taken place within a culture of expertise that connects them to a shared form of life. Within this culture, it is simply assumed that politics is a preserve of professionals and requires specialized forms of expertise. This is true in several senses. Issues have become more complex and technical; the policymakers who deal with them are more highly trained; the environment in which these professionals work tends to favor specialized forms of knowledge; and the process of getting policies implemented is more complex, requiring greater attention to the management of perceptions. To the extent that modern presidential communication is organized and implemented by communication experts, it has become more impersonal and rational, and ultimately, less connected to the values and experiences of ordinary Americans. Put simply, modern presidential communication imagines a political world devoid of ordinary Americans.

But wait, an astute observer may ask, this conclusion may be true of other modern presidents. But wasn't Ronald Reagan known at least as much for his populist rhetoric as for his success in "going public?" After all, during his five-week campaign for tax reform, Reagan cast himself as the "people's lobbyist." He called his tax reform plan a "second American revolution" that would make the rich pay their fair share and reinstate fairness and equality in the tax system for working people. With a conservative twist, he lambasted "big government," declaring that the "power to tax [was] the power to destroy" basic American values. This rhetoric seems to speak for and to the American people—doesn't it?

In my estimation, it does not. If we think of presidential communication as a kind of accounting—a justification for taking action—then motivation becomes a key indicator of its meaning. Why is an action acceptable? Because it is motivated by "good" intentions. Think back, for instance, to Eisenhower's public addresses. In those speeches, Eisenhower seeks to justify various aspects of his policies, from his budget proposals to relations with the Soviets. In his justification of these proposals, the president constructs a world in which government actors respond to "facts" to devise appropriate policies. In other words, in his rhetoric, the government acts on behalf of the people. For all its attacks on "big government," Reagan's rhetoric takes a similar form: he is acting on behalf of the people against the "liberal establishment" and their "tax and spend" orthodoxy. In populist rhetoric, however, officials do not act for the people. Rather, the people act for the people. And they act not based upon "facts," or some political theory (like supply-side economics), but based upon common sense. Reagan's rhetoric, in other words, took on populist trappings, but fundamentally it was not motivated by a populist imagination.

This is not to say that populism isn't important to modern presidential communication. In the last thirty years, it *has* become an important counterpoint to crafted talk. And, to the extent that he mimicked its form (if not its meaning), Reagan played a small role in its ascendancy. However, the rise of populism had distinctive organizational roots, and other presidents, namely, Carter and Clinton, did more to institutionalize it in presidential communication. These developments are the subject of the next chapter.

## Chapter Four

"Feeling Your Pain": Presidential Communication in a Populist Era

AS WE MOVE into the twenty-first century, a culture of expertise remains dominant in American presidential communication. In many ways the Clinton years read like a testimony to its staying power.[1] The 1990s featured "war rooms," "oppo research," and "triangulation"; "Harry and Louise" and the "Contract with America"; Rush Limbaugh and Matt Drudge. Like all modern presidents, Clinton used the latest communications technology to hone his messages. He worried incessantly about issues of framing (famously going so far as to quibble over the meaning of the word "is" during a legal deposition), and he crisscrossed the country giving more minor speeches in support of his policies than any prior president.[2] All of this is testament to the fact that the institutional configuration of American politics has remained basically the same since the end of the Second World War. And yet, for all its pervasiveness, the culture of expertise seems peculiarly unpopular. Few public officials admit to being expert politicians. Indeed, the decade of Clinton and Gingrich also saw the rise of Ross Perot and John McCain, presidential hopefuls whose popularity rested precisely on their refusal to practice crafted talk. It seems that the more crafted talk has become entrenched in presidential politics, the less it is respected.

Why should this be the case? Because, I think, of a resurgence of populism in the last quarter century. Populism has a long pedigree in American political culture, stretching back to the anti-Federalists.[3] Over this time, its basic intuition—that the "the people," threatened by "elites"—has been appropriated by different groups for different purposes. One finds, for instance, groups as diverse as 1830s Jacksonians and post–World War Two neoconservatives embracing a populist worldview. When one thinks of populism today, neoconservative demagogues (think Pat Buchanan) often come to mind. But equating modern populism with the Buchanans of the world would be a mistake. It is a much broader movement. New Social Movements (NSMs) of the 1960s and 1970s initiated the modern embrace of populism.[4] Suspicious of what Habermas has called the "instrumental reason" of the administrative state, NSM leaders advocate a politics based on the authentic common sense of ordinary people.[5] Part of their appeal involves an explicit rejection of crafted talk, which they take to be one of the most obvious manifestations of "instrumental reason." For NSM leaders, the professionalism, technicism, and means-end forms of rationality characteristic of crafted talk constitute a threat to "the people." Here, "the people" are defined not by class or ideology, but by a "postmaterialist" search for personal meaning and identity.[6] Seeking to devise forms of communal life that foster personal and collective authenticity, "the people" have been stymied by a self-serving professional class who wield crafted talk in the service of manipulation and control.[7]

Interestingly, however, populism has not underwritten a new institutional configuration of American political life. As I say, American politics continues to be driven by the presidency-led administrative state and the coterie of professional organizations that move in its orbit. Instead, populism has come to the fore in a more surreptitious manner, by infusing the very institutions—interest groups, think tanks, foundations, political parties, bureaucracies—that it ostensibly works against.[8] Populism now circulates precisely through the parties and the federal bureaucracies, through the interest group and think tank communities, and the community of experts who work as presidential aides and consultants. It has become so pervasive that it no longer confronts an identifiable antagonist: few political actors admit to being a member of the professional, elite, political class. Today, presidential hopefuls typically claim to be "real" people intent on combating the technicism of Washington politics. In this sense, modern populism serves as a meditation on us (rather than them), on "personhood" as much as "peoplehood."[9]

Having said this, the populist sensibility has not simply hollowed out the cultural core of these institutions. Crafted talk remains a powerful current in presidential communication. Rather, populism and crafted talk have blended in complicated ways. This mixing has thrown longstanding assumptions and expectations about presidential communication into doubt. For contemporary presidents, what it means to be professional or authentic, to be self-expressive or "on message," are not always clear. Put another way, by insisting that presidents be real, populism troubles the expectation that they be professional (and vice versa). In this chapter, then, I describe contemporary presidential communication as riven by a conflict between competing assumptions about how it ought to be practiced.

Perhaps no form of presidential communication demonstrates this conflict better than presidential town meetings. Such meetings have long embodied the populist ethos of participatory democracy. But no modern president had ever risked the intimacy, immediacy, and spontaneity characteristic of this form until Jimmy Carter took office.[10] Thus, when President Carter stepped to the podium in the town hall of Clinton, Massachusetts, on March 16, 1977, to conduct his first presidential town meeting, he innovated a new form of presidential communication.[11] Presidents Reagan and Bush refused to follow Carter's lead. But President Clinton resurrected the form in a series of town meetings during his first term of office. The town meetings of Presidents Carter and Clinton, I think, do more than register the influence of a populist sensibility in modern presidential rhetoric. They show the blending of this sensibility with crafted talk. This is to say, on the one hand these meetings register deeply felt intuitions about the proper role of intimacy, informality and authenticity in presidential communication; on the other hand, they are organized by communication experts to satisfy the goal all modern presidents share: to advance a legislative agenda. In this clash of populism with crafted talk, presidential town meetings provide a unique insight into the state of contemporary presidential communication.

Political Communication through a Populist Lens

Populism has erupted in different places at different times. The term was first coined in the 1870s–1880s—apparently independently—by the Russian Narodnichestvo and the People's Party of the United States. But one can already see its basic terms in the anti-Federalist opposition to the American Constitution, and during the twentieth century it has been embraced by groups as diverse as European right-wing authoritarian movements and Latin American left-wing socialist causes. Given this diversity, it is not surprising that scholars struggle even to name the phenomenon: ideology or syndrome? Rhetoric or discourse? Reactionary or progressive? Agrarian or urban?[12]

Like other constitutive concepts we have encountered (the "rhetorical presidency"; "progressivism," etc.), populism orients understanding in a particular direction. Canovan, for instance, notes that all populist movements share a "rhetoric," an "anti-elitis[m]" that "exalts 'the people' and stresses the pathos of the 'little man.'" More recently, Kazin has argued that populism is less a "rhetoric" than a "language," one "whose speakers conceive of ordinary people as a noble assemblage not bounded narrowly by class, view their elite opponents as self-serving and undemocratic, and seek to mobilize the former against the latter."[13] However, while all forms of populism exalt the people and castigate elites, this says nothing about who these groups are and what values are at stake. The "people" versus "elites" are merely "empty signifiers," as Westlind describes them, which mean something only when taken up at specific moments.[14] "The people," might be Russian peasants or the American middle class, farmers or factory workers. Elites may be a plutocracy or a liberal intelligentsia. Traditions under threat—pastoral agrarianism or democratic self-expression may vary across cultures and time periods. Thus, while populism constitutes the world in a particular fashion, its substantive definition must be worked out by specific groups in opposition to particular power blocs.

It is here that we must ask about the particular character of the populism favored by NSMs.[15] How do these movements define "the people?" Which of their traditions or values are threatened and by whom? At first glance, these questions seem unanswerable. NSMs span the ideological spectrum—from conservative Christians to radical leftist ecologists. Not surprisingly, they embrace divergent worldviews and traditions. However, underneath this diversity NSM theorists have gleaned a concern that all NSMs seem to share.[16] NSMs on both the right and the left share a sense that a highly rationalized public life threatens to squelch values and identities that do not conform to its means-end forms of reasoning. As Melucci puts it, this concern has led NSMs on a "search for identity, [a] quest for self that addresses the fundamental regions of human action: the body, the emotions, the dimensions of experience irreducible to instrumental rationality."[17] This "quest for self" distinguishes the NSM idiom from prior populist vernaculars.[18] Within modern populism, "the people" are defined not by class or ideology, but by culture and psychology. Rooted in values and identities that emanate from their everyday lives, "the people" are threatened by forms of instrumental rationality—including crafted talk—wielded by elites ensconced in dominant political and economic institutions. Literally in defense of their selves, NSMs across the political spectrum—from the peace movement to the Christian movement—struggle against the logic of control and management that lies at the heart of crafted talk.[19] To engage in this struggle, they have developed a shared cultural vocabulary.

Conviction, and cognate terms such as conscience and commitment, are a key group of terms within this vocabulary. In contrast to the impersonality and professionalism of crafted talk, NSMs argue that political communication must be rooted in personal beliefs. The Civil Rights Movement—a model for subsequent NSMs—made this argument to great effect during the 1950s and 1960s.[20] Civil Rights leaders encouraged Americans to "Let your conscience be your guide." Martin Luther King Jr. preached that the problem of civil rights ultimately was spiritual in nature: "we must meet the forces of hate," he argued, "with the power of love; we must meet physical force with soul force....";[21] and groups like the Students for Non-Violence Coordinating Committee (SNCC) argued that a proper democratic politics must emanate from personal conscience. "Call it a comprehension of ... identity," SNCC activist James Farmer said, "an intuition of the expanding boundaries of ... self, which, if not the same thing as freedom, is its radical source."[22] These appeals share a sense that a good politics must ultimately flow from personal conviction. This notion has a long history in Western politics. But it had a particular appeal in the postwar period, a time when crafted talk defined conventional politics. Compared to Eisenhower's careful hedging on the issue, and Kennedy's insistence on treating Civil Rights as one "technical [read political] problem" among others, the idea offered individuals disgruntled with the status quo a way of imagining an alternative mode of relating to one another. In the ensuing years, it has linked ethnic groups with environmentalists, feminists with anti-nuclear activists.

With this stress on conviction, NSMs foreground the role of the private sphere in public life. As Carl Oglesby, a leader of Students for a Democratic Society (SDS), put it, "Direct experience is the only 'incontrovertible' guide to personal and political behavior."[23] In part, NSMs grasp the private sphere so tightly because they find only alienation and anomie in a public life dominated by crafted talk. "The essential challenge," Students for a Democratic Society (SDS) leader Tom Hayden argued, "is ... to quit the acquiescence to political fate, the confidence in business-as-usual futures, and realize that in a time of mass organization, government by expertise, success through technical specialization, manipulation by the balancing of official secrecy with the soft sell technique ..., the time has come for the reassertion of the personal."[24] But NSMs' embrace of the personal also stems from a deep conviction that private life represents an important reservoir of political meaning. As one participant in the women's movement put it, "personal life [does] not merely reflect politics; it [is] politics."[25] In slogans like "the personal is political" (coined by the women's movement), and "think globally, act locally" (coined by the environmental movement), the populism of NSMs encourages "the people" to view their everyday lives as wellsprings of political action.

Finding political meaning in one's private life is not an easy exercise. For modern populists, it involves a process of discovery. As SDS put it in its founding document, The Port Huron Statement, it means *discovering* a "way that is one's own" rather than simply "having one's way."[26] Pat Robertson, no friend of the student movement, nonetheless shares this vocabulary of discovery. Writing of his turn to Christianity, he writes that, "There was just this incredible emptiness in my heart and I was looking for something better. What I wanted was just not in [conventional rewards and pleasures] ... and I didn't know what it was."[27] This sense of discovery has resonances with the progressive concept of "refined" public opinion. Just as "true" public opinion is educated, so one's "true" convictions are not self-evident. They must be realized in careful contemplation. But unlike progressives, who imagined a "refined" public opinion emerging out of an educational process of moral leadership and publicity—a kind of top-down transfer of knowledge— modern populism conceives of education as inside-out—delving into oneself to find one's "real" convictions. Whether connecting that "real" self to nature, God, or simply community, the point of this inner quest is to find a core set of convictions that integrates personal and collective authenticity.

This search for authenticity has resonances with other vocabularies in modern American public life. Certainly, it touches on a therapeutic language of self-help that has emerged during the twentieth century.[28] To the extent that it can be turned to the act of consumption, it also connects with modern media culture.[29] Observing these relationships, one might argue that the "quest for self" intrinsic to modern populism is little more than a corruption of public life—politics as therapeutic consumption. There is much to be said for this view. However, it will not do to conflate modern populism with these other cultural currents. While the three vocabularies have obvious links, modern populism has a distinctive shape and feel. More specifically, it has a deep connection with spirituality and religion. Doug Rossinow's argument about the New Left, that in this movement "wholeness, or authenticity ... displaced the more traditional [religious] objectives of salvation and even goodness," is an apt characterization of NSMs generally. Within modern populism, self-realization is important to the extent that it leads one to experience a spiritual sense of community, akin to the Christian feeling of agape.[30] In other words, the ultimate goal of authenticity is to discover a common humanity, not one's solitary, inner self.

It is in the connection between self and community that one finds the political dimension of modern populism. To borrow a term from Wini Brienes, the modern populist grammar imagines a "prefigurative politics"—a form of politics that prefigures and embodies a desired society.[31] The idea is that a properly organized community will allow all individuals the opportunity to discover themselves, and in discovering themselves they will find a connection to others deeper than mere self-interest. The problem is that modern society is not organized to foster authenticity. Instead, it engenders enormous social injustice that prevents whole groups of people from realizing their best selves. This fact implies that a "quest for self" must of necessity involve political participation. Since within modern populism, no one can be free in a society in which some are unfree, the only way to achieve personal authenticity is to work for social justice. It is only in this work that essential bonds between people can be discovered, and thus that authenticity can be achieved. In this manner, within the vocabulary of modern populism, self-understanding is linked to community through the concepts of participation and social justice.

But how is a just community to be achieved? This is really to ask, how are people supposed to work toward social justice? This question raises a certain ambivalence within modern populism. One answer stresses the importance of modeling personal and collective authenticity in everyday life. Society achieves social justice by acting it out both individually and collectively. The idea here is to develop forms of action that avoid the self-interest and technicism of conventional politics. After all, what good is it to achieve a given end—say, social justice—if in the process individuals must take actions that contradict their values? SDS member Dan McKelvey captures the sense of this approach when he asserts that, "One cannot divorce means from ends for no other reason than because men's consciousness and values are shaped in part by their actions and their perceptions of their actions. We must strive to create ... a certain mode of relating to other people which will serve as a counterweight to the manipulative, dehumanized, coercive relations which we so rightly criticize in the society around us."[32] In practice, this view translates into decentralized, small-scale, highly participatory organizations that emphasize process as much as results of decision making. For instance, during the 1970s many feminist organizations revolved around consciousness-raising groups whose purpose, a leader of one such group instructed its participants, was to "share ... feelings" and let these feelings "lead ... to ideas and then to action."[33] The group itself existed solely to promote a process of self-discovery. Ella Baker, a leader of SNCC (whose study groups provided a model for women's consciousness raising groups), articulates the root sensibility of this approach when she says that organizations are useful only to the extent that they get "people ... to understand that they cannot look for salvation anywhere but to themselves."[34]

The intuition here, much like that of the progressives, is that the good community exists somewhere beyond self-interest, power, and compromise, in a space where the core values of individuals merely express the democratic values of the broader community.[35] But unlike the progressives, modern populists believe that these core values can be realized by ordinary people in their own self-examination. There is no need for a morally upright, technically competent, class of public leaders to serve as models of preferred values. At the same time, modern populism is not open to the charge leveled against earlier forms of populism—that it is essentially conservative or reactionary.[36] As Jean Cohen writes, "what is at stake in the new forms of resistance ... is not the defense of a traditional sociocultural world (communal, ascriptive, diffuse) but of an already ... modernized life world (associational, achievement-oriented, differentiated)."[37] This is to say, NSMs seek not a return to, but a diversity of, core identities and values. Faced with the totalizing threat of crafted talk, modern populism imagines a thoroughly democratic public life that opens itself to many forms of self-expression.

The difficulty, of course, is that placing one's faith wholly in diversity and self-expression tends to produce inefficient, uncoordinated organizations. Sara Evans describes SNCC staff meetings as little more than "anarchic democracy."[38] Ella Baker recounts that in these meetings "the right of people to participate in the decisions that affect their lives ... began to be translated into the idea that each person working had a right to decide what ought to be done. So you began to do your own thing."[39] Subsequent movements experienced a similar tension. In internal conversations that privilege personal authenticity, organizations often lose sight of their ultimate goal: social justice.

Typically, this tension works itself out in NSMs through a process of professionalization. Plagued by disorganization and inefficiency, NSMs, like all social movements, eventually dwindle down to a few highly committed individuals. Finding themselves leaders of social movements with no movement behind them, these individuals reorganize. As John McCarthy and

Mayer Zald note, since the 1970s they have been subsidized in this task by several sources: an enlarged pool of middle class contributors; government programs; philanthropic foundations; and a mass media that eases access to potential supporters. The ironic result, McCarthy and Zald conclude, is the "professionalization" of social movements: "Movement leaders in this matrix become social movement entrepreneurs. Their movements' impact results from their skill at manipulating images of relevance and support through the communications media."[40] As mass support for social movements wanes, movement leaders gravitate to the arena of conventional politics. And as they do, the populist sensibility that animates their activities insinuates itself into professional political organizations.

In the process, modern populism and crafted talk have blurred. Consider, for instance, the rise of the "new right."[41] Inspired by a belief that the liberal state threatened cherished values (both political and religious), conservative organizations began to mobilize in the 1950s. The result was a conservative social movement that eventually grew into think tanks, philanthropic foundations, and interest groups circulating around national politics. As the movement has ebbed, these conservative organizations have embedded themselves within the political process. While retaining a populist sense that government ought to respond to the values of ordinary Americans, these organizations press their cause through the organizational structure of conventional politics: direct mail campaigns, satellite television and talk radio, fundraising drives through church networks, political action committees (PACs), and think tanks, among others. At the height of the conservative revolution, the 1994 Republican takeover of Congress, Newt Gingrich could rely on a network of conservative organizations so cohesive that it was capable of distributing a "cheat sheet"—a list of terms (like "tax & spend") by which to refer to Democrats—to thousands of conservative politicians, from members of city councils to state houses.[42] Working toward a day when the national government can be returned to "the people," these conservatives nonetheless have adopted a strategy that would make any modern professional political actor proud.

This transformation of the conservative movement is only one (albeit compelling) example of a larger trend. As the grassroots infrastructure of the political parties has fragmented, and the political process become detached from the everyday lives of ordinary Americans, only the most committed—or ambitious—individuals remained. But given that all of these actors are professional manipulators of crafted talk, it is difficult to distinguish conviction from ambition. In other words, as professional populists came to head interest groups and write policy papers for think tanks; as their groups came to represent the core constituencies—the "base"—of party support throughout the country; as they began to staff Capitol Hill as legislative aides for members of Congress and Congressional committees, and to work at the parties' national headquarters; as they began to run for political office themselves—the difference between conviction and professionalism has blurred. Today, all members of the Washington Community use every means at their disposal to frame issues in ways that serve their interests. All rely on mass media to organize and mobilize constituencies. And thus, all rely on rationalized means to achieve their ends, whatever those ends might be.

Curiously, however, the core of the populist vocabulary has survived its integration into conventional political institutions. Indeed, the notion that political actors should be "real" people, represent "the people," work against political experts who just don't "get it," is widely accepted. Granted, members of the Washington Community may scoff at the notion in private. But in public, a populist grammar holds great sway. Whatever their private beliefs, the public actions of political actors are in part shaped by the expectations of modern populism. This is especially true in presidential politics. Think, for instance, of reactions to Michael Dukakis' performance during a 1988 televised presidential debate. Much to his detriment, he insisted on answering a hypothetical question about the rape of his wife with an unemotional recitation of policy. Recall reactions to George H. W. Bush's display of ignorance during a 1992 town meeting debate when he did not know the average price of a loaf of bread; or, to Al Gore's "wooden" personality during the 2000 presidential campaign. Today, it is the rare politician who does not take into account the assumptions and expectations of populism.

This cultural strand, therefore, exercises a powerful force in contemporary presidential communication. Institutionalized as a set of assumptions about what presidential communication ought to be, it represents an alternative gravitational force to crafted talk. Its terminology— conviction, self-discovery, authenticity, community, participation, social justice—encourages us to view presidential communication as an expression of self. By making politics deeply personal, this vocabulary disrupts the ease and comfort with which politicians once grappled with the "technical problems" of politics. The result is at times contradictory and ironic: Bob Dole, a career Washington politician, runs for the presidency in 1996 as a simple, ordinary man from Kansas. At others it is excruciating to watch: Al Gore's long refrain about the death of his sister during the 1996 Democratic convention speech; and at others it is merely hilarious: Gerald Ford attempting to eat a tamale with its husk still attached during the 1976 presidential campaign. At all times, however, modern populism produces great anxiety about an institutional environment grounded in a professionalism and expertise. The town meetings of Jimmy Carter and Bill Clinton illuminate the terms on which this anxiety has been expressed over the past quarter century.

Getting Real: President Carter's Town Meetings[43]

It is fair to say that Jimmy Carter never would have become president had Richard Nixon not abused his presidential prerogatives. But it is just as fair to say that Carter would not have won had he not been so comfortable with the new populism. During the 1976 presidential campaign, Carter presented himself as an authentic person who could reestablish the public's trust in the presidency, someone, he was to say repeatedly during the campaign, who would "never lie" to the American people. He promised Americans not an efficient government but a "Government as Good as Its People." As president, Carter continued to link himself to "average Americans." He chose to walk to the White House rather than ride in a limousine during his inaugural parade. He suspended the playing of "Hail to the Chief" on his entrance at public functions. He addressed the public in a nationwide television speech dressed in a cardigan sweater, sitting in front of a three-log fire. He mandated that at least 10 percent of guests at state dinners were to be "average Americans." He briefly toyed with the idea of setting up a toll-free phone line to the White House in which citizens could get help on their problems with government, and with asking others to call him "Mr. Carter" rather than "Mr. President."

At the same time, Carter and his advisers were professional politicians. As early as 1972, when he was still governor of Georgia, political advisers such as Hamilton Jordan were suggesting that Carter was perfectly placed to take advantage of the populist mood.[44] Five days before Nixon officially resigned from office, on August 5, 1974, Carter's inner-circle had already devised a detailed plan for the coming presidential campaign. They combined a military-like assault on Democratic party elites with a populist style that stressed small, informal events. In a scene repeated across the country, Carter landed in a small town, spoke at the most prominent local venue, stayed the night with a local citizen, and awoke early the next morning to start the process over again. As he entered office, Carter moved quickly to institutionalize his interactions with ordinary Americans in a "People Program." This program—designed, as Midge Costanza, its first director, put it, to "ensure that President Carter is not isolated from the people and that the government responds to their ideas"—included call-in radio shows, White House tours, the designation of a White House mailbox for the public, and town meetings.[45]

Carter was not the first to use ask-the-president forums. Both Eisenhower and Nixon experimented with the format.[46] However, Carter was the first to engage ordinary Americans in spontaneous, unrehearsed Q&A sessions, and to make these engagements a routine aspect of his presidency. Although he was often accused of using them as "gimmicks," the president evidently believed in them very strongly. Looking back on Carter's four years in office, Gregory Schneiders, a presidential assistant who organized these events for a time, recalls that the president "really meant all those corny things he said ... in the White House."[47] The depth of his commitment is apparent in the design of his presidential library, where a town meeting display occupies a good deal of the building's bottom floor. Long after it became clear that the town meetings served little political purpose, and media consultants like Gerald Rafshoon had lost interest, Carter continued to hold them. In the end, over his four years in office, he held seventeen of these events across the country.

In many ways then, Carter's town meetings were organized according to the modern populist expectation that a good politics is rooted in the everyday lives of "real" people. Most obviously, they were held in small towns across the country. The first of them took place in Clinton, MA, population 13,000. Subsequent meetings took place in Yazoo City, MS; Nashua, NH; Aliquippa, PA; Portsmouth, NH; Bardstown, KY; Burlington, IA; Tampa, FL; Dolton, IL; and Merced, CA. Purposely "off the beaten track," as one aide involved in selecting the sites put it, these towns evoked a "real" America outside the Washington beltway.[48] The town's citizens often turned out to greet the president parade-style along the town's main street. For the town meeting in Clinton, MA, a pastoral painting featuring a country road winding through trees toward a tranquil lake served as a backdrop to the stage. At the town meeting in Merced, the walls of the gymnasium were lined with placards that read, "A Big Howdy from a Small Town."[49] As if to accentuate the intimate atmosphere, Carter often took off his jacket and rolled up his shirtsleeves when answering audience questions. And, to stress his intention to get close to real Americans, Carter made it a point to stay overnight in the home of townspeople like Catherine Thompson of Clinton, MA, even going so far as to write a note explaining why her children were late for school.

Getting real also meant avoiding television. Unlike forms of crafted talk, which depended heavily on television, Carter's town meetings virtually ignored the medium.[50] Most of these events were held in high school gymnasiums, and one (in Burlington, Iowa) was held outside, on a grassy hill overlooking a bluff. Selection of these sites indicates that television was not a prime consideration in the development of the meetings. Poorly lit, and unable to carry sound very well, gymnasiums are not ideal environments for broadcasting a televisual event. Given where they were held, it is not surprising that only three of the town meetings in my sample (in Clinton, Yazoo, and Aliquippa) were broadcast live.[51] The first was broadcast nationwide, while the other two were broadcast regionally; all three were aired on the public broadcasting system (PBS), not on the networks.

In keeping with their assumption that the events would be "genuine" engagements between the president and the public, Carter's aides did little to control the composition of local audiences.[52] For some of the town meetings, the White House simply ran ads in local newspapers that announced the president's visit and provided coupons to be filled out and returned by readers. Readers who turned in their coupons were entered into a raffle for available seats. For other meetings, the president's visit was advertised and tickets given out on a first come, first served basis. Unlike Eisenhower's Q&A sessions, which were organized by advertising agencies and the Republican National Committee, or Nixon's, which were wholly controlled by his staff, Carter clearly wanted these events to reflect his commitment to genuine interactions with ordinary Americans.

Not surprisingly, given that audience questions were not screened— individuals merely had to walk up to a microphone—the exchanges had none of the staged feel of crafted talk. Audiences asked questions that mirrored their diversity. Of the 152 questions asked of the president, nearly 20 percent were uncodifiable into any particular category. In Yazoo, MS, the president was asked successively about "Public Law 93-641," and about "how it feels to be President" (pp. 1321–1323). Questioners asked about the Middle East peace process and about local redevelopment programs. They spoke on behalf of the homeless, the children of America, taxpayers, and small business people, among others. One woman told of the personal dilemma of paying for her children's college education (Dolton, p. 1947). Another wanted to know how she could get direct-dial telephone service in her county (Bardstown, p. 1343). Questioners complained about the cost of groceries

(Clinton, p. 394). An engineer launched into a long discussion of his plans to conserve energy through the invention of new traffic lights (Dolton, p. 1951). Audience members joked with the president: "Mr. President, excuse me if I'm nervous, but the last time I won anything in a government raffle, I was drafted" (Portsmouth, p. 708); "I'm a professional window cleaner. Do you have any dirty windows in the White House? The motto of my company is: 'We brighten your outlook" (Burlington, p. 1499). During a long exchange, the president and a part-time farmer in Merced engaged in easy banter about the laziness of family members (Merced, p. 1314). On two occasions (in Portsmouth and Tampa) audience members held up protest banners, heckled the president and others in attendance, and held town meetings of their own outside the gymnasium. The diversity and intimacy of these questions register a basic assumption of the format as a whole: as a Clinton, MA, audience member put it, Carter was "one of us, a man of the people...." This is to say, the entire exercise was grounded in a shared sense that Carter would engage with audiences as one American speaking to another.

An implication of this assumption was that Carter should not rely on expertise or professionalism when answering questions. But if not professionalism, then on what could Carter base his responses? One answer was his personal experience. The president talked (in Clinton, MA) about the price of groceries at the White House: "I know from firsthand [about the cost of food]. We've been really watching the food bill.... I'm in the same boat as you." To a question about federal set-aside programs for minorities asked in Yazoo, MS, he talked about his experience as a small businessman: "When I came home from the Navy in 1953, I started a business and I needed ... to get a loan...." To a question (asked in Nashua, NH) about the separation of church and state, he shared intimate details about his religious life: "I worship daily. The last thing I do every evening is to have a private worship service with my wife...." With its stress on the mundane details of everyday life—which we all share—this kind of response placed Carter in the same intimate sphere as his audiences.

Carter also distinguished himself as a "real" person by stressing the ethical dimension of issues. This comes out clearly in his responses to questions that asked about locally important issues like the closure of military bases or the performance of a local government agency. To such questions, a savvy political answer might have been to tell audiences what they wanted to hear. However, Carter made a concerted effort to do precisely the opposite. To a question about local telephone service (asked in Bardstown, KY), Carter made it clear that he could not "help Bullitt County get better telephone service. I'm not guaranteeing you any results...." When criticized by a Merced, CA, farmer about the grain embargo on the Soviet Union, Carter was unapologetic: "The most important responsibility of any President ... is to keep our Nation strong and at peace, and I don't believe that we can keep our Nation at peace ... without our Nation being strong ... morally and ethically.... [T]he only way you can keep that moral and ethical strength is to condemn aggression...." The implicit claim behind such responses becomes clear in the president's response to a question about a base closure near Clinton, MA: "I never promised in order to get votes that I would keep a particular military base open. I would like to make a judgment in every instance on what I think is best for our country...." As this last response suggests, by insisting that he would make decisions based upon his convictions, Carter wished to separate himself from the strategic mindset of conventional politics. As with any "good" person, Carter implicitly communicated to his audience, personal ethics, not political expediency, guided his decision making.[53]

Finally, Carter occasionally admitted that his audiences were more informed than he was about particular issues. As he stated in his opening remarks at the first town meeting in Clinton, MA, "I've got a lot to learn and I'm eager to learn. I don't claim to know all the answers and the day I leave the White House and another President takes over, I still won't know all the answers." Of course, during press conferences presidents sometimes made a similar admission, but typically with very different results. Think, for instance, of Wilson's refusal to answer questions to which he did not have an answer—and reporters' sense that he was stonewalling. Or, think of Eisenhower's candid admissions of ignorance—and the conventional wisdom within Washington that he was unprepared. The same candidness that was interpreted as defects on these occasions seemed emancipatory and participative in the context of the town meetings. As Carter himself put it at the end of his town meeting in Dolton, IL, "We get a lot of good ideas coming out to meet people like you, and I think the sense that I get is that we are all partners." In a press conference—a typical format during the heyday of crafted talk—the expectation is that the president should have command of facts and details. In part, this expectation defines what it means for presidents to act as professional communicators. When they don't have this command (think Ronald Reagan), reporters and other observers in the Washington Community begin to doubt a president's abilities. Given their populist assumptions, town meetings carry no such expectations. At least to a point, confessing ignorance brings a president closer to audiences, engages them in a personal manner, and even includes them as partners in governance.

In both form and substance, then, one can see that Carter's town meetings were not organized according to the dictates of crafted talk. The White House did all of the things typically done in preparation for presidential trips: advance people were sent; researchers were asked to produce guides containing local facts and issues; speechwriters were mobilized to prepare opening remarks. But the occasions were not stage-managed in the way that crafted talk demands. Locations were purposefully "off the beaten track." Audiences were not carefully chosen and their questions were not screened. The president often referred to personal experiences and was not drilled in facts and details as he typically was for press conferences.

Perhaps most tellingly, the favor of the national news media was not curried. These occasions, in other words, were not standard efforts to manage public opinion through the news. Instead, White House aides devoted most of their attention to making these events genuine, authentic interactions between the president and local people. Their assumption was that these meetings ought to be intimate and familiar, that they should give ordinary Americans a sense of participation in government. For its time, this was a revolutionary idea. The previous twenty-five years had witnessed the institutionalization of a diametrically opposed assumption: that politics was a domain of experts who required little assistance from the American people. Carter's town meetings demonstrate that, after roughly twenty years of struggle by NSMs against this very principle, a populist idiom had reached the center of American politics.

If Carter's town meetings demonstrate this fact, they also show that populism had made only limited headway against crafted talk. In 1977, the institutions of crafted talk—bureaucracies, think tanks, academic institutions, political and media consulting firms, interest groups, the national news media—retained tight control over basic expectations and assumptions of presidential communication. President Carter was still the "leader of the free world," engaged in constant negotiations with the Soviet Union. When not engaged by the "People Program," his staff used crafted talk to burnish the president's image and frame his legislative initiatives. Pollsters and political consultants (especially Pat Cadell and Gerald Rafshoon) generally exercised a great degree of control over the president's communication practices. If not as organized (or successful) as the spin control of the Reagan period and beyond, Carter's overall style of political communication exhibited many of the traits of crafted talk.

One can see these traits in the town meetings themselves. Consider, for instance, the structural arrangement of these events. It is true that they were held in out-of-the-way places. But each was organized as a kind of political rally. Advertised as intimate gatherings, an average of nearly 1,500 people attended these meetings. The audience resembled a crowd more than a small gathering of "real" people, and the meetings had the feel of campaign events more than intimate discussions with the president. Often, gymnasiums were so full that people in the back took to holding placards or signs for the president to read. For his part, Carter rarely moved from behind a lectern located in the middle of a raised stage. The lectern came complete with the presidential seal, a representation of the president's unique status. The effect of this arrangement was to accentuate the position of the president, who stood before the audience as a singular, stationary performer, while diminishing the individuality of the audience members, who remained faceless within an audience of over a thousand people. Rather than a "real" person speaking to average Americans, the structure of these meetings portrayed Carter as "the President," performing in front of an audience.

Further, the location of the town meetings in small towns often hid the mundane political motives behind these presidential trips. All of the meetings were part of longer "swings" through key states, or were overshadowed by more "presidential" addresses held elsewhere. The president's first town meeting, for instance, occurred as part of a two-day trip in which the president was slated to visit Massachusetts and West Virginia to curry the favor of Senate Majority Leader Robert Byrd and House Speaker Thomas P. "Tip" O'Neill Jr. And after visiting Clinton for a day, the president went on to give a widely publicized address at the United Nations. His trip to Aliquippa, PA, was intended as a show of support for former Pittsburgh mayor Peter F. Flaherty, a gubernatorial candidate that year who had supported Carter's presidential campaign. A visit to Portsmouth, NH, initiated his 1980 presidential campaign. His Bardstown, KY, meeting made up for Carter's cancellation of a scheduled appearance at the National Governor's Association meeting in Louisville earlier that month (which was widely viewed as a snub to Kentucky's Democratic governor, Julian Carroll), and served as a backdrop for selling his proposal to increase coal production as part of his energy program.

Interactions between the president and audiences also contradict basic populist assumptions. For example, questioners almost never approached

Carter as particular people, preferring to speak in the voice of the "average American." A questioner during the Clinton town meeting began this way: "Bill Clinley, 26 Cotchelay Street. Mr. President ... *we* ask that despite many pressures which are exerted upon you to mold your programs to conform to special interests.... *[W]e* have faith that you will always place *our* interests above all of these (italics mine)" (Clinton, p. 394). Another questioner, after Carter's Camp David summit with Menachem Begin and Anwar Sadat, took time to "commend [Carter] on [his] splendid efforts.... I think I can speak for the majority of Americans in saying that we are extremely proud..." (Aliquippa, p. 1606). Still another, in a query about natural gas, framed his question this way: "Do you think you and we, the people, can get the Congress to listen to you and to us and help us get an energy program that will keep us the richest and the greatest and the freest nation on Earth? [italics mine]" (Tampa, p. 1577). The framing of such questions resembles that of letters written in reaction to FDR's fireside chats—a time when Americans first learned to exercise a voice of mass citizenship. But while this frame sounded appropriate in that context, it rang false in a town meeting, where the expectation was that participants were individuals, not part of a mass citizenry.

The fact that audiences asked questions that had no clear connection to their everyday lives further illustrates their unease with populist expectations. Ninety-seven of the 152 questions (or 62 percent) that participants asked the president were about policy issues that had no direct connection to the questioner. That is, a majority of audience members preferred to ask about public issues that affected all Americans rather than about issues that affected only themselves or people like themselves. For instance, after identifying herself as a housewife from Burlington, Iowa, one woman asked the president: "What is being done to hold Mexico responsible for harming wildlife and ecology and a regional economy in South Texas?" (Burlington, p. 1496). A semi-retired pharmacist from Dolton, IL, was going to ask the president about "an immediate freeze on wage prices," but as that question had already been asked, he turned to his "alternate question on Cuba" (Dolton, p. 1943). During the ninety minutes Carter spent answering questions from high school students in Nashua, NH, not one of the questions were oriented to issues peculiar to teenage students. Instead, the students asked about issues such as Middle East arms sales, civil service reform, national health care, and the budget. In all, only fourteen of the 152 questions asked of Carter (or 9 percent) were based in the personal experience of the questioner. As much as the populist mood of these occasions stressed informality and individuality, audiences refused to step away from their more conventional role as mass citizens.

Given that two-thirds of the questions involved policy issues, it is not surprising that Carter tended to reply in these terms. His town meetings were littered with discussions of some law, federal action, legislative proposal or policy idea. He talked about zero-based budgeting, the Strategic Arms Limitation Treaty (SALT), federal regulations of nuclear power plants, energy policy, and ways of achieving better coordination between federal, state, and local agencies. Often, he would begin a response by reflecting on a personal experience, as when he answered a question on nuclear power plants (during the Nashua, NH, town meeting) by noting that his "own background in graduate school [was] as a scientist," but then go on to provide a more technical, policy-oriented response: "I can't decide that [whether a particular nuclear plant is safe] and I don't have the authority nor the desire to do so. Some states, as you know, through referenda or through action by the State legislatures, have put very tight constraints on the location of power plants...."

But the president often went beyond merely responding to individual questions. On some occasions, his answers betray an impulse to use these meetings for purposes other than merely interacting with his immediate audiences. For example, at times—particularly when asked foreign policy questions—he spoke over the heads of his immediate audience to communicate with wider constituencies. During the Clinton, MA, town meeting, he was asked what he "personally fe[lt]" must be done to secure peace in the Middle East (p. 386). Instead of directing his comments to the questioner, he offered a diplomatic lecture on the "prerequisites for peace," ending with an appeal to Israeli and Palestinian leaders: "we offer our good offices ... [to] get all of the parties to agree to come together to Geneva." The president not only instructed (rather than conversed) with the audience member, he used the question, much as he might in a press conference, as a platform to issue a message to political actors outside this forum. At other times, Carter set himself apart as a role model for others to emulate. To a question about inflation (Portsmouth), the president began his response by saying: "the first thing we can do, I as President, is to set an example..." (p. 704). To a question about how Americans might conserve energy, (Burlington), he asserted that "I try to run 4 or 5 miles every day..." (p. 1500), the implication being that if he could do it, others should try as well. Finally, at the end of nearly every town meeting, the president engaged in an awkward round of moral cheerleading: "We're the strongest nation on

Earth," he told his audience in Dolton, IL, "Militarily, we're the strongest; economically, we're the strongest.... [L]et's don't ever forget that the United States of America is the best place on Earth to live. It's the greatest nation on Earth..." (p. 1953). In all of these ways, Carter acted not as an "average" American—no different from other Americans—but as the "President," a singular actor. And as the "President," his answers sought to achieve some end—whether speaking to international constituencies or propping up flagging national morale—that lay outside the moment.

All of these dynamics suggest that audiences and the president shared nonpopulist expectations about their respective roles in interacting with one another. Where modern populism demands a certain egalitarianism of action—every person must participate in politics to discover communal ties—Carter's town meetings often were grounded in assumptions of conventional politics. Carter often justified his actions by referring to his responsibilities as the "President," while audiences clearly viewed their role as nonparticipatory. Put another way, where modern populism imagines an inside-out educational process in politics—individuals discovering their convictions through self-examination—Carter's town meetings often proceeded through a more conventional process of opinion management. This was most evident on the many occasions when the president ended responses by asking for the name and address of questioners so that he could send them additional materials—a Congressional address or legislative proposal—for further reading. Here, Carter invites these individuals to participate in politics not through personal reflection, but through the careful review of technical materials.

Taken together, the blending of populist and rationalist assumptions embedded in Carter's town meetings make for puzzling engagements. On the one hand, the meetings were organized according to the populist expectation that the president ought to present himself as a real person; they suggested that it was legitimate for "average Americans" to interact with, rather than simply applaud for, their president; and they indicated that presidential leadership might be done not through crafted talk, but through genuine, intimate interactions in face-to-face settings. On the other hand, it is clear that neither audiences nor the president were comfortable with the implications of this expectation. Advertised as intimate affairs, the events resembled something like campaign rallies. Audiences tended to defer to the president, to speak in the anonymous tones of the "average American," and to ask policy-oriented questions of a kind one might find in any meeting of professional political actors. Standing on a stage above his audience, behind a lectern with the presidential seal, the president laid out policies, legislation, rules, and guidelines. On occasion, he addressed his answers to constituencies outside the gymnasiums or acted as a kind of national moral cheerleader. The result was a breakthrough of sorts in modern presidential communication—no president had ever dared to engage in such spontaneous, intimate affairs, and certainly none had done so without the networks in tow. But it was a curious, often contradictory, innovation.

This ambiguity is reflected in news coverage of the meetings. White House reporters found it difficult to fit the events into conventional news formats. Were they speeches? Photo opportunities? Campaign rallies? Reporters vacillated. At times, they covered the meetings as traditional news events: "Carter States Panama Canal Objectives"; "Carter Threatens 'Drastic Action' in Coal Stalemate"; "Carter Bars Cuba Recognition for Now."[54] In this mode, reporters framed the meetings as something like press conferences, that is, as occasions on which Carter made some newsworthy comment. Audiences fell into the background of this coverage—often, they were not even identified—as reporters evaluated the president's comments against current policy commitments, the statements of other political actors, or his own previous statements. For instance, in his report on the president's visit to Dolton, IL, Don Irwin noted that "in his reply to a man who asked why Washington did not admit that 'Cuba's form of government is here to stay,' Carter made no mention of maneuvers that a Navy and Marine Corps force will conduct...." Similarly, in her report on the president's visit to Bardstown, KY, Helen Dewar couched Carter's comments in the context of others made by Labor Secretary Ray Marshall, recent actions taken by the UMW-BCOA bargaining committee, and the opinions of a White House source. For Irwin and Dewar, the meaning of the town meetings lay in the production of news by the president.

On occasion, however, reporters suggested precisely the opposite, that the interactions had no newsworthy purpose other than to serve Carter's political goals. In other words, reporters sometimes framed the meetings as political events. "It was a colorful [evening]," Edward Walsh wrote of the first town meeting in Clinton, MA, "and from the White House's point of view, [a] successful evening...." Of Carter's visit to Bardstown, KY, Walsh wrote that the event was "pure Carter populism," but one intended to "to use the backdrop of the nation's largest coal producing states for an appeal for enactment of his energy program...." David Broder noted that during his visit to Aliquippa, PA, the president "endured the rituals of a town meeting ... including the now customary little girl's hug and an unexpected invitation to become an honorary member of a local Girl Scout troop." As these quotes indicate, reporters sometimes approached the town meetings as little more than political puffery. "The main point the President was trying to make," of the Clinton, MA, town meeting, Robert Shogan concluded, "had less to do with any of the specific issues raised than with the simple fact that he was appearing in this unpresidential setting." And Eleanor Randolph opined of the Bardstown meeting that "at [what] seems to be a standard event in the Carter Presidency—the President easily deflected questions on his troubles with the strategic arms limitation treaty, the rights of refugees, and even one complaint about local telephone service."[55] The frame of this coverage had a cynical implication, namely, that the president would organize supposedly "genuine" interactions with the public so that he could use audiences as stage props to satisfy a self-interested political goal.

Finally, reporters sometimes interpreted the town meetings as campaign events. "Jimmy Carter began his campaign for reelection today," *The Washington Post* reported of the president's visit to Portsmouth, NH, "where presidential campaigns always begin—the nation's first primary state." Viewing the events through this prism, reporters emphasized their pageantry and puffery, and located their meaning in the context of the next presidential election. "Tonight's event ... was called a 'town meeting,'" Edward Walsh reported of Carter's visit to Clinton, MA, "but it was in no sense a genuine New England town meeting and more closely resembled a carefully planned campaign appearance...." Steven Weisman wrote of Carter's visit to Dolton, IL, that it "was the climactic public event of a two-day swing through the Middle West ... that had both governmental and political overtones. Before leaving for the high school ... Mr. Carter showed that he was obviously buoyed by the laudatory remarks directed at him last night by Mayor Jane M. Byrne of Chicago, who stands to influence the way the Illinois delegation will vote at the Democratic convention next summer." Don Irwin went so far as to ignore any specific reference to the town meeting at all, preferring to focus on the wider political context as the president "tested political currents in [the] little state that will hold 1980's lead-off presidential primary...."[56] As in the political frame, this coverage stressed the politics that lay behind the pageantry of these events. However, because this politics was rooted in a conventional goal—winning elections—this coverage bore less of the cynicism of the politics frame. In convening these meetings, Carter's purpose may have been self-interested, this coverage assumed, but it was self-interest in the service of a legitimate political goal.

If anything, the networks leaned even more toward covering the town meetings as political or campaign events. One reason has to do with simple logistics. Given that most of the town meetings were held in the early afternoon, network reporters had little time to package their reports. Instead, they typically transmitted pictures of Carter's day as a whole back to New York, and the meetings were reported in the context of the day's activities. Thus, all three networks reported on the president's meeting with citizens in Yazoo, MS, in the context of the several speeches he gave during his swing through the South. Similarly, they couched the president's Tampa, FL, town meetings in the context of his earlier visit to Atlanta, GA. Taken as a whole, it was difficult not to see the town meetings as one instance in daylong political exercises. When not covering them in these political terms, network reporters framed the town meetings as campaign events. For example, all three networks led their coverage of the president's July 4, 1980, visit to Merced with a "Campaign '80" caption. In contrast to print reporting, little of the network coverage focused on the news value of the president's remarks. Indeed, on the day after these events—a time which print reporters used to reflect on their news value—network reporters had already moved on the next location: none of the town meetings received network television coverage on the day after they took place.

Print and television news coverage register the ambivalence of the meetings as a whole. Much like participants themselves, reporters struggled to develop a coherent sense of the expectations embedded in these meetings. Were they authentic encounters between the president and citizens, or were they merely instances of crafted talk? Like the participants, reporters generally came to view these meetings in conventional terms. Just as few citizens engaged with the president on terms of equality, so the reporting captured the meaning of these meetings in conventional frames. Just as audiences refused to act as equal participants in these exercises, so the news coverage virtually ignored their participation. Just as the president separated himself from citizens—standing on a platform behind a presidential seal—so the coverage highlighted his actions, words, and intentions. Every one of the newspaper photos of these events isolate Carter standing on a platform, looking outward to a cheering audience. In the end, Carter's town meetings have the curious distinction of being organized and designed to foster authenticity and participation, but ultimately achieving neither.

Taken as a whole then, Carter's town meetings demonstrate the shallowness of populism's roots in presidential communication. So removed had presidential communication become from ordinary people that Carter's limited populist intention to be "real" to the American people was utterly remarkable. However, neither Carter, his audiences, nor the news media were prepared to go much beyond this wave at authenticity. In these meetings, one finds great interest in a new form of presidential interaction with the public, but great confusion as well.

However, as President Clinton's town meetings indicate, by the 1990s populism's roots in the presidential communication had deepened, and thus begun to trouble more profoundly the assumptions of crafted talk.

Getting Personal: President Clinton's Town Meetings

It is likely that Bill Clinton came to the town meeting format less as a matter of principle than of political survival. From the very beginning of his presidential candidacy, he was caught in a ferocious Washington spin cycle. During the early primary period of the 1992 presidential election, Clinton received what Meg Greenfield called the "worst press I've known a candidate to get."[57] Stories about his drug use, his purported liaisons with Gennifer Flowers, and his draft status as a college student dominated press coverage. By the end of the election, the spin cycle had shifted. One study found that in the last two months of the campaign, Clinton received over 60 percent favorable coverage in the *Washington Post*, a mirror opposite of the 60 percent negative coverage which President Bush received.[58] Surviving the withering press coverage of the early campaign, Clinton dubbed himself "The Comeback Kid" and rode into the White House confident that he had solved the puzzle of the news media. However, the Washington spin cycle was not done with him. The new president never had a honeymoon period with the Washington Community.[59] After only days in office he was besieged by interest groups on both the left and the right. Conservatives in Congress kept up a steady stream of criticism on the radio and television talk show circuit while liberals rushed to negotiate their concerns with the new president.[60] Before his first week in office had ended, reporters were suggesting that Clinton was "embarrassingly unprepared for battle," that he was "risking disaster," "stumbling," and "incredibly inept."[61]

In this context, Clinton's turn to town meetings and other outside-the-beltway venues can be understood as a matter of political expediency.[62] It is important, however, to note the wider significance of the president's move to populist forms of communication. Baby boomers inspired by NSMs had been insinuating themselves into the Washington Community since the 1970s.[63] By the 1990s, the vocabulary of modern populism had made great inroads in presidential politics. But as the first baby-boomer president, Clinton represented something of a watershed event in this process. It seemed, finally, that all of the Washington Community—on both the left and the right—had become populists. Where Carter's populism represented something of an aberration, Clinton's rise to the presidency crystallized a process that had been under way for over two decades. It therefore gave Washingtonians pause as they took stock of what had transpired. What did it mean, they wondered, that even the president is an ordinary person now? As with other populist forms, the town meeting—no doubt embraced by Clinton for self-interested reasons—served as a kind of meditation on the meaning of modern populism for presidential communication.

The format also resonated with a cultural populism characteristic of emerging "new media": television and radio talk shows; television news magazines like *60 Minutes* and *PrimeTime Live*; cable channels like MTV and the Comedy Channel; print and television tabloid shows; and the Internet. As Richard Davis and Diana Owen argue,

> The new media ... differ qualitatively from the traditional media in the populism they not only articulate, but seem to embody. Populist themes are recurrent in the new media. The new media are unabashedly anti-big government and anti-incumbent. They also claim to shear away the filter traditional news media have constructed between the governors and the governed.... The new media's very existence should be able to offer ordinary citizens the opportunity to participate in politics far beyond opinion polls....[64]

Like Carter's events, Clinton's town meetings carried a strong expectation that ordinary people should participate in the political process. However, by the 1990s, this expectation was connected to a wider enthusiasm for new media. Moving in these larger cultural currents, Clinton's town meetings gained added significance. Much more than Carter's efforts, Clinton's interactions with the public were celebrated as a manifestation of a new, more intimate relationship between political leaders and citizens.[65]

The structure of Clinton's engagements with citizens indicates the strength of their connection with new media. Where Carter's events were designed without consideration for television, Clinton's town meetings were explicitly organized as media events. Cities for these events were chosen not because they were out of the way, but because they served as regional media hubs—Atlanta rather than Aliquippa, Detroit rather than Dolton. The events were held in local news studios rather than high school gymnasiums. Satellites connected three or four audiences dispersed throughout the region to the events. On nine occasions, local news directors organized the town meetings and reporters moderated the proceedings. For the tenth, Clinton chose Ted Koppel and his news show, *Nightline*, to moderate a nationally broadcast town meeting from Tampa, Florida.

Moreover, where Carter's town meetings were modeled on the political rally, Clinton's events took their cue from the daytime television talk show. Organized along the lines of women's consciousness-raising groups, these shows surrounded guests by a circle of relatively small audiences and a roving host. The idea of these talk shows, as Livingstone and Lunt put it, is not only to erode boundaries between audiences and participants, experts and ordinary people, but also to celebrate "the ordinary person and the authenticity of direct personal experience."[66] Clinton obviously wished to infuse his meetings with a similar feeling. His town meetings included an audience of no more than a few hundred seated in rows set low and near to the stage. Only a few feet separated the president from audience members. Wide-screen monitors beamed audiences linked by satellite into the forum. Clinton had nothing more than a stool on stage with him; instead of standing behind a lectern, he carried a microphone, walking around the stage to get closer to questioners. Audience members were not forced to move down an aisle to a fixed microphone to address the president. Instead, local news journalists walked down the aisles, handing the microphone to questioners along the way. At times, for questions asked from the front row, Clinton would even relinquish his own microphone. Like new media then, Clinton's town meetings embodied a series of populist expectations: that interactions ought to be intimate; that they ought to be rooted in personal experience; that they ought to based on sharing between people rather than lecturing from a single person to an audience; and that all participants ought to participate equally.

One can also see these expectations in the pattern of interactions between questioners and the president. Over the ten town meetings, audiences asked 270 questions of the president. Seventy-one of these questions, or 34 percent of the total, were framed in terms of the personal experience of the audience member. A woman's question during the May 17, 1993, San Diego town meeting is indicative of these queries:

> I'm really frustrated with the welfare system. Right now, I'm a single parent, and I just moved into the apartment. Since I moved into the apartment, my benefits have been cut, and I figured I'd try to make a better life for my child and myself, so I started to go to school. Since I've been going to school, I can't get any child care benefits.... What changes are you willing to make within that welfare system so that people such as myself can make a better life for their child and themselves?

As the form of this question suggests, personal experience often served as a warrant for audience questions. Over these ten meetings, individuals asked questions on the basis of their experience as HIV positive men, as parents of children with preexisting medical conditions, as mothers and fathers whose children had been shot to death at school, as former gang members and out-of-work single mothers. To emphasize the role of personal experience, news directors sometimes initiated events by showing video segments that dramatized the experiences of particular audience members.

At times, Clinton also acted on this expectation. For instance, in the most commonly remarked upon aspect of his interactions with audiences, he often acknowledged the emotional power of their stories. "I feel terrible for what happened to you," he told an audience member (during the October 3, 1993, Sacramento town meeting) whose brother had been murdered. On other occasions, Clinton worked more actively with these personal experiences. For example, he sometimes attempted to weave the personal stories of audience members into a larger point. "Let me just say," he said in the middle of the Sacramento town meeting, "if you take what he said, plus what the young man here who wanted the job for his friends, plus what the young man said whose brother got shot in school—it goes back to the bigger point: The problems you see that you're all horrified about today have been festering and developing over a generation in America...." At other times, he drew out the importance of a particular personal story to illustrate a policy issue. For example, at the Kansas City town meeting (April 7, 1994), a woman asked how Clinton's health care proposal would help a person like herself, someone who had been on state assistance and had a child. Clinton responded:

> I want to make sure everyone who's listening understands this.... For awhile, she was on public assistance.... What she's asking is—o.k., I had insurance, but nobody took me anyway; how are we going to fix that? The answer is that under our program....

The president also sometimes invited the audience to draw larger lessons from the personal stories they told. For example, during the Sacramento town meeting (October 3, 1993) a church-based community organizer described his efforts to reduce crime in his community and asked what the administration planned to do in this regard. Clinton responded that he would "like for the [community organizer] to have a chance to say ... what [he] thought ought to be done," after which the audience member was allowed to offer his suggestions.

As these examples indicate, at times the president clearly shared a sense that the town meetings ought to be occasions on which people built collective knowledge by sharing personal experiences. Like Carter, he often admitted that he didn't "ha[ve] all the answers." But he went beyond Carter's vague assertion that he wanted to "partner" with ordinary Americans. At the May 9, 1994, town meeting, he told the audience:

> I don't pretend for a moment to have all the answers. All I can tell you is that I've done my best to find them with the help of a lot of brilliant people.... They came up with a plan.... *But I think what we need to do is talk about how we can solve this problem.* That's what I've been in the business of doing all my life. (italics mine)

This notion—that talking is itself an end, and not simply a means of political activity—flows directly from the vernacular of modern populism. Talk, Clinton implies, is even more important than the plan created by the "brilliant people" (read: experts) he consulted. Through talk we discover answers within and across ourselves. Such answers are more legitimate and "real," Clinton suggests, precisely because they are not handed down from experts to citizens.

One other way that Clinton borrowed from populism was that he rarely embodied the role of the "President," a role distant from the ordinary experience of average Americans. One can see this in the many occasions that he sought to share his perspective with audiences. To a question about why he had not sought more middle-class tax cuts as he had promised during the campaign (Charlotte, April 5, 1994) the president began this way: "After the election, the deficit by the previous administration was revised upward. So here's what I had to do. Do I go through with a whole middle-class tax cut and let the deficit balloon ... or do I tell the American people the truth?" (p. 595). Here, instead of assuming the identity of "the President" (in which case, he might have responded, "As President, I think it is best that..."), Clinton tried to put the audience into his shoes: here is the situation with which I was faced; here were my options; can you (audience) now see why I have not asked for more tax cuts? On such occasions, Clinton offered to share his role as president with others so that they might understand his situation and perspective. Where someone like TR justified his actions in part by constituting himself as the public's representative, or someone like Ike championed the expertise of technocrats, Clinton accounts for his actions by erasing the line between the "president" and ordinary citizens.

Not surprisingly, given their status as professional observers of politics, media and political critics did not appreciate this populist sensibility. They derided the events as "therapeutic, personal-problem-solving support group[s]" that put "a premium on empathy." They characterized Clinton as a kind of "starved animal, feeding on the questions from the audience as if they were the stuff of life and breath," and they concluded that, on the whole, his town meetings were "profoundly antipolitical."[67] The sense of this judgment was that Clinton used town meetings to make himself appear as a populist, when in fact he only turned to this form of communication to satisfy personal political goals. In other words, the president's town meetings were little more than a devious exercise in crafted talk.

I do not think this is the right conclusion. The critics are certainly correct to note the many elements of crafted talk strewn throughout these events. For instance, consider once again their structural arrangement. When the White House agreed to do a town meeting, it asked local news stations, as one report put it, to "assemble a representative audience."[68] But no modern White House would leave it at that. White House aides encouraged local stations to hire Jean Bowman, a freelance producer who had previously worked in the Advance Office of the White House, to help them prepare these events. Bowman counseled the stations on audience selection, camera positions, and stage construction. She conducted a long dress rehearsal in which she stood in for the president, mimicking his mannerisms and movements, and briefed the audiences moments before the meetings began.[69] No detail was too small to be worried over, from the kind of stool provided for the president to the color of the drapes hanging in the background.[70]

Further, to convene an audience of "real people" doing "real things" news directors naturally turned to the tool with which they were most familiar: demographic marketing analysis.[71] For instance, the local news station in San Diego advertised the meeting as an opportunity to ask "a question" of the president. Audience members were selected from the questions submitted through mail, telephone and fax machines. Paul Sands, the local news director, then took it upon himself to match particular kinds of people with questions on "newsworthy topics: people who've lost real jobs; public school teachers and students who are hurt by budget cutbacks; people who work in the military; people who are tired of paying higher taxes." In this way, the questions would have, as Assistant news director Jeff Godlis put it, "pertinence and coherence," while at the same time make for "good television."[72] Don North, News Director of the local Kansas City station, went through a similar process. Faced with selecting 100 audience members from a pool of roughly 1,000 questions submitted to the station, North looked for "diversity" and "challenging questions." And, to eliminate the tedium of similar questions, he conferred with the news directors of the other stations involved in the town meeting to be sure that no question was duplicated.[73]

The result of this selection process was that questions were less personal than representative. As I suggested above, a great many of the questions asked during the town meetings were based on personal experience. However, looked at more closely, it is clear that many more were "representative," that is, were asked by someone who obviously represented a social type.[74] Indeed, the news people who organized these events ensured that this would be the case. For instance, during the April 8, 1994, meeting in Minneapolis, MN, the local news anchor/moderator introduced a man as "providing the perspective of tonight's program of the small business person in small town America." On another occasion (May 17, 1993), the moderator gave this introduction: "Mr. President, you mentioned laid-off defense workers. Well, coincidentally, we just happen to have a couple, both of whom are laid-off defense workers." Doug Casey, anchor of the local Rhode Island news station, introduced a questioner during the May 9, 1994, town meeting as "a woman from Providence [who] has an artificial leg that has always been paid for under her medical plan. Another moderator that evening provided a more simple introduction: "She's a working mother, and she has a question about child care."[75]

By having audience members represent some larger demographic group, the Clinton town meetings deviate markedly from populist expectations. Local stations had carefully selected questions and the persons asking them. Moreover, audience members had days to prepare their delivery of the question they were chosen to ask. Identification of questions with individuals was so important to these occasions that to help reporters identify audience members, a seating chart on which members of the studio audience and their questions were listed was given to the Kansas City moderators.[76] Thus, the questions seemed "rehearsed" and "prescreened" to Tom Shales, *The Washington Post*'s television critic, because in fact they were.[77] Paradoxically, then, to the extent that personal stories were made to stretch beyond the individual experience of the questioner, they risked losing the sense of authenticity, and hence the legitimacy, which gave them their peculiar power. The demographic sensibility used to choose audience members, ostensibly to ensure that the town meetings would make "good television" by forming a diverse studio audience, robbed the populist expectations of much of their motive force.

For his part, Clinton often violated the populist expectation that he ought to ground his contributions in personal experience. Indeed, for all his talk of others' pain, he did not reveal much about himself in these meetings. Recall that President Carter mentioned a personal experience in 14 percent of his answers. For a supposedly more "personal" president, Clinton only mentioned a personal experience in 24 of the 207 answers he gave to audience questions. Usually, these references were very brief—only a line or two—and offered less as an act of sharing than as an indication of how much he cared about an issue or as a justification for his actions on an issue. For instance, to a question concerning donor organs, new medical technologies and his health care proposal (April 7, 1994), Clinton began with this claim: "Well, let me mention—let me talk about this from two or three different points.... [I]t's an issue I'm very sensitive to now. As you know, I just lost my mother a few months ago; my father-in-law died last year. My family's been through this personally...." And during the May 9, 1994, Cranston, RI, town meeting Clinton was asked how he felt about a particularly egregious example of juvenile violence. To justify his assertion that he "cared a lot about this," Clinton reviewed a few salient features of his past: "My first job in public life was as an attorney general in my state, dealing with criminal procedures. Then I was governor and I had to enforce the criminal laws in my state, including the capital punishment law...." After establishing his credentials for caring, he moved into the core of his response: "Now, I think you have two or three options...." To a question about how he planned to improve the public school systems (Sacramento, October 3, 1993), Clinton reversed this order, first outlining his plans, and then, toward the end of his answer, justifying his proposals by stating that in his experience of spending "twelve years working on the public schools," he understood that this is what ought to be done.

Instead of contributing his personal experiences to the larger conversation, Clinton preferred to outline his proposals and policies. The tone of this approach was set at the beginning of the meetings, during his opening remarks. Given a few minutes to speak at the beginning of every town meeting (except the last), Clinton used this time to list the things he had done, or was about to do, as president. In his first year in office, he claimed in remarks before the April 5, 1994, question and answer session, he had "imposed some discipline" on the federal budget," invested in "growth for the jobs of the 21st century," kept "economic renewal going," and passed a major education bill. In his second year, he was proposing to "improve the political system" with lobby reform, to "deal" with welfare and healthcare reform, and to negotiate a crime bill. Before the May 9, 1994, meeting, Clinton used a series of charts to summarize the health care dilemma and his proposals to solve it.

This tone was carried through to the form of his answers during the meetings. To most every experience divulged by the audience, Clinton outlined a policy or plan. In fact, a great many (25 percent of the total) were put in the form of lists of such plans. Some of these lists were fairly simple. The president's answer to a question on illegal immigration and health care (May 17, 1993) consisted of only two points. Another list, addressed to a question about how his health care reform proposal would handle the issue of malpractice, consisted of three things: "We propose to do three things: number one, develop more alternative-dispute-resolution mechanisms; number two, limit the amount of contingency fees [for lawyers]; and number three ... develop ... a set of medical practice guidelines...." But sometimes Clinton's answers became very complex. A four-part answer to a question concerning the issue of handguns in public schools (May 9, 1994) was so complex that the moderator felt compelled to break in: "Do you think you [audience member] can remember all that?" After the audience laughter died down, Clinton summarized his position: "Sure you can. Get the assault weapons off, take the handguns away from the kids, metal detectors and other security devices at schools, teach kids nonviolent ways to resolve their differences, and organize every school."

This last example illustrates particularly well that Clinton relied on a list-form device to organize his answers. To every question-type, Clinton simply memorized a list of pertinent policies or proposals. For instance, during the Nightline town meeting (September 23, 1993), an audience member who was introduced as a retired educator with AIDS rambled on about how difficult it was to receive treatment under medicare. As Koppel moved to cut him off, the president interjected: "I know what you're—can I get to the—I know the question. First of all..." It was not difficult to predetermine the kinds of questions which demographically selected audiences would ask. For each of these question types, Clinton memorized a list of appropriate programs. In this case, all that Clinton needed was the key words "AIDS" and "medicare" to produce an appropriate answer—even without a question being asked. At the end of the San Diego town meeting (May 17, 1993), the president said he "thought you [the audience] were going to ask me about the problems with the sewage treatment in Tijuana." Without waiting for a direct question, he went ahead and listed a series of proposals for solving this problem. On another occasion (April 8, 1994), after an audience member was introduced as a self-employed farmer, but asked a question about organ donation, the president briefly answered his question, then said: "Now, let me also say to you since you were introduced in a slightly different way—as a farmer who's self-employed, who already had a medical problem, who has folks working for you on the farm. Farmers, in my opinion...."

These examples indicate that Clinton's answers were less than spontaneous, and that he conceived of his audiences more as a demographically sampled strata of voters than as a group of individual citizens with personal, unique stories. This seems to support the critics' conclusion that the meetings were mere shams—they were nothing more than crafted talk dressed up in the latest style.

However, allowing all of these points, by focusing on the crafted nature of these events the critics risk missing the larger institutional context in which they took place: the gradual growth of populism throughout the organizational environment of national politics in the preceding twenty-five years. Clinton was able to turn to a populist form like the town meeting only because its assumptions about politics held such power in the collective imagination. A more reasonable conclusion is that Clinton's town meetings represent the same curious blend of populism and crafted talk that characterized Carter's events. At times, participants followed along with these populist expectations. They shared personal experiences; they interacted in informal, intimate ways; they built collective understanding of issues by linking personal stories; they sought to draw others into their perspective. At others, the events veered into the assumptions of crafted talk. Audience members were invited to represent demographic groups, and the president offered policy prescriptions rather than his own personal experiences. The right conclusion here is not that the populism in these meetings merely served as a shell for crafted talk. Rather, it is that the participants—Clinton included—tried to dance to two different tunes. Moving along with populist expectations at one moment, they suddenly would jerk around to the beat of crafted talk.

For their part, the Washington press was utterly unhelpful in thinking through these nuances. As the president himself suggested in response to a question about why he stopped doing town meetings in 1994,

> One of the things I noticed is I'd go out and do these town hall meetings, and we'd have thirty or forty questions, and there would be one where there would be a little spark to fly, and that would be the only thing that would get any kind of real legs out of it, so that if the American people drew any conclusion, they would think that I

was here making the problem I'm trying to combat worse. And that may be the
reason we kind of stopped doing them.... (June 1, 1995)

On another occasion (February 10, 1993), he indicted reporters for their apparent cynicism, arguing that he and the press just "didn't see the world the same way." Clinton's point was not that he never thought in the terms of crafted talk (and reporters did), but that he sometimes also thought in the terms of modern populism (and reporters never did).

Evidence from news coverage of the town meetings supports this conclusion. Like the rest of the public, the Washington press greeted these events as new, fascinating forms of political communication. As Table 4.1 shows, the three newspapers in my sample put coverage of the first town meeting on the front page. This trend continued off and on through the first four town meetings. However, by the fifth town meeting, on March 15, 1994, only the *Los Angeles Times* continued with its front-page coverage. And by the sixth town meeting—as the events lost their initial luster and it became clear to reporters that there was little news to be found in them—the coverage almost stopped. Of the last four meetings, the three newspapers published a total of seven stories between them, and none appeared before page seven.

Table 4.1: Newspaper Coverage of Town Meetings by Placement

Date/Paper	NYT	WP	LAT
Feb. 10, 1993	A1	A1	A1
May 17, 1993	A14	A8	A1
Sept. 23, 1993	A1	A17	A1
Oct. 3, 1993	A14	A7	A3
Mar. 15, 1994	B6	A3	A1
Apr. 5, 1994	A18	A4	A14
Apr. 7, 1994	A18	A9	A17
Apr. 8, 1994	A7	A7	A32
May 9, 1994	—	—	—
June 1, 1995	—	A10	—

Network coverage had a similar pattern. Counting coverage of the town meetings on the day of their broadcast and the day after, I found that these productions were mentioned on only fourteen of the forty-nine possible network news broadcasts (see Table 4.2). And the segments in which town meeting coverage appeared often included two to four other items. For instance, the two minutes and forty seconds which ABC gave to the town meeting on February 10, 1993, also included coverage of Clinton's plans to cut White House jobs, and comments from Labor Secretary Robert Reich &

Interior Secretary Bruce Babbitt. Thus, like the print press, the networks covered the town meetings, but they obviously did not consider these events very newsworthy in their own right.

But the quantity of coverage devoted to the town meetings was less important than its quality. Much more than with Carter's events, Washington reporters insisted on viewing Clinton's meetings as little more than a sales job. This frame was set very early in the coverage, even before the first meeting. Announcing Clinton's intention to hold his first town meeting a week later, George Condon's short piece ran under the headline: "Clinton

Table 4.2: Network News Coverage of Town Meetings by Time[78]

Date	ABC	CBS	NBC
Feb. 10, 1993	2:40	2:20	1:20
Feb. 11, 1993	—	—	3:30
May 17, 1993	—	—	—
May 18, 1993	5:00	2:30	2:00
Sept. 23, 1993	—	—	—
Sept. 24, 1993			
Oct. 3, 1993	—	(not recorded)	—
Oct. 4, 1993	—	—	—
March 15, 1994	2:20	4:00	2:00
March 16, 1994	—	—	—
Apr. 5, 1994	—	1:40	—
Apr. 7, 1994	2:50	—	—
Apr. 8, 1994	2:10	—	—
Apr. 9, 1994	2:10	(not recorded)	—
May 9, 1994	—	—	—
May 10, 1994	—	—	—
June 1, 1995	(not available)	(not available)	(not available)
June 2, 1995	(not available)	(not available)	(not available)

Plans Detroit Sales Pitch." Its first paragraph suggested that Clinton was a "salesman not yet ready to display his wares but eager to close the sale."[79] *The Washington Post* said Clinton was preparing to "stump" for his health care reform plan, while *The New York Times* alternately called the impending occasion a "show" or a "revival meeting."[80] Instead of efforts to speak honestly and directly with the American people about their country's problems, the national press routinely interpreted these affairs against the backdrop of Clinton's political struggles and strategies. "With his economic program and his presidency under fire," Dan Halz wrote of the May 18, 1993, town meeting, "President Clinton lashed back at critics today...." And the president's call for stricter gun control during the October 4, 1993, meeting in Sacramento was explained by David Lauter as a strategy "seized" by Democratic strategists "as a potential tool to reach middle-class Americans concerned about their security."[81]

If anything, interpretations like these were even more pronounced in the television news coverage. For instance, although only one of the eighteen questions asked of Clinton during the March 15, 1994, town meeting concerned the Whitewater investigations, it was this question that the networks used to peg their stories that evening. Brit Hume of ABC led off the two minute twenty second segment with Clinton's "counterattack" against the Republicans and the question asked at the town meeting. The rest of the segment consisted of responses from Senator Bob Dole, and Congressmen Newt Gingrich and Lee Hamilton. The CBS and NBC coverage took much the same form. The first question asked of Clinton during the May 17, 1993, town meeting in San Diego challenged him to "name one country that has ever taxed and spent itself back into prosperity." Though this was the only question of its kind that evening, the networks again used it as a peg for their coverage the next evening. Juxtaposed to scenes of Clinton in campaign mode visiting various communities in Los Angeles and comments from other politicians and consultants about his policies on taxes, the inclusion of this one interaction painted the town meeting as a political and none too harmonious affair. The town meetings were thus either ignored by the national media, or interpreted in strictly political terms.

Understood more broadly, reporters' constant references to the town meetings as a "pitch," a "campaign," or a "sales job," was framed wholly in the terms of crafted talk. They talked of the president's "battle" with Republicans, of "counterattacks" and "sales pitches." But they never interpreted the meetings as genuine interactions between Clinton and the public. Indeed, they virtually ignored Clinton's argument that the town meetings were designed to "give people the chance to directly connect with the person who was elected..., to let people tell their personal stories."[82] The sense of the coverage was that Clinton held these events for strictly political reasons, and that it was the reporters' job to pierce the administration's efforts at spin control. In the process, reporters ignored the presence of alternative assumptions in these meetings.

Of course, the president was of little help in reinforcing the importance of the populist idiom to his leadership. As I've made clear, he himself often approached the town meetings as a form of crafted talk. In fact, Clinton stopped these meetings not because members of the studio audiences and viewers at home disliked them—many people expressed an interest in participating in and watching more of these events.[83] Rather, he stopped them because they did not help raise his polling numbers.[84] Just as he began these events to help him win the 1992 presidential election, Clinton stopped them when it became clear that they would not be useful in his immediate negotiations with other political actors. Inspired by the talk show format, which itself was modeled on women's consciousness raising groups, which in turn owed their genesis to the study groups of the Civil Rights movement, Clinton's town meetings were ended due to a typically professional political concern: low poll numbers.

Professionalism and Authenticity

What are we to make of the curious state of contemporary presidential communication? The evidence from the Carter and Clinton town meetings indicates that presidential communication today draws from two cultural reservoirs: a culture of expertise and a populist culture. Both Carter's and Clinton's town meetings were structured to satisfy expectations of intimacy and authenticity, *and* to conform to the White House's goal of mobilizing public opinion behind its policies. Audiences felt perfectly comfortable grounding their questions and opinions in their personal experiences, and in assuming that the president was the political agent responsible for acting on their concerns. For their part, Presidents Carter and Clinton wanted to appear as average Americans just as they sought to use the events in the pursuit of their presidential goals.

Not surprisingly, this rhetorical form makes a great many Americans frustrated with contemporary presidential communication. But this frustration arises not because presidential rhetoric contradicts conventional assumptions, but because the assumptions themselves are contradictory. In other words, frustration with conventional presidential communication is not a struggle of us versus them. It is a struggle within ourselves over what we can and should expect of presidential rhetoric. As such, it is part of a larger struggle in contemporary American politics. Consider, for instance, the following: fights over whether term limits are good because they keep politicians close to the people or bad because they reduce the ability of legislators to gain needed knowledge and experience; struggles within the Democratic party over campaign finance reform pitched between a conviction that it is the right thing to do and an unwillingness to "unilaterally disarm" in their fight against Republicans; interest groups led by individuals whose political commitments stem from deeply felt convictions, but whose everyday activities center on routine practices of crafted talk; political consulting firms that specialize in crafted talk, but work only with candidates who embrace their political values; a public that expects political candidates to be polished speakers but also authentic individuals who speak from the heart; reporters who pounce on every wayward word of political leaders but denounce the stagedness of crafted talk; novice politicians elected precisely because they are not political professionals, then trounced from office because they are not political professionals.

We might think of this situation in terms of Stephen Skowronek's diagnosis of modern presidential politics.[85] According to Skowronek, political time (the temporal evolution of regimes) has been stymied by a "thickening" of institutions in historical time. This is to say, the bureaucracies, interest groups, consulting organizations, and media organizations that ring the administrative state have a vested interest in the culture of expertise from which they spring. For Skowronek, the thickening of these organizations has prevented the old (New Deal) regime from falling, and a new one from ascending. The result is a curious stalemate, in which the old regime has been discredited, but a new one has yet to take its place. In my estimation, this political deadlock has been accompanied by a kind of cultural stagnation. The "thickening" of institutions in Washington has engrained crafted talk deeply in to the everyday practices and roles of the Washington Community. But the vocabulary is not seamless. Indeed, some of the very organizations that have "thickened" Washington politics dedicate themselves to fighting the assumptions of crafted talk. Populist expectations have seeped in to these cracks and crevices, doing enough to trouble any easy acceptance of a culture of expertise, but not enough to articulate a new practice of presidential communication.

In the wake of stalemate, we are likely to see the kind of volatility produced by any occasion on which people genuinely do not know how to proceed. Skowronek perceives volatility in Clinton's zigzag across the ideological spectrum of Washington politics, here co-opting a conservative idea, there linking it with a left-liberal policy prescription. Town meetings are a similar expression of volatility. At one moment populist, at another rationalist, these events show presidents groping for traction in a cultural climate in which the longstanding expectations of crafted talk no longer resonate, and populist appeals seem politically ineffective. Should one "be real" or "be professional?" How would we know the difference? Our inability to answer such questions makes for deep dissatisfaction with the current state of presidential communication.

Conclusion

Culture and Presidential Communication

WE BEGAN this study with the question of why presidential communication matters. The fact that it matters seems beyond dispute. I know of no competent observer who doubts its centrality to presidential politics, or to American politics generally. But why does it matter? What is it good for? How should it be done? What counts as doing it well? As we conclude, it seems fitting to ask what the intervening pages contribute to our understanding of these questions.

Their broad contribution, I think, is to show that Americans have answered these questions quite differently at different historical moments. For instance, progressives understood presidential communication as a kind of embodiment of public opinion. When they addressed audiences, Presidents Roosevelt and Wilson understood themselves to be modeling a particular ideal of citizenship. In contrast, FDR engaged in little of this modeling activity. Instead, he used the romantic realism of media culture to invite a heterogeneous mass audience to imagine itself as a competent and responsible actor in American civic life. In the years after World War II, new professional and bureaucratic assumptions changed the meaning of the rhetorical presidency yet again. No longer understood as a kind of modeling activity, or as a melodramatic tale intended to inspire and invite citizens into the public arena, postwar presidential communication became a highly staged effort to manage public opinion. This sense of presidential communication remains resonant in contemporary presidential communication. But in recent years it has been accompanied by a resurgent populist sensibility. Contemporary populism insists that presidential rhetoric is, or ought to be, a form of self-expression.

Thus, while the idea of the rhetorical presidency has held great fascination over the last hundred years, its precise meaning has varied a great deal.

One key to apprehending this variation, I think, is to see presidential rhetoric as a cultural practice. As Raymond Williams reminds us, "culture is one of the two or three most complicated words in the English language."[1] In all its earliest usages, culture was a noun of process: to tend or to make things grow (as in "to cultivate"). The rhetorical presidency is cultural precisely in this sense: its meaning grows out of assumptions and expectations that arise between people as they observe and engage in the practice. These assumptions include notions about the roles, purposes, obligations, and responsibilities pertinent to the practice. It is only in the context of such cultural assumptions that the rhetorical presidency gains meaning.

The other key to interpreting variation in presidential rhetoric is to recognize that these assumptions are neither located solely in people's heads nor floating in the ether of political life. Here, I have suggested that a twist on Habermas' notion of "institutions of public life" is useful.[2] The salons, coffeehouses, taverns, and newspapers that served as conduits for Habermas' eighteenth-century bourgeois public sphere have their correlates in twentieth-century American politics. Cultural assumptions about the presidency arise, and are embedded within, institutions of political life. For instance, during the progressive era, churches, women's groups, journalism, and universities exercised a profound influence on how the rhetorical presidency was understood. Institutions like these provide the material and human resources through which assumptions about presidential communication gain force and perpetuate themselves over time. Imbued with institutional legitimacy, particular assumptions are translated into taken-for-granted ways of apprehending the practice of presidential rhetoric as a recognizable activity. This institutional dimension reinforces the sense of presidential rhetoric as a social practice. Its form and meaning do not flow from the predilections of particular presidents, but rather from the conceptual investments of individuals and groups interacting within a political community.

Does this mean that presidents have no control over their speech, that their personal communication skills, personalities, and political interests have no influence on how they conduct their rhetorical activities? Of course not. To suggest otherwise is to misconstrue how culture works. Presidents are perfectly free to say anything they wish in any way that they wish. Their freedom is limited only by boundaries of intelligibility. To see this clearly, we might think of presidential rhetoric as entwined within rules (assumptions or expectations) about how it ought to be done. Such rules are ingrained in the very practice of communication, which means that, for the most part, presidents follow the rules simply by "doing" rhetoric. However, at some point, what they say, and/or how they say it, may cease to be intelligible to others. In such instances, doubt is raised about whether the president is "doing" presidential communication correctly. What did he just say (or not say)? Can you believe that he said it in that way (or did not say it at all)? Why isn't he doing his rhetoric in this way? These moments of doubt introduce a rhetorical dimension into the idea of presidential rhetoric.

Consider, for instance, President Wilson's interactions with reporters. Wilson approached his press conferences with the idea that they gave him an opportunity to model, and therefore to shape, public opinion. As he understood it, his job was to represent the public interest. Reporters were merely there to act as conduits between himself and the public. This quintessentially progressive understanding of rhetoric utterly puzzled reporters. On their view, Wilson did not represent the public—they did. It was their job to question the president closely, and to provide their readers with information necessary to make informed, independent, judgments. In this clash of expectations, reporters simply did not recognize Wilson's rhetoric as a legitimate instance of "doing" presidential communication. President Wilson was perfectly free to conduct himself in any way he wished during his press conferences. But in contradicting reporters' expectations, he raised doubt in reporters' minds, and this doubt ultimately required him to account for his behavior. His freedom to speak as he wished, in other words, depended on his ability to pull it off, to convince reporters that he really was "doing" presidential rhetoric in a way that conformed to their expectations.

As a routine matter, doubt sufficient to cause a crisis of recognition rarely surfaces with regard to presidential rhetoric. Of course, observers sometimes quibble at the edges. Professional commentators, for instance, sometimes argue that President G. W. Bush does not use the rhetorical power of his office often enough—that is, that he lets others in his administration do the rhetorical job that is properly his. But this criticism is directed more at the manner than the meaning of the president's rhetoric. Both Bush and his critics share the sense that presidential rhetoric is supposed to manage public opinion. They merely disagree about his record of satisfying this expectation. More substantial doubt would entail questioning whether presidential rhetoric really ought to be about the management of public opinion. This kind of doubt rarely surfaces for several reasons. As a kind of accounting behavior, presidential communication always contain a moral dimension. In other words, it foregrounds a persuasive appeal against a background of assumptions about roles, purposes, obligations, and responsibilities of the office. Presidents typically win the office precisely because they stray very little from these assumptions. That is, for most presidents, abiding by prevailing assumptions means nothing more than being themselves. Thus, there is a kind of institutional self-selection built into the process of presidential selection. Moreover, if a more maverick president happened to win the office, the common sense of the professional communicators who surround him would likely hem in his more radical departures from conventional wisdom. This is especially the case for more recent presidents, who come to the office at a time when presidential communication is more professionalized, and impersonal, than ever before.

Still, some historical moments present presidents with more treacherous cultural terrains than others. At such moments, presidents may find it difficult to abide by prevailing expectations because the expectations themselves are confused. Today, for example, the idea of the rhetorical presidency is entangled with two opposing cultural strands: crafted talk and populism. Both resonate profoundly among the inhabitants of the institutions that currently dominate national politics. And, because this institutional environment has "thickened," to borrow a term from Stephen Skowronek, neither set of expectations seems on the verge of dissipating.[3] Contemporary presidents, therefore, confront a situation in which they are expected both to manage public opinion and to do so in a way that conveys the sense that they are ordinary, real people. This can be tricky business. Any hint that one's rhetoric stems from political calculation or expediency can easily violate the expectation that one is speaking from one's heart. At the same time, any effort to simply "be real" that ignores the need to manage public opinion risks its own kind of failure.

Consider, for instance, President Bush's favored political slogan, "compassionate conservatism." Though the events of 9/11 and after have pushed the term to the margins of the Bush presidency, it remains a signal caption for the president's philosophy of public life. The first thing we may note about this slogan is that it ideally illustrates the dynamics of crafted talk. Its genealogy extends through the institutional environment of professional politics. It made its debut in the news in a 1981 press conference of Vernon Jordan, then-president of the National Urban League.[4] Responding to a question regarding the Reagan administration's policies with respect to urban centers, Jordon stated, "I do not challenge the conservatism of this administration.... I do challenge its failure to exhibit a compassionate conservatism...."[5] Jordan used the term to criticize Republicans. Other Democrats thought it might serve their own party's interests. After

Mondale's resounding electoral defeat in 1984, James R. Jones, a Democratic House member from Oklahoma, argued that "we [Democrats] should adopt the slogan of compassionate conservatism. We can be fiscally conservative without losing our commitment to the needy...."[6]

Meanwhile, the term was introduced in Republican circles by a group of conservative intellectuals and journalists led by Jack Kemp. During the 1980s, it was variously linked to California Governor Pete Wilson, Senator Bob Dole, and perennial presidential candidates Pat Buchanan and Steve Forbes. After Dole's 1996 election defeat, Kemp continued to promote the slogan through his nonprofit organization *Empower America*, a so-called Republican "idea factory" devoted to selling its particular version of Republican social policy. Others hawked the term as well. Myron Magnet, editor of *City Journal*, a magazine published by the conservative Manhattan Institute, promoted the idea in several publications. The term finally came to George W. Bush courtesy of Marvin Olasky, a University of Texas Journalism professor and fixture on the conservative circuit of foundations, institutes, think tanks, and publications. An advocate of "compassionate" but conservative social policies, Olasky became one of Bush's informal advisors as early as 1993 and wrote *Compassionate Conservatism: What It Is, What It Does, and How It Can Transform America* (2000), a book widely considered to be an outline of Bush's political philosophy.

Why is the term so resonant among professional politicians? Because it cleverly conjoins two seemingly opposed words in a way that defines one's competitors as "uncompassionate" and aligns oneself with the compassionate sensibilities of key demographic constituencies, namely, minorities and suburban women. During the 2000 election, Bush used the slogan to great effect, at once distancing himself from his Republican challengers and Democrat Al ("wooden," "unfeeling," "wonkish") Gore, and in the same moment reaching out to women and Hispanic voters.

At the same time, we cannot ignore the fact that the term, with its stress on compassion, is extraordinarily resonant for good reason. Professional politicians might have latched onto a wide variety of marketing gimmicks, but this one (and not others) has stuck. Why? Because compassion is one of a series of interlocking terms (sincerity; authenticity; humanity; ordinariness) that hold great power in the populist culture of contemporary presidential politics. As a populist term, compassionate conservatism appeals to our sense that political agendas ought to be justified in terms of the compassion and authenticity of the person or group offering them.

It is, in a nutshell, a brilliant bit of contemporary presidential communication that evokes a complicated response. Is it merely a slogan designed to obscure and manipulate? Or is it an authentic representation of the president's personal convictions? How would we know the difference? Our difficulty in answering this last question explains a good deal of why Americans are so frustrated with the state of contemporary presidential communication. Obviously, we want our presidents to be good professional communicators. (In this regard, witness the longstanding adulation of President Reagan as the "Great Communicator.") But just as obviously, we wish presidents to be themselves—and to be like us. One imagines that these contradictory requirements must frustrate presidents as well. After all, they are obliged, at once, to fashion professional public appeals, and to do so in a way that seems expressive of their personal convictions. Solving this riddle once would be difficult in the best of circumstances. Doing so routinely, as presidents must, seems well nigh impossible. In the end, the entire enterprise seems designed to produce unhappiness and frustration on all sides.

Let me conclude with a note on historical change. It is a subject on which I have said little in the preceding chapters. However, assuming for the moment that I have accurately diagnosed contemporary presidential communication, it is worth asking whether Americans are fated to experience an endless conflict between their desire for authenticity and professionalism in presidential communication. Or, to put the matter in more conceptual terms, to ask how a "structural transformation" of contemporary political life could occur. Habermas' study of the transition from the bourgeois to the modern public sphere suggests one answer. In his narrative, conceptual transformation follows fundamental changes in the institutional structure of public life. At such moments, old assumptions no longer seem compelling to individuals and groups confronting new problems and possibilities. Moreover, moments of crisis render formerly dominant institutions weak and ineffective, thus opening an opportunity for new institutions to grow and thrive. Think, for instance, of the demise of progressivism. In the presidential campaign of 1912, all three candidates—Wilson, Roosevelt, and Taft— embraced a progressive platform. By the early 1920s, however, progressivism had nearly disappeared from public life. What had happened in the intervening decade? World War I. After the shock, hysteria, and upheaval of that war, overtly religious conceptions of public life no longer seemed appropriate. Moreover, vigorous use of publicity seemed more dangerous after the hysterical public outbursts stoked by Wilson's Committee on Public Information. After the crisis of the war, this is to say, the world looked different, leading political actors to turn to new assumptions about public life.

We can imagine other, less cataclysmic, paths to change. For instance, incremental change may occur when dominant institutions seek to co-opt new problems, constituencies, or situations. Think here of what has happened to the use of media culture in politics over the last half century. Initially, the romantic realism of media culture contained a great deal of openness to the needs and interests of audiences. In part, this was due to the fact that it was new and relatively undeveloped. Further, media producers had few of the demographic tools with which to target audiences with any precision. For this reason, they tended to imagine mass audiences in a gross rather than demographic sense. They assumed that their products ought to appeal to everyone, not to a demographically important slice of the population. The transformation of this assumption was slow, but decisive in the post–World War II period, when media culture lost much of its openness. We might think of this transformation as incremental rather than fundamental, but over time it altered the role of media culture in presidential communication.

Technology represents another path to change. Habermas himself assigns great weight to the role of media industries in transforming the bourgeois public sphere. Clearly, by opening new possibilities, new technologies may offer political actors new rhetorical opportunities. But we should be cautious here. Technology is rarely an independent agent of change. Instead, it usually contributes to a process of change that is propelled by other economic, political, cultural, or social forces. Consider the case of modern mass media, which are sometimes taken to have directly caused the rise of the rhetorical presidency. The notion, for instance, that modern presidential rhetoric would be impossible without television is common. While in some sense true, we should keep in mind that the invention of television, and other modern mass media, was accompanied by other socioeconomic forces—the maturation of industrialism; urbanization and then suburbanization; the transfer of political power from Congress to the presidency—all of which also contributed to the rise of the rhetorical presidency. And even then, it took the deepest economic depression in modern times to sweep aside older institutional forms and make room for the growth and extension of media culture in public life.

We ought to be similarly cautious about the transformational potential of the most recent technology to make its way into presidential politics, the Internet. As of this writing, the Internet's impact on American politics is of intense interest among scholars. On the view I am suggesting here, this phrasing of the question—the Internet's impact on politics—is miscast.

Technologies do not have the kind of general effects presupposed by the question. Rather, they have specific effects that are contingent upon context. The technology may open new possibilities, but how political actors make sense of, and respond to, these opportunities—indeed, even how they define an opportunity—is determined in culture. In this regard, it strikes me that uses of the Internet in presidential communication are being shaped by the two great forces in contemporary American political culture: the drive toward rationalization, and the opposite, though equally fervent, drive toward self-expression. On the one hand, professional political actors see in the Internet new ways to manage presidential communication with ever greater precision. For instance, the medium opens the possibility of reaching potential donors with greater accuracy, and of targeting presidential messages more precisely to the specific interests and assumptions of particular demographic groups.[7] On the other hand, the technology has also been sutured into the populist impulse of contemporary presidential politics. As an illustration, one has only to point to the spontaneous, grassroots, "virtual" movement that placed Howard Dean at the front of the Democratic primary race in the 2004 election. Thousands of Dean supporters found the Internet attractive because it gave them an opportunity to maneuver around the professional world of conventional presidential politics and make their voices heard. They were attracted to Dean for similar reasons: he was a "real" candidate who refused to shape his rhetoric to the demands of professional handlers. His guttural growl after the Iowa caucus epitomizes the self-expressive instincts of modern populism. No one knows how these processes will work themselves out. I suggest, however, that we are more likely to find answers in cultural context rather than in characteristics of the medium.

Another way of putting this is that, however presidential communication may change in the future, and whatever our particular worries might be about these changes, they will be changes caused by us, and they will be our worries. If I were to condense the approach I have offered in these pages into a single claim, it would be the following: presidential communication matters because we assume that it matters. Who "we" are is contingent on time and place, and on the character of the institutions we build and inhabit. But still, at bottom, the meaning of presidential communication is embodied in us, in the roles, values, and purposes through which we attach meaning to the activity. In the end, it is a thoroughly human social practice.

Notes

Introduction

1. Lyn Ragsdale, *Vital Statistics on the Presidency*; Samuel Kernell, *Going Public*.

2. John Maltese, *Spin Control*.

3. See, for instance, Richard Neustadt, *Presidential Power;* Samuel Kernell, *Going Public;* James Ceaser, Glen Thurow, Jeffrey Tulis, & James Bessette, "The Rise of the Rhetorical Presidency"; Jeffrey Tulis, *The Rhetorical Presidency*.

4. For reviews, see Mary Stuckey and Frederick J. Antczak, "The Rhetorical Presidency: Deepening Vision, Widening Exchange"; Theodore Windt, "Presidential Rhetoric: Definition of a Discipline of Study"; Martin Medhurst, Ed., *Beyond the Rhetorical Presidency*; and Richard Ellis, Ed., *Speaking to the People*.

5. Terence Ball, *Transforming Political Discourse,* 16.

6. Richard Neustadt, *Presidential Power*, especially Chapter 3, "The Power to Persuade."

7. For reflections on the impact of Neustadt's work on the study of the presidency, see "A symposium: 'Neustadt's *Presidential Power* twenty years later: the test of time.'"

8. Richard Neustadt, *Presidential Power*, 28.

9. Hence, the rise of the "personal presidency," see Theodore Lowi, *The Personal President.*

10. Samuel Kernell, *Going Public*.

11. For my purposes, the terms "going public" and "public presidency" are interchangeable. Both refer to the model of presidential communication rooted in Neustadt's bargaining theory of presidential communication.

12. Samuel Kernell, *Going Public*, 105.

13. See, for instance, Paul Brace and Barbara Hinckley, *Follow the Leader*; Pamela Johnston Conover, "Presidential Influence and Public Opinion"; Benjamin Page and Robert Shapiro, "Presidential Leadership of Public Opinion"; Lyn Ragsdale, "The Politics of Speechmaking, 1949–1980"; Lyn Ragsdale, "Presidential Speechmaking and the Public Audience"; Lee Sigelman, "Gauging the Public Response to Presidential Leadership."

14. For a synthesis and exhaustive summary of this literature, see George Edwards, *On Deaf Ears*. Other important works include Jeffrey Cohen, *Presidential Responsiveness and Public Policy-Making*; George Edwards, *The Public Presidency*; Richard A. Brody, *Assessing the President*; Samuel Kernell, "Explaining Presidential Popularity"; John E. Mueller, *War, Presidents, and Public Opinion*; Brace and Hinckley, *Follow the Leader*.

15. For evidence that they do so, see Elmer Cornwell, *Presidential Leadership of Public Opinion*; Michael Grossman and Martha Joynt Kumar, *Portraying the President;* John Maltese, *Spin Control*.

16. See Terry Moe on the general issue here, who writes that the "organizing principle" which pulls together much of the work inspired by Neustadt is the "personal presidency:" "The common notion is that all relevant variables explain presidential behavior to the extent that, via causal chains that are lengthy and complicated, they ultimately affect the thinking of the man who is president." Quote comes from Moe, "Presidents, Institutions, and Theory," 346.

17. James Ceaser, et al., "The Rise of the Rhetorical Presidency," 161.

18. Jeffrey Tulis, *The Rhetorical Presidency*, 4. See also Woodrow Wilson, *Constitutional Government*.

19. This point offers a response to the claims of a growing literature on nineteenth-century presidential rhetoric. Much of this literature intends to show that, despite arguments to the contrary, nineteenth-century presidents often used rhetorical appeals in the same way as twentieth-century presidents. However, according to the rhetorical presidency model, the key difference between the two centuries lies not in the use of rhetoric itself, but in the institutional assumptions about its place in the political system. Nineteenth-century presidents may have used rhetoric, but they were not expected to do so, and others did not evaluate their presidencies on their rhetorical skills or success. On nineteenth-century presidential communication, see Richard Ellis, Ed., *Speaking to the People*; and Karen Hoffmann, "'Going Public' in the Nineteenth Century."

20. For a discussion of this point, see David Crockett, "George W. Bush and the Unrhetorical Rhetorical Presidency."

21. The agenda-setting literature is now quite extensive. For an early summary, see Maxwell McCoombs, "Agenda-Setting Research: A Bibliographic Essay." For a more recent review, see Everett M. Rogers and James W. Dearing, "Agenda-Setting Research."

22. For an excellent summary, see Timothy E. Cook, *Governing with the News*, especially ch. 6. Also see Bartholomew Sparrow, *Uncertain Guardians*.

23. For data on the president's ability to set media agendas, see Leon Sigal, *Reporters and Officials;* Edward J. Epstein, *News From Nowhere;* Joseph S. Foote, *Television and Political Power*; Frederic T. Smoller, *The Six O'clock Presidency*.

24. Recent research suggests that these advantages are withering. With the rise of cable television, it seems that presidents no longer command the kind of media attention they once enjoyed—and thus are less able to set public and policy agendas. See Samuel Kernell and Matthew Baum, "Has Cable Ended the Golden Age of Television?"

25. David Zarefsky, "Presidential Rhetoric and the Power of Definition." For more extended discussions, see Edward Schiappa, *Defining Reality*; Murray Edelman, *The Symbolic Uses of Politics*; and William Riker, *The Art of Political Manipulation*.

26. See George Edwards, "Presidential Rhetoric: What Difference Does It Make?"

27. Mary Stuckey and Frederick J. Antczak, "The Rhetorical Presidency."

28. Among rhetoricians, a debate has waged for several decades between rhetorical critics with their emphasis on texts over context, and rhetorical historians, who insist on the priority of context over text. For examples, see Michael Leff and Fred Kauffeld, Eds., *Texts in Context*; Thomas W. Benson, Ed., *American Rhetoric: Context and Criticism*; and Bruce E. Gronbeck, "Rhetorical History and Rhetorical Criticism—A distinction."

29. Martin Medhurst, "Introduction: A Tale of Two Constructs," xv, xvi.

30. Clifford Geertz, *The Interpretation of Cultures*, 14.

31. Much of this tradition is inspired by the work of Kenneth Burke. See his *A Grammar of Motives*; and *A Rhetoric of Motives*. More immediately, Michael Calvin McGee's work has been especially influential. See his "A Materialist's Conception of Rhetoric"; and "In Search of 'The People.'" Also see Celeste Condit & John Louis Lucaites, *Crafting Equality*; Kathleen Turner, Ed., *Doing Rhetorical History;* James Boyd White, *When Words Lose Their Meaning*.

32. Stephen Skowronek, *The Politics Presidents Make*.

33. Stephen Skowronek, *The Politics Presidents Make*, 4. For a similar view of the presidency, see Harvey Mansfield, Jr., *Taming the Prince*.

34. For a more general argument in this vein, see Lawrence Jacobs and Robert Shapiro, *Politicians Don't Pander*.

35. Marvin Scott and Stanford Lyman, "Accounts," 46.

36. A point made by W. Lance Bennett, "The Paradox of Public Discourse," 794. See also Patricia Day and Rudolf Klein, *Accountabilities*; and John March & Johan Olsen, *Democratic Governance*.

37. On the nature of social rules, see Anthony Giddens, *The Constitution of Society*.

38. Douglass North, *Institutions, Institutional Change, and Economic Performance*, 4.

39. For a general discussion, see Walter Scott, "Institutions and Organizations."

40. John Searle, *Speech Acts*, 33–34.

41. Jürgen Habermas, *The Structural Transformation of the Public Sphere*.

42. A good starting point for learning more about this criticism is Craig Calhoun, Ed., *Habermas and the Public Sphere*.

43. Habermas uses this term as a section heading. See *Structural Transformation*, 31–43.

44. Kenneth Burke, *A Grammar of Motive*; and Robert Wuthnow, Ed., *Vocabularies of Public Life*.

45. On this point, see Anthony Giddens, *The Constitution of Society*; and William Sewell, "A Theory of Structure."

46. Ludwig Wittgenstein, *Philosophical Investigations*, ¶71.

47. Hannah Pitkin, *Wittgenstein and Justice*, 48.

48. Ludwig Wittgenstein, *Philosophical Investigations*, ¶217.

49. Clifford Geertz, *The Interpretation of Cultures*, 17.

50. As Thomas Farrell argues, forms of communication "may be understood as ... narrative succession[s] of discursive anticipations, each attempting to project, explain, and integrate what is subsequent.... The capacity of any discourse to enter a partisan world, anticipate its prospective resistances, and offer meaningful integration to its forthcoming results becomes the rhetorical test of form itself." Farrell, "Knowledge in Time," 128

51. For a useful comparison of FDR's rhetoric with that of President Hoover, see Davis W. Houck, *Rhetoric as Currency*.

Chapter One

1.   Two standard histories on progressive presidential communication are George Juergens, *News from the White House*; and Stephen Ponder, *Managing the Press*.

2.   James Pollard, *The Presidents and the Press*, 569.

3.   George Juergens, *News at the White House*, 27–34.

4.   For other analyses of Roosevelt and Wilson's relationship with the press, see Elmer Cornwell, *Presidential Leadership;* and John Tebbel and Sarah Miles Watts, *The Press and the Presidency*.

5.   In an analysis of Roosevelt and Wilson's rhetoric during the 1912 presidential campaign, Robert Alexander Kraig argues that their rhetoric differed in fundamental ways. Most generally, he finds Roosevelt's a forward looking vision that fully embraced the modern liberal state, while Wilson's rhetoric harkened back to a nineteenth-century image of American society. This interpretation does not necessarily contradict my own. It is perfectly possible for Roosevelt and Wilson to disagree on the substance of politics, but to do so using a common progressive vocabulary. See Kraig, "The 1912 Election and the Rhetorical Foundations of the Modern Liberal State."

6.   See, for instance, Peter Filene, "An Obituary for the Progressive Movement" and Daniel Rodgers, "In Search of Progressivism." Other relevant works on the nature of progressivism include Jean Quandt, *From the Small Town to the Great Community;* Richard McCormick, "The Discovery that Business Corrupts Politics"; Richard Hofstadter, *Age of Reform;* Robert Wiebe, *The Search for Order, 1877–1920;* Samuel P. Hays, *The Response to Industrialism: 1885–1914;* Gabriel Kolko, *The Triumph of Conservatism: A Re-interpretation of American History, 1900–1916;* James Weinstein, *The Corporate Ideal in the Liberal State, 1900–1918;* and Martin Sklar, *The Corporate Reconstruction of American Capitalism, 1890–1916*. For a recent overview of the literature, see Sidney M. Milkis and Jerome M. Mileur, Eds., *Progressivism and the New Democracy*.

7.   Eldon Eisenach, *The Lost Promise of Progressivism*, 19.

8.   Daniel Rodgers, "In Search of Progressivism," 123. Also see J. Michael Hogan, "Introduction: Rhetoric and reform in the progressive era"; and Eldon Eisenach, *The Lost Promise of Progressivism*, 19.

9.   Hofstadter, *The Age of Reform*, 185. On progressivism and the news, also see Herbert Gans, *Deciding What's News;* Michael Schudson, *The Power of News;* Douglas Birkhead, "The Progressive Reform of Journalism."

10. The literature on this period is very large. I have found the following general histories useful: Carl Degler, *The Age of the Economic Revolution, 1876–1900;* Henry May, *The End of American Innocence;* Harold Faulkner, *The Quest for Social Justice*. Other important works on the period include Morton White, *Social Thought in America;* James Kloppenberg, *Uncertain Victory;* Thomas L. Haskell, *The Emergence of the Social Sciences*; Burton J. Bledstein, *The Culture of Professionalism*; Dorothy Ross, *The Origins of American Social Science;* Daniel Czitrom, *Media and the American Mind;* John Aldrich, *Why Parties?*; Michael McGerr, *The Decline of Popular Politics*.

11. David Mark Chalmers, *The Muckrake Years*, 9. Also see Louis Filler, *The Muckrakers*; and Arthur Weinberg and Lila Weinberg, Eds., *The Muckrakers*.

12. On the religious dimension of progressivism, see Robert Crunden, *Ministers of Reform*; and Wilson Carey McWilliams, "Standing at Armageddon: Morality and Religion in Progressive Thought."

13. Herbert Croly, *The Promise of American Life*, 400.

14. Edward Ross, *Social Control,* 103.

15. On the influence of organic thinking on American thought, see Richard Hofstadter, *Social Darwinism in American Thought*; A.J. Beitzinger, *A History of American Political Thought*; and Ralph H. Gabriel, *The Course of American Democratic Thought*.

16. On the influence of Liberal Protestantism on progressive thought, see Andrew Feffer, *The Chicago Pragmatists and American Progressivism*; and Jeffrey Lustig, *Corporate Liberalism*. On the German idealist strains in progressive thought, see Arthur Vidich and Stanford Lyman, *American Sociology*.

17. Woodrow Wilson, "The Nature of Democracy in the United States," Public Papers of the Presidents, Woodrow Wilson [hereafter referred to as PPW], v. 5, 63.

18. Walter Weyl, *The New Democracy,* 137.

19. Eldon Eisenach, *The Lost Promise of Progressivism*, 76. Eisenach finds these terms sprinkled throughout the writings of Arthur Hadley, Charles Horton Cooley, and Franklin Giddings.

20. John Dewey, *Democracy and Education,* 99.

21. James Kloppenberg, *Uncertain Victory*, 357.

22. The passage appears in a letter from Roosevelt to Trevelyan, dated June 19, 1908, in TR Letters, v. 6, 1088.

23. Woodrow Wilson, "A Lecture on Democracy," PPW, v. 7, 359.

24. Lincoln Steffens, *The Autobiography of Lincoln Steffens*, 515.

25. Woodrow Wilson, *Constitutional Government,* 68.

26. Frederic Howe, *The Confessions of a Reformer*, 5.

27. George E. Mowry, *The Era of Theodore Roosevelt,* 104–105.

28. Of course, most progressives did not experience this as a contradiction. Convinced of the moral correctness of their cause, they believed that new centralized forms of authority merely made the connection between political authority and public opinion more direct. On this view, centralization confirmed rather than limited popular sovereignty and participation.

29. For a more extensive list, see John Buenker and Edward R. Kantowicz, Eds., *Historical Dictionary of the Progressive Era.*

30. Robert Park, *Society: Collective Behavior, News and Opinion*, 149. Quote may be found in Jean Quandt, *From Small Town to the Great Community*, 68–69.

31. Walter Lippmann, *Public Opinion*, 358.

32. See Ted Curtis Smythe, "The Reporter, 1880–1900."

33. See Frank L. Mott, *The News in America*, 22.

34. Frank L. Mott, *The News in America*, 71.

35. On the role of stories in news reporting, see Robert Darnton, "Writing News and Telling Stories"; Karl Manoff, "Writing the News (By Telling the 'Story')"; and Andie Tucher, *Froth & Scum*.

36. Robert Park, "Introduction," and Shelley Fisher Fishkin, *From Fact to Fiction*.

37. On this point, see Douglas Birkhead, "The Progressive Reform of Journalism."

38. Michael Schudson, *Discovering the News,* 65.

39. See Thomas Cochran, "Media as Business."

40. See Howard Good, "The Journalist in Fiction," Michael Schudson, *Discovering the News*, 69.

41. Frank L. Mott, *News in America*, 158. Also see Michael Schudson, *The Power of News*, 53–71.

42. On the history and meaning of the interview, see Michael Schudson, *The Power of News*, 72–93; Barbie Zelizer, "Saying as Collective Practice"; and John Heritage, "Analyzing News Interviews."

43. Joseph Alsop and Stuart Alsop, *The Reporter's Trade*, 5.

44. On the detached style of journalism, see Michael McGerr, *The Decline of Popular Politics*, ch. 5.

45. Michael Schudson, *Discovering the News*, 85.

46. Phillips' essay first appeared as a series beginning with the March, 1906 edition of *Cosmopolitan Magazine*.

47. See Samuel Kernell, *Going Public,* 56; Tebbel and Watts, *The Press and the Presidency,* 319; F.B. Marbut, *News from the Capital*; and Donald Ritchie, *Press Gallery*.

48. Quote comes from Louis Filler, *The Muckrakers*, 60.

49. Quote comes from Donald Ritchie, *Press Gallery*, 192.

50. As examples of this reluctance, see Richard Hofstadter, *The American Political Tradition and the Men Who Made It*, 225–227; George E. Mowry, *Theodore Roosevelt and the Progressive Movement*, 9–10; Henry Pringle, *Theodore Roosevelt,* 208; Lewis Gould, *The Presidency of Theodore Roosevelt*; H.W. Brands, *T.R.* For a contrary view, see Leroy Dorsey, "Preaching Morality in Modern America: Theodore Roosevelt's Rhetorical Progressivism."

51. Roosevelt's rhetoric has received a good deal of attention from rhetoricians. Much of this work has focused on the key rhetorical tropes and genres one may find in his political speeches. See especially a series of essays written by Leroy Dorsey: "Preaching Morality in Modern America," "The Frontier Myth in Presidential Rhetoric," "Theodore Roosevelt and Corporate America, 1901–1909: A Reexamination," *Presidential Studies Quarterly*, 25 (1995): 725–737; Dorsey and Rachel Harlow, "'We Want Americans Pure and Simple.'" Also see Daniel O. Buehler, "Permanence and Change in Theodore Roosevelt's Conservation Jeremiad."

52. Theodore Roosevelt, "Character & Success," *TR Works*, v. 1, 98–99.

53. Theodore Roosevelt "Social Evolution," *TR Works*, v. 12, 340.

54. Letter to Steffens, dated June 12, 1908. In *TR Letters*, v. 6, 1072. On Roosevelt's moralism, see Hofstadter, *The American Political Tradition*, 226; Henry May, *The End of American Innocence*, 108; and Wilfred Binkley, *The Man in the White House*, 39.

55. See Steffens, *The Autobiography of Lincoln Steffens*; and Harry A. Stein, "Theodore Roosevelt & The Press."

56. On Roosevelt's iconic status, see David Francis Sadler, *Theodore Roosevelt;* Richard Collin, *The Image of Theodore Roosevelt in American History & Thought*; Kathleen Dalton, "Why Americans Loved Teddy Roosevelt"; and Bruce Miroff, *Icons of Democracy*.

57. See Elmer Cornwell, *Presidential Leadership*, 23–24.

58. An analysis of Roosevelt's tour on behalf of his conservation policies is particularly appropriate because it was the issue of conservation through which Roosevelt devised the notion that he was a "steward" of the public interest. See Roosevelt, *Autobiography*, 420; Gifford Pinchot, *Breaking New Ground*, 303; Paul R. Cutright, *Theodore Roosevelt;* Samuel P. Hays, *Conservation and the Gospel of Efficiency,* 134; Stephen Ponder, "'Publicity in the Interest of the People'"; Christine Oravec, "Science, Public Policy, and the 'Spirit of the People'"; David Buehler, "Permanence and Change in Theodore Roosevelt's Conservation Jeremiad."

59. On the Commission and Pinchot's involvement in this trip, see Pinchot, *Breaking New Ground*, 328–329; Samuel P. Hays, *Conservation and the Gospel of Efficiency*, 106–108; Harold T. Pinkett, *Gifford Pinchot*, 107–110; and M. Nelson McGeary, *Gifford Pinchot*, 94–98.

60. Transcripts of these speeches can be found in *TR Works*, v. 12, 1364–1470. Hereafter, I will refer to them by the place in which they were delivered.

61. On this aspect of progressive thought, see Richard Hofstadter, *The American Political Tradition*, 204–205; George E. Mowry, *The Era of Theodore Roosevelt*, 101; Henry F. May, *The End of American Innocence,* 9.

62. Many observers have argued that Roosevelt led primarily through embodiment rather than persuasion. Writing in 1909, George Chandler believed that Roosevelt "owed a large measure of his strength with the nation at large to one quality: representativeness." Quoted in Richard Collin, *The Image of Theodore Roosevelt*, 77. John Dewey addressed the same theme when he wrote that Roosevelt was a "living embodiment" of his generation "rather than its representative." Dewey, "Theodore Roosevelt," 115. Finally, historian Peter Rechner concludes that "Roosevelt's most characteristic achievement was his sense of being the embodiment not only of the collective will but of the collective identity of the nation." Rechner, "Theodore Roosevelt and Progressive Personality Politics," 57.

63. Richard Collin, *The Image of Theodore Roosevelt*, 1–2.

64. Henry F. May, *The End of American Innocence*, 108.

65. Nicholas Roosevelt, *Theodore Roosevelt,* 39.

66. Allen White, *The Autobiography of William Allen White*, 297.

67. David Barry, *Forty Years in Washington*, 263.

68. This section is based on an analysis of news coverage in seven newspapers: *The New York Herald Tribune, The New York Times, Washington Evening-Star, The Washington*

Post, The Kansas City Star, The Chicago Daily Tribune, and The Los Angeles Times. The sample includes 203 stories written between September 23, 1907, one week before the trip, and October 23, 1907, the day Roosevelt arrived back in Washington, D.C.

69. George Juergens, *News from the White House*, 66. Elmer Cornwell makes the same point: "He [TR] could play favorites ... because the precedent had not yet been established that all must be treated alike in the White House." In Elmer Cornwell, *Presidential Leadership*, 19–20.

70. As Charles Thompson writes, "It belongs to this side of his character that he [TR] was never interviewed in a proper sense. A real interview is an unpremeditated thing, in which the reporter asks what questions he pleases, and takes the answers with merciless accuracy.... No one ever heard of an interview being given by Roosevelt..." in *Presidents I've Known and Two Near Presidents*, 118–119. See also Steffens, *Autobiography*, 509; and Isaac Marcosson, *Adventures in Interviewing*, New York: John Lane Co., 1920, 87.

71. For episodes, see David Barry, *Forty Years in Washington*, 267–269; and Oscar King Davis, *Released for Publication*, 128.

72. Archie Butt, *Taft and Roosevelt*, 30. See also Oscar King Davis, *Released for Publication*, 123–124; and Lewis Gould, *The Presidency of Theodore Roosevelt*, 20.

73. See David Barry, *Forty Years in Washington*, 271; Robert L. Spellman, "Cooperation on a Secondary Story: Oscar King Davis and the President"; and Harry Stein, "Theodore Roosevelt and the Press," 94–107.

74. On Roosevelt's press bureaus, and Pinchot's activities in particular, see Stephen Ponder, *Managing the Press*, Ch. 3.

75. Theodore Roosevelt, *Autobiography*, 464.

76. Gifford Pinchot, *Breaking New Ground*, 329.

77. Stephen Ponder, *Managing the Press*, 42–43.

78. Michael Schudson, *The Power of News*, 55.

79. On three of these five days, three newspapers used the Associated Press wire reports: *Washington Post* and *New York Times* on October 1st; *Washington Post*, *Los Angeles Times*, and *New York Times* on October 2nd, and *Los Angeles Times* and *Washington Post* on Oct. 5th. In one sense, this accurately reflects how Roosevelt's trip was covered in local newspapers across the country. However, in another sense, it clearly reduces the amount of variation in the coverage. Nonetheless, because each newspaper made independent editorial decisions as to headlines, framing, and length, it is useful to include the stories separately.

80. "National Pays Honor to William McKinley's Memorial at Unveiling of His Monument at His Old Home," *New York Herald Tribune*, Oct. 1, 1907, 3.

81. "Gentle Rebuke by Roosevelt," *Chicago Daily Tribune*, Oct. 1, 1907, 1.

82. "To Dead McKinley," *Washington Post*, Oct. 1, 1907, 3.

83. But see "World's Greatest Waterway Endorsed by President," *New York Times*, Oct. 6, 1907, 18. This article appeared in the Sunday edition of the *New York Times* and provided the most in-depth coverage of the proposal from an engineering perspective.

84. See, for instance, Roger Streitmatter, "The Impact of Presidential Personality on News Coverage in Major Newspapers." This tendency was least true of *New York Herald Tribune*, which framed nearly all of its coverage in terms of the 1908 presidential election and Roosevelt's decision to enter the race.

85. Headlines in *New York Times*, *Chicago Daily Tribune*, *Washington Evening-Star*, and *Los Angeles Times*, respectively.

86. See, for instance: a picture showing Roosevelt arriving at a train station by car, *New York Herald Tribune*, Sept. 26, 1907, 3; a picture showing Roosevelt and his wife driving in a car, *Washington Post*, Sept. 30, 1907, 3; a picture with the caption "Down the Mississippi River with the President," *Los Angeles Times*, October 2, 1907, 1; a picture showing Roosevelt boarding his boat in Keokuk, Iowa, with the caption: "President and Party Boarding the Mississippi, Keokuk, Iowa," *New York Herald Tribune*, Oct. 4, 1907, 3; and a six-column wide picture of Roosevelt arriving in St. Louis, *New York Herald Tribune*, Oct. 5, 1907, 3.

87. "The President En Route," *Chicago Daily Tribune*, Oct. 1, 1907, 1.

88. "On Way West," *Los Angeles Times*, Oct. 1, 1907, 1.

89. "President Roosevelt Ready for the CaneBrake Hunt," *New York Herald Tribune*, September 23, 1907, 3.

90. In, respectively, *New York Herald Tribune*, Sept. 27, 1907, 6; "The President Still Sticks to the Trail of Big Law Breaker," *Chicago Daily Tribune*, Oct. 2, 1907, 1; "The President's Dream of a Successful Hunt," *Washington Evening-Star*, October 11, 1907, 1.

91. Letter to Trevelyan, dated September 9, 1906, *TR Letters*, v. 5, 400.

92. Letter to Alfred Henry Lewis dated February 6, 1906, *TR Letters*, v. 5, 156–57.

93. "The Schoolmaster," *Washington Post*, Oct. 3, 1907, 3.

94. During a later, post-presidential hunting trip in Africa, Roosevelt refined his technique. He not only banned reporters (except for a select few) from his trip, he signed an agreement with *Outlook Magazine* to publish his own account of the trip. See, Gary Rice, "Trailing a Celebrity."

95. See, respectively, "Where the President Was Last Seen," *Washington Evening-Star*, October 7, 1907, 1; *Washington Post*, Sept. 30, 1907, 4; *Washington Evening-Star*, October 6, 1907, 1; and *Washington Evening-Star*, October 4, 1907, 1.

96. See, respectively, *Los Angeles Times*, October 17, 1907, p. 4; *New York Times*, October 20, 1907, p. 8; and *Washington Evening-Star*, October 20, 1907, 1; *Washington Post*, October 15, 1907, 4.

97. Gabriel Kolko characterizes Wilson as a "conservative" who embraced progressive proposals only when they conformed to a wider business-oriented agenda. See Kolko, *The Triumph of Conservatism,* 204. Similarly, Eldon Eisenach describes Wilson as a "reactionary" who defined the "prevailing system of party and constitution" against the efforts of true progressive reformers. See Eisenach, *The Lost Promise of Progressivism*, 123–127.

98. PPW, v. 6, 229.

99.   See, for instance, PPW, v. 7, 352–356; David Ryfe, "'Betwixt and Between;'" Jeffrey Tulis, *The Rhetorical Presidency*; and Teri Bimes and Stephen Skowronek, "Woodrow Wilson's Critique of Popular Leadership."

100.   Wilson, *Constitutional Government*, 68. Also see Robert Eden, "Opinion Leadership and the Problem of Executive Power," and Jeffrey Tulis, *The Rhetorical Presidency*.

101.   On this point, see Roland Young, "Woodrow Wilson's Congressional Government Reconsidered," 205; and Howard Gillman, "The Constitution Besieged." Mary Stuckey explores the racial repercussions of Wilson's rhetoric in "'The Domain of Conscience.'"

102.   On Wilson's views of newspapers, see "The Modern Democratic State," PPW, v. 5, 72; and "The Nature of Democracy in the United States," PPW, v. 6, 225.

103.   Wilson, *Constitutional Government*, 102.

104.   Oliver Newman letter to Ray Stannard Baker, undated, Reel 80, R.S. Baker Papers, Library of Congress.

105.   For other confrontations between Wilson and reporters during the 1912 presidential campaign, see Em Bowles Alsop, *The Greatness of Woodrow Wilson*, 28; and James Kerney, *The Political Education of Woodrow Wilson*, 343–44.

106.   Stockbridge, "How Woodrow Wilson Won His Nomination," *The Current History Magazine*, July, 1924, 564.

107.   This episode is recounted in Charles Thompson, *President's I've Known and Two Near Presidents*, 274.

108.   He officially stopped conducting regular press conferences in July 1915.

109.   The following analysis is based upon a sample of twenty press conferences conducted during Wilson's first three years in office, and coverage of these press conferences in eight newspapers: *The New York Times, The New York Herald Tribune, The Washington Post, The Washington Evening-Star, The Chicago Daily Tribune, The Kansas City Star, The Los Angeles Times, and The San Diego Union-Tribune.* All references to press conferences occur in PPW, v. 50.

110.   Ray Stannard Baker, *Woodrow Wilson, Life and Letters*, v. 3, 230.

111.   Lowry's interpretation of the conference is the most cited. See Edward Lowry, *Washington Close-Ups,* 19. However, a *New York Times* story the day after the first conference praised Wilson for making a "big hit" with the press, and for appearing so "unaffected" and "honest." (March 16, 1913, 1) Historians George Juergens and Robert C. Hilderbrand explain the discrepancy in these two reports by suggesting that Wilson's actions during and after WWI soured journalists to him, and tainted their memory of his early days in office. For this argument see Hilderbrand, *Power and the People,* 95–96; and George Juergens, "Woodrow Wilson and the Press." This is plausible. It is equally likely, however, that the press conferences were truly stunted affairs, and that the *New York Times* article is registering appreciation for the institution of regular press conferences rather than for Wilson's performance within them. Hilderbrand himself proposes this view in his introduction to the collected press conference transcripts, and it is one to which I will subscribe in this chapter.

112.   Letter from Oulahan to Baker, dated March 15, 1929, in R.S. Baker papers, reel 81, Library of Congress.

113.   PPW, v. 50, 5.

114.   PPW, v. 50, 48.

115.   PPW, v. 50, April 2, 1914, 437.

116.   On the construction of neutrality in news interviewing, see Steven Clayman, "Displaying Neutrality in Television News Interviews."

117.   David Greatbatch, "Aspects of Topical Organization in News Interviews," 441.

118.   These quotations may be found in PPW, v. 50, 103, 563, and 682, respectively.

119.   PPW, v. 50, September 8, 1913, 218, and March 23, 1914, 427, respectively.

120.   In a commencement address at the U.S. Naval Academy on June 5, 1914, Wilson admonished the cadets to "not to get the professional point of view.... There is nothing narrower or more unserviceable than the professional point of view—to have the attitude toward life that it centers in your profession. It does not." In PPW, v. 30, 145.

121.   Rosten, *The Washington Correspondents*, 14. Stephen Hess makes a similar observation of Washington reporters in the 1970s. He writes that these reporters seem to have a "natural interest ... in the politics of government, as opposed to the management of government." in *The Washington Reporters*, 101.

122.   Elmer Cornwell, "Presidential News."

123.   For instance, on May 9, 1913, the headline of the right hand lead story in *New York Herald Tribune* read: "Reform Currency at this Session, Urges Mr. Wilson." One assumes from this headline that Wilson is the main actor of the story. However, though the first paragraph of the story details the President's impending actions, the subsequent ten paragraphs of the story concern actions in Congress. From the headline, it seems as though Wilson is a major newsmaker; from the story's content, this is clearly on a partial truth. President Wilson did make news; but usually only in the context of a story whose main action and characters were elsewhere.

124.   PPW, v. 50, December 22, 1914, 657.

125.   *New York Herald Tribune*, December 23, 1914, 3.

126.   In his remarks to the Gridiron Club of Washington on April 12, 1913, Wilson remarked that newspapermen "are taking it for granted every day that it is incredible that there is not a fight on somewhere.... Now I want you gentlemen of the press to believe in the incredible. There ain't no friction. And there ain't gonna be no friction." PPW, v. 27, 296.

127.   *New York Times,* January 4, 1914, 2.

128.   These stories can be found in, respectively, *Chicago Daily Tribune*, October 24, 1913, 1 and *The San Diego Union*, October 24, 1913, 4.

129.   David Lawrence, *The True Story of Woodrow Wilson*, 340.

130.   Elmer Cornwell, *Presidential Leadership*, 37.

131.   Elmer Cornwell, *Presidential Leadership*, 41.

132.   Joseph Blum, *Joseph Tumulty and the Wilson Era*, 61.

133.   See Robert Hilderbrand, *Power and the People.*

134.   See Robert Jackall and Janice M. Hirota, *Image Makers.*

135. See Elmer Cornwell, who writes that the Committee "cannot be taken as evidence that the President had lost any of his earlier aversion to the seamy side of such activity." In *Presidential Leadership*, 55.

136. See Lary May, *Screening Out the Past*; and Jean Quandt, *From the Small Town to the Great Community*.

137. See Robert Jackall and Janice M. Hirota, *Image Makers;* and John A. Thompson, *Reformers and War*.

138. See Robert M. Crunden, *From Self to Society*; Gustav Le Bon, *The Crowd*; Patrick Brantlinger, *Bread & Circuses*; and Ray Eldon Hiebert, *Courtier to the Crowd*.

139. On progressive reactions to the war, see Gary Gerstle, "The Protean Character of American Liberalism." On the demise of progressivism generally, see Arthur Link, "What Happened to the Progressive Movement in the 1920s?"

140. Walter Lippmann, *Public Opinion*.

141. John Dewey, *The Public and Its Problems*, 137; 109, respectively.

142. John Dewey, *The Public and Its Problems*, 126.

143. John Dewey, *The Public and Its Problems*, 174.

Chapter Two

1. James W. Davis, *The American Presidency*, 140.

2. See the various places where Neustadt identifies FDR as a "master" of the presidency, *Presidential Power,* 87, 132, 137, respectively.

3. Theodore Lowi, *The Personal President,* especially chapter 3.

4. Fred Greenstein, "Change and Continuity in the Modern Presidency," 47.

5. Samuel Kernell, *Going Public,* 249.

6. The term "fireside chat" was first coined by the manager of the CBS Washington bureau in 1933.

7. This interpretation is scattered throughout the literature. See James MacGregor Burns, *Roosevelt,* 199; Frank Freidel, *Franklin D. Roosevelt,* 99; William Leuchtenberg, *FDR and the New Deal*, 330; Theodore Lowi, *The Personal President,* 65; Winfield, *FDR and the News Media*, 104.

8. The phrase "soothing conciliation" comes from Kenneth Cmiel, *Democratic Eloquence,* 259; The Jamieson quote comes from *Eloquence in an Electronic Age,* 55. For an alternative view, see Elvin Lim, "The Lion and the Lamb." Lim develops an operational definition of intimacy based upon several variables, and then quantifies the appearance of these variables in the speeches of Presidents Hoover and FDR. Contrary to conventional wisdom, he finds that FDR's chats were no more intimate than those of Hoover. While this finding does not necessarily mean that the conventional wisdom is wrong—Lim's definition of intimacy may be incorrect, and in an any event Lim does not contest the fact that contemporary listeners interpreted FDR's speeches as more intimate than those of Hoover—it does suggest that more work needs to be done in understanding the nature of the appeal in the fireside chats.

9.   But see Joy Hayes, *Radio Broadcasting and Nation Building in Mexico and the United States, 1925–1945.* For a study of letters written to FDR generally, see Leila Sussman, *Dear FDR.*

10.   Warren Susman, "The Culture of the Thirties," 158.

11.   Warren Susman, "The Culture of the Thirties," 157.

12.   See Susan Strasser, *Satisfaction Guaranteed.*

13.   See Robert Jackall and Janice Hirota, *The Image Makers.*

14.   David Chaney, *Fictions of Collective Life,* 136.

15.   At this point, one might make two objections to the line of argument I have pursued. First, one might argue that mass culture is solely manipulative, that it has no other purpose but to deceive. Put crudely, but I think fairly, this is the view of critical theorists such as Max Horkheimer and Theodor Adorno (see their *Dialectic of Enlightenment*) and their followers who suggest that the most important aspect of media culture is its economic value to the capitalist organizations that produce it. Here, I would simply say that this view has been repudiated by a wealth of audience studies which show consumers using media culture to make sense of their everyday lives. For a review, see Will Brooker and Deborah Jermyn, *The Audience Studies Reader.* A second objection is more historical: can't one claim that all mass culture, in the 1930s and beyond, responds to the interests and experiences of audiences? In this sense, mass culture of the 1930s is no different from that of later decades. My response is yes and no. Mass culture is by definition polysemic. However, I argue that its mode of address has changed significantly since the 1930s. Producers have more technologies for shaping audience tastes. Audiences themselves have become savvier consumers of mass culture, leading producers to adopt a more ironic, knowing tone. And the media landscape is much larger than in the 1930s, taking up more of our everyday lives. Increasingly, responding to the social experience of consumers means precisely responding to their experience of media consumption—a postmodern condition of simulacrum and specularism. Compared to contemporary media culture then, I argue that media culture of the 1930s had a distinctive register, offered a particular set of symbolic resources, and conveyed a unique mode of address.

16.   See David Bordwell, "Standardization and Differentiation," 101; Barry King, "Stardom as Occupation," 166; and Francesco Albertoni, "The Powerless 'Elite.'"

17.   See Richard de Cordova, *Picture Personalities;* Joshua Gamson, *Claims to Fame;* Cathy Klaprat, "The Star as Market Strategy."

18.   Richard Dyer, *Heavenly Bodies,* 17.

19.   David Chaney, *Fictions of Collective Life,* 146.

20.   I mean this in the same sense that Kenneth Burke refers to literature as "equipment for living." See Burke, "Literature as Equipment for Living."

21.   Walter Lippmann, *A Preface to Morals,* 6.

22.   On realism, see Stanley Corkin, *Realism and the Birth of the United States;* Amy Kaplan, *The Social Construction of American Realism;* and David Shi, *Facing Facts.* On romanticism, see Lionel Trilling, *The Liberal Imagination;* Richard Chase, *The American Novel and Its Tradition;* Quentin Anderson, *The Imperial Self;* and Michael Davitt Bell, *The Development of Romance.* For a useful review of this literature, see

George Dekker, "The Genealogy of American Romance." See also the bibliographic essay provided by Emily Miller Budick in her *Nineteenth-Century American Romance*. On melodrama, the seminal text is Peter Brooks, *The Melodramatic Imagination*.

23.   Peter Brooks, *The Melodramatic Imagination*, 41.

24.   See Stephen Neale, *Cinema and Technology,* for a discussion of cinema's technical qualities.

25.   For a discussion of photography's cultural authority, see Susan Sontag, *On Photography*, New York: Dell, 1977.

26.   See, for instance, Leo Charney and Vanessa R. Schwartz, Eds., *Cinema and the Invention of Modern Life*.

27.   The great theorist of cinema realism is Andre Bazin. See his *What Is Cinema?*

28.   On broadcasting's "liveness," see Paddy Scannell, *Radio, Television and Modern Life*. Most of the literature on "liveness" in broadcasting refers to television. See Jane Feuer, "The Concept of Live Television"; David Barker, "'It's Been Real"; and James Friedman, Ed., *Reality Squared*.

29.   On these sociodramas, see Roland Marchand, *Advertising the American Dream*, ch. 1.

30.   Tom Gunning, *D.W. Griffith and the Origins of American Narrative Film*. On the development of the Hollywood idiom, also see David Bordwell, et al., *Classical Hollywood Cinema*; and Jane Gaines, Ed., *Classical Hollywood Narrative*.

31.   The new vernacular required a new method of acting. In a change from the "grand and lofty" style of acting characteristic of nineteenth-century theater, movie actors were trained to act as if they were not acting at all. The new method emphasized natural speech and simple gestures and sought to demonstrate the inner emotions of characters. In this way, acting became more personal and intimate. Actors represented real rather than ideal people so that viewers could understand and interpret the psychological motivation of the characters. On this change, see Benjamin McArthur, *Actors and American Culture, 1880–1920*.

32.   For discussions of advertising on radio, see Susan Smulyan, *Selling Radio*; and John W. Spalding, "1928: Radio Becomes a Mass Advertising Medium." For discussions of various broadcasting genres, see Michele Hilmes, *Radio Voices;* Wayne Munson, *All Talk;* Susan Smulyan, "Radio Advertising to Women in Twenties America," and Morleen Getz Rouse, "Daytime Radio Programming for the Homemaker, 1926–1935."

33.   Paddy Scannell, *Radio, Television and Modern Life*, 164.

34.   A point made in another context by Stanley Cavell in *Senses of Walden*, 61–65.

35.   See Lizabeth Cohen, "Encountering Mass Culture at the Grassroots," for a discussion of this process in Chicago of the 1920s.

36.   Data for this analysis include the eight fireside chats delivered during FDR's first term in office and a random sample of 380 letters (of approximately 10,000 housed at the Franklin D. Roosevelt Library (FDRL) written by ordinary people in reaction to the chats. Both sets of data can be found at the FDRL in Hyde Park, NY. The first of the chats was broadcast on March 12, 1933, and the last on September 6, 1936. For convenience, I have numbered the letters 1–380, and will refer to them in the text by these numbers.

37. Quote is in Arthur Schlesinger, Jr., *The Coming of the New Deal*, 558.

38. See Thomas Doherty, *Pre-Code Hollywood: Sex, Immorality, and Insurrection in American Cinema, 1930–1934*, New York: Columbia University Press, 1999, 77–92 for a discussion of FDR's use of newsreels.

39. See Alfred B. Rollins, *Roosevelt and Howe*.

40. Quoted in Donald Horton and R. Richard Wohl, "Mass Communication and Parasocial Interaction," 36.

41. Quoted in Arthur Schlesinger, *The Coming of the New Deal*, 12.

42. Frances Perkins, *The FDR I Knew*, 71.

43. Erving Goffman, "Radio Talk," 241.

44. Leo Rosten, *The Washington Correspondents*, 71.

45. Much of this information is taken from Robert Fine, *FDR's Radio Chatting*. Also see James Ragland, "Franklin D. Roosevelt and the Man in the Street"; and John Sharon, "The Psychology of the Fireside Chat."

46. James Ragland, "Franklin D. Roosevelt and the Man in the Street," 65. On his radio broadcasts generally, see Robert J. Brown, *Manipulating the Ether*.

47. Quote taken from Arthur Schlesinger, Jr., *The Coming of the New Deal*, 572.

48. Indeed, although the chats, and FDR generally, garnered enormous public adulation, they also sparked great antagonism. For every two people who loved the president, another could not stand to hear his name spoken in her presence. On FDR's critics, see Clyde P. Weid, *The Nemesis of Reform;* and Gary D. Best, *The Critical Press and the New Deal*.

49. For a comparison of President Hoover and FDR's rhetoric, see Davis W. Houck, *Rhetoric as Currency*.

50. Arthur Schlesinger describes this last phrase on personal initiative as a "concession" to business leaders worried that FDR was leading the country toward socialism. However, statements like this one occur throughout the chats, indicating that they are part of a wider effort by FDR to individualize and personalize the unprecedented government presence in economic and social affairs. See Schlesinger, *The Coming of the New Deal*, 498–99.

51. Letter from Early to Hays, dated April 20, 1933, President's Personal Files, 1A, Box 2 "Presidents Personal Life 1932–35," FDRL.

52. Sharon, "The Psychology of the Fireside Chat."

53. Letter dated March 20, 1935. Found in the President's Personal Papers, Box 1, "Speech Materials and Suggestions, 1935," FDRL.

54. One letter-writer wrote the following in response to FDR's sip of water: "When the speaker uttered the parenthesis about the glass of water ... the human element of the speech was immeasurably reinforced." From my sample of public reaction letters, #133.

55. William Leuchtenberg, *FDR and the New Deal*, 330.

56. Ragland, "Franklin D. Roosevelt and the Man in the Street," 72.

57.   James MacGregor Burns, *Roosevelt,* 538

58.   Patrick Maney, *The Roosevelt Presence,* 81.

59.   For an assessment of reporters' relation with the president, see Graham White, *FDR and the Press*, 1979.

60.   Raymond Clapper, "Why Reporters Like FDR," 14–17.

61.   Erik Barnouw, *History of Broadcasting in the United States*, v. 2, 8.

62.   Letter #51.

63.   Letters #63 & #75, respectively.

64.   Unlike other kinds of fan-mail letters, letter-writers to the president seemed to have been more middle-class, educated, and male, characteristics shared by listeners of public affairs programs generally. See Frederick Lumley, *Measurement in Radio*; Leila Sussman, *Dear FDR;* and Robert McElvaine, *Down and Out in the Great Depression.*

65.   Letters #110, #180, #150, #143, #126, #139, #127, #297.

66.   Letter #377.

67.   Letter #s 40, 74, 81.

68.   Letter #s 168, 200, 210, 136.

69.   Letter #s 43, 173, 29, 30, 4, 15.

70.   Letter #s 77, 183.

71.   Kenneth Cmiel argues that this style developed in the clash between aristocratic and populist political practices vying for public legitimacy in the nineteenth century. As the lower classes entered politics, they championed informality and plainness as ways of undermining traditional codes of deference. Increasingly, the simple and colloquial blended with the refined and formal to create "middling styles" of political rhetoric. By the end of the nineteenth century, people viewed these styles as open, democratic and typically American patterns of political speech. See Cmiel, *Democratic Eloquence.*

72.   Scannell, *Radio, Television, and Modern Life*, 24, 171–172, respectively.

73.   Letters #143, #192, #342.

74.   Letter #22.

75.   Hadley Cantril, "The Invasion from Mars."

76.   Leila Sussman, *Dear FDR*, 135, 139.

77.   Letter #165.

78.   Letter #116.

79.   Letter #233.

80.   Letter #292.

81.   Letter #112.

82.   See, for instance, James W. Cook, *The Arts of Deception;* Karen Halttunen, *Confidence Men and Painted Women.*

83.   James W. Cook, *The Arts of Deception*, 28.

84. Letters #110, #86, #88, #127, #83, #184.

85. Letters #236, #152, #179.

86. Letters #70, #98, #278, #148.

87. Letters #27, #219, #221, #296.

88. Letters #195, #197, #255.

89. Letters #250, #284, #240, #313, #97.

90. William Stott, *Documentary Expression and Thirties America.*

91. Susman, "The Culture of the Thirties," 157.

92. It is this intuition which has led Joy Hayes to argue that the fireside chats—and the public reactions letters they elicited—constitute an example of nationalism in the making. See Hayes, "Radio Broadcasting and Nation-Building," ch. 5.

93. Kateb, "Walt Whitman and the Culture of Democracy," 212, 214.

94. The sentimentalism that pervaded much of nineteenth-century American mass culture represents an important precursor to this mode of address. See Glen Hendler, *Public Sentiments.*

95. Letter #s 125, 260, 1, 137, 91, 144, 147, 186, 263, respectively.

96. Letter #s 278, 9, 175, 130, 177.

97. Letter #s 102, 117, 120.

98. Letter #s 233, 277.

99. Clifford Geertz, "Deep Play," 449.

100. Bruce Miroff, *Icons of Democracy,* 233.

101. On the inevitable comparisons between FDR and other modern presidents, see William Leuchtenberg, *In the Shadow of FDR.*

Chapter Three

1. This is true in the sense that, excepting Richard Neustadt's study, every major early statement on the subject was written in the 1980s. See, for instance, Samuel Kernell, *Going Public*; Jeffrey Tulis, *The Rhetorical Presidency*; James Ceasar, et al., "The Rise of the Rhetorical Presidency"; Kathleen Hall Jamieson, *Eloquence in an Electronic Age*; Theodore Lowi, *The Personal President.*

2. Hayden White, *Tropics of Discourse.*

3. On the early growth of the administrative state, see Stephen Skowronek, *Building a New American State; and* John A. Rohr, *To Run a Constitution.*

4. Ronald Jacobs and Robert Shapiro, *Politicians Don't Pander.*

5. Ronald Jacobs and Robert Shapiro, *Politicians Don't Pander*, xv.

6. Robert Entman, "Framing: Toward Clarification of a Fractured Paradigm," 52. On the process of framing generally, see Robert Entman and Andrew Rojecki, "Freezing Out the Public"; Daniel Kahneman and Amos Tversky, "Choices, Values, and Frames"; Zhongdang Pan and Gerald M. Kosicki, "Framing Analysis"; Vincent Price, et al.,

"Switching Trains of Thought"; Thomas Nelson and Donald Kinder, "Issue Frames and Group-Centrism in American Public Opinion"; Dietram Scheufele, "Framing as a Theory of Media Effects"; William Gamson and Andrew Modigliani, "Media Discourse and Public Opinion on Nuclear Power"; Shanto Iyengar and Donald Kinder, *News that Matters;* and Jon Krosnick and Donald Kinder, "Altering the Foundations of Support for the President Through Priming."

7.   On the nature of the priming process, see especially Shanto Iyengar and Donald Kinder, *News that Matters*; Shanto Iyengar and Donald Kinder, *Is Anyone Responsible?*; and Vincent Price, et al., "Switching Trains of Thought."

8.   See, for instance, the elevated picture of the presidency developed by the first generation of presidency scholars: Wilfred Binkley, *President and Congress*; Clinton Rossiter, *The American Presidency*; Austin Ranney, *The Doctrine of Responsible Party Government*; and Louis Koenig, *The Chief Executive*. Rossiter ends his volume by proclaiming that, with all of the urgent problems facing the country, "we have never been in more obvious need of presidential manipulation of all the techniques that are available to him to mold public opinion, goad Congress, and inspire public officials at all levels." Clinton Rossiter, *The American Presidency*, 264.

9.   Lewis J. Paper, *The Promise and the Performance*, 158. Also see, Hugh Heclo, "The Executive Office of the President."

10. See Hugh Heclo, *A Government of Strangers,* 38.

11. Data from Paul C. Light, *Thickening Government.*

12. Jonathan Rauch, *Demosclerosis,* 84.

13. Numbers can be found in Harrison W. Fox and Susan Webb Hammond, "The Growth of Congressional Staffs," 115-116.

14. Number taken from David Ricci, *The Transformation of American Politics,* 1–2; and James Allen Smith, *The Idea Brokers,* xiv.

15. In one of the first studies of Washington reporters conducted in 1936, Leo Rosten found that 60 percent of the Washington reporters he polled knew how their newspapers wanted stories played. By 1960, that number had dropped to 9 percent. See Rosten, *The Washington Correspondents,* 220–222. Quoted in William Rivers, *The Other Government,* 15.

16. On the ramifications of this routine for democracy, see Herbert Gans, *Democracy and the News.*

17. Leon Sigal, *Reporters and Officials,* 124.

18. A good review of the literature on presidential-press relations in the modern era can be found in Timothy Cook, *Governing with the News,* Chapter 6.

19. On the relation of presidents and television news, see Charles A. H. Thomson, *Television and Presidential Politics,* 13; Sig Mickelson, *From Whistle Stop to Soundbite,* 12; and Daniel Sies, "The Presidency and Television."

20. Figures can be found in Frederic T. Smoller, *The Six O'clock Presidency,* 45–46.

21. Quoted in Lawrence Wittner, *Cold War America,* 202.

22. See Martha Joynt Kumar and Michael B. Grossman, "Political Communications from the White House"; and Joseph Pika, "Interest Groups and the Executive."

23.   Samuel Kernell, *Going Public,* 27.

24.   Paul Lazarsfeld, et al., *The People's Choice*; Bernard Berelson, et al., *Voting*; Angus Campbell, et al., *The Voter Decides*; and Angus Campbell, et al., *The American Voter.*

25.   Phillip Converse's essay, "The Nature of Belief Systems in Mass Publics," is perhaps the most famous of this work. See V. O. Key, *The Responsible Electorate,* for a dissenting view.

26.   Joseph Schumpeter, *Capitalism, Socialism, and Democracy.*

27.   David Truman, *The Governmental Process*; Robert Dahl, *A Preface to Democratic Theory.*

28.   This interpretation is confirmed by work on how presidents and other political professionals use public opinion polls. On their face, such polls purport to give policymakers a sense of how the public would like political issues to be handled. For the most part, however, policymakers do not use polls in this way. Because they consider themselves to be experts, and the public uninformed about policymaking issues, policy and political professionals generally ignore the substantive results of polls. Instead, they use polling data to determine how well their rhetorical strategies are working to manage public preferences, and for guidance on how they might revise these strategies to work more effectively. See Lawrence Jacobs and Robert Shapiro, "Presidential Manipulation of Polls and Public Opinion," and "Issues, Candidate, Image, and Priming"; Susan Herbst, *Reading Public Opinion;* Philip J. Powlick, "The Sources of Public Opinion for American Foreign Policy Officials."

29.   E. E. Schattschneider, *The Semisovereign People.* The distance from Roosevelt's flattery of public opinion in the chats is remarkable.

30.   On this process, see Stanley Kelley, Jr., *Professional Public Relations and Political Power*; Sidney Blumenthal, *The Permanent Campaign;* Larry Sabato, *The Rise of Political Consultants;* Dennis W. Johnson, *No Place for Amateurs.*

31.   In the notion of crafted talk, I mean to refer specifically to the president's policymaking rhetoric; that is, to rhetoric intended to support some policy goal. Of course modern presidents engage in other forms of rhetoric, perhaps most importantly ceremonial rhetoric whose function is social cohesion and/or value maintenance. While this "priestly function" of the presidency, as some have called it, is interesting and important, it lies outside the terms of my discussion here. But see, James Fairbanks, "The Priestly Function of the Presidency"; Michael Novak, *Choosing Our King*; Charles Henderson & Robert S. Alley, Eds., *So Help Me God*; & Richard Pierard & Robert Linder, *Civil Religion & the Presidency.*

32.   On the history of presidential speechwriting, see Kurt Ritter and Martin Medhurst, *Presidential Speechwriting*; and Kathleen Hall Jamieson, *Eloquence in an Electronic Age.*

33.   This is in line with the findings of Roderick Hart, *The Sound of Leadership*; and Barbara Hinckley, *The Symbolic Presidency.* In content analyses of presidential speech (in Hart's case, all public speeches, in Hinckley's case, state of the union addresses), both authors find that over the twentieth century presidents increasingly speak in the institutional voice of the office rather than as particular individuals.

34.   On the history of communication as a scientific discipline, see Christopher Simpson, *Science of Coercion;* Jesse G. Delia, "Communication Research"; J. Michael Hogan,

"George Gallup and the Rhetoric of Scientific Democracy"; and Stephen Chaffee and Joseph Hochheimer, "The Beginnings of Political Communication Research in the United States."

35.   The culmination of this trend toward specialization is accreditation. It is no surprise to learn that, during the 1990s, universities and colleges around the country began to offer certificates, and even master's degrees, in political management.

36.   This is not to say that modern presidents avoid speaking in moral terms. Rather, it is to say that strategic thinking serves as the guiding assumption of crafted talk. At one time, morality served as the constitutive basis of presidential thinking. In crafted talk, it has become one style of talk within a form of presidential communication that is generally animated by strategic concerns.

37.   Edward Bernays, "The Engineering of Consent," 114.

38.   There is an excellent literature on the rhetoric of the Cold War, some themes of which I have borrowed in the following passages. See, for instance, Martin J. Medhurst and H. W. Brands, *Critical Reflections on the Cold War*; Shawn Parry-Giles, *The Rhetorical Presidency, Propaganda, and the Cold War, 1945–1955*; Martin J. Medhurst, et al., *The Cold War as Rhetoric*; Lynn Boyd Hinds and Theodore Otto Windt, Jr., *The Cold War as Rhetoric; and* David J. Tietge, *Flash Effect.*

39.   On Eisenhower's views of the Cold War, see Robert R. Bowie, *Waging Peace.* On his corporatism, see Robert Griffith, "Dwight D. Eisenhower and the Corporate Commonwealth."

40.   Other studies of Eisenhower's rhetoric include Martin J. Medhurst, Ed., *Ike's War of Words*; Martin J. Medhurst, *Dwight D. Eisenhower;* Ira Chernus, *Eisenhower's Atoms for Peace;* Shawn Parry-Giles, *The Rhetorical Presidency, Propaganda, and the Cold War, 1945–1955.*

41.   See John Tebbel and Sarah Watts, *The Press & the Presidency*, 465.

42.   Emmett Hughes, *The Ordeal of Power*, 131–132.

43.   Letter to William Phillips, dated June 5, 1953. In *Eisenhower Papers,* v. 14, 275.

44.   Quoted in *Foreign Relations Series of the United States*, 1952–54, v. 2, no. 1, 267–68; Walter L. Hixson, *Parting the Curtain*, 22.

45.   "Every significant act of government should be so timed," Eisenhower said during the 1952 presidential campaign, "and so directed at a principal target, and so related to other governmental actions, that it will produce the maximum effect." Quote taken from "Extract from Address by Dwight D. Eisenhower, delivered at San Francisco, Wednesday, October 8, 1952," C.D. Jackson Papers, Box 2, Robert Cutler, DDE Library.

46.   Quoted in Shawn Parry-Giles, "Militarizing Propaganda," 113. Also see Scott Lucas, "Campaigns of Truth"; and Herman, "The Career of Cold War Psychology."

47.   Delivered on April 16, 1953, and December 8, 1953, respectively.

48.   Quoted in David Barkin, "Eisenhower's Secret Strategy: Television Planning in the 1952 Campaign," *Journal of Advertising History*, 9 (1987), 19. Original quote comes from Siguard Larmon letter to Eisenhower, dated July 18, 1952, In William E. Robinson Papers, Box 9, Siguard Larmon folder, Eisenhower Library.

49. For instance, Arthur Larson (Eisenhower speechwriter, former undersecretary of labor, and beginning in 1958, head of USIA) recalls that in response to the Sputnik launches Eisenhower asked him to devise a series of "fireside chat" speeches, a public relations campaign that failed to materialize only because the President suffered a stroke on November 26, 1957. See Arthur Larson, *Eisenhower,* 156. In reference to one of the President's meetings with public relations professionals, Ann Whitman (his Secretary), wrote in her diary that, "For whatever it is worth, the whole business worried me because it sounded so fascist—you think this way, you say this in answer to that, etc...." In the Whitman Papers, ACW Diary, Box 1 #3, September 29, 1953, DDEL.

50. On this board, see Craig Allen, *Eisenhower and the Mass Media,* 41. Eisenhower found it difficult to find an industry leader to accept the position. After some months, he decided to include these activities in the job description of his press secretary, Jim Hagerty.

51. Eisenhower experimented with many other television formats. He held televised cabinet meetings, televised chats with individual members of his cabinet, and coffee klatsches with ordinary voters. Eventually, he also settled on televised news conferences. But the televised address remained a staple format throughout his presidency.

52. Memo from Lodge to Major General Wilton B. Persons, dated November 12, 1953, White House Central Files, 101-Z.

53. Data for this section include fifteen of Eisenhower's televised addresses. Excluding inaugural and State of the Union speeches, Eisenhower delivered 29 such addresses while in office. I winnowed this list to fifteen by excluding those delivered before a live audience, those that included other speakers (Eisenhower cabinet members), and those that dealt solely with the President's trip to a foreign locale. All fifteen may be found in the *Public Papers of the Presidents Series*, which is organized by date and year. In the text, I will refer to them by PPE [for Public Papers, Eisenhower], title of speech, date, and page number.

54. In PPE, "Radio Address to the American People on the National Security and Its Costs," May 19, 1953, 309.

55. In PPE, "Radio and Television Address to the American People on the State of the Nation," April 5, 1954, 373.

56. PPE, "National Security and Its Costs," May 19, 1953, 306; "Achievements of the Administration and the 83rd Congress," August 6, 1953, 555; "State of the Nation," April 5, 1954, 375.

57. Quotes from PPE, "National Security and Its Costs," May 19, 1953, 306; "Security in the Free World," March 19, 1959, 57; and "Administration's Purposes and Accomplishments," January 4, 1954, 3.

58. See PPE, "National Security and Its Costs," May 19, 1953, 82; "Achievements of the Administration and the 83rd Congress," August 6, 1953, 159; "Administration's Purposes and Accomplishments," January 4, 1954, 4; "Security in the Free World," March 16, 1959, 57; "Address to the American People on the Tax Program," March 15, 1954, 317; "Address to the American People on the State of the Nation," April 5, 1954, 377; "Address to the American People on the State of the Nation," April 5, 1954, 379–380.

59.   PPE, "Cost of Government," May 14, 1957, 341; "Farm Bill Veto," April 16, 1956, 394; "Security in the Free World," March 16, 1959, 281; "Science in National Security," November 7, 1957, 794; "Tax Program," March 15, 1954, 317; "Achievements of the 83rd Congress," August 23, 1954, 755.

60.   See, for instance, PPE, "Administration Purposes and Accomplishments," January 4, 1954, 2; "The Situation in the Middle East," February 20, 1957, 147; "National Security and Its Costs," May 19, 1953, pp. 312–313; "Cost of Government," May 14, 1957, 346; "Security in the Free World," March 16, 1959, 282; "Tax Program," March 15, 1954, 315; "Achievements of the 83rd Congress," August 23, 1954, 751; "State of the Nation," April 5, 1954, 373.

61.   On the impact of rational language on the political process, see Murray Edelman, "The Influence of Rationality Claims on Public Opinion and Policy."

62.   One may see this language throughout Eisenhower's speeches, but see PPE, "National Security and Its Costs," May 19, 1953, 308; "Achievements of the Administration and the 83rd Congress," August 6, 1953, 548; "Need for Mutual Security in Waging the Peace," May 21, 1957, 391; and "State of the Nation," April 5, 1954, 377.

63.   PPE, "Tax Program," March 15, 1954, 313; "Cost of Government," May 14, 1957, 343.

64.   Quotes in "Memorandum of Appointment," dated September 2, 1955, Ann Whitman Papers, ACW Diary, Box 6, September, 1955 (6); Letter from Larmon to Eisenhower, dated March 11, 1954, Ann Whitman Papers, Name Series, Box 20, Sig Larmon (3).

65.   PPE, "Achievements of the 83rd Congress," August 23, 1954, 748; "The Need for an Effective Labor Bill," August 6, 1959, 569.

66.   Quotes in PPE, "Tax Program," March 15, 1954, 316; "State of the Nation," April 5, 1954, 373; "Science in National Security," November 7, 1957, 794; "State of the Nation," April 5, 1954, 381.

67.   Quoted in PPE, "Developments in Eastern Europe and the Middle East," October 31, 1956, 1060; "Cost of Government," May 14, 1957, 342; "National Security and Its Costs," May 19, 1953, 313; "Situation in Little Rock," September 24, 1957, 691.

68.   Eisenhower memorandum dated November 23, 1953 to Sherman Adams, Henry Cabot Lodge, Leonard Wood Hall, George Magoffin Humphrey, Thomas Edwin Stephens, and Arthur Ellsworth Summerfield. In *Eisenhower Papers*, v. 14, 686.

69.   Marian D. Irish, "The Organization Man in the Presidency," 272.

70.   C. Wright Mills, *The Power Elite*.

71.   See, for instance, William Lee Miller, "Can Government Be Merchandised?" Norman Graebner, "Eisenhower's Popular Leadership"; Goodman Ace, "Fireside Chitchat," 31.

72.   James Reston, "The Fireside Chat: A Discussion of How Presidential Report Has Declined When the Need Seems Greatest," *New York Times*, May 24, 1956, 16.

73.   For other instances, see *Washington Post*, "Refusing to Race," October 10, 1957, A14; Doris Fleeson, "The President and the Satellite," *Washington Evening-Star*, October 10, 1957, A10; James Reston, "The President's Speech," *New York Times*, November 8, 1957, 12.

74. For an example of conservative criticism, see David Lawrence, "After Six Months," *US News & World Report*, v. 35, July 17, 1953, 108; for liberal criticism, see "The Shape of Things: The President Vanishes," *The Nation*, v. 177, Sept. 19, 1953, 221.

75. These kinds of potshots got so bad that Hugh Scott, a Republican House member from PA, implored his Republican colleagues to "stop picking on the President!" In "Let's Stop Picking on the President!" *The American Magazine*, v. 156, Sept. 1953, 19.

76. T.R.B., "Washington Wire," *The New Republic*, v. 129, December 21, 1953, 2.

77. See, for instance, *The New Republic*, v. 129, Nov. 16, 1953, 7; *Time*, v. 62, Nov. 30, 1953, 52; *The Commonweal*, v. 59, Dec. 11, 1953, 247; *The New Republic*, v. 130, March 8, 1954, 2; *The Nation*, v. 178, March 13, 1954, 211.

78. Interestingly, this drumbeat of criticism did not put a dent into Eisenhower's popularity with the public. Throughout his presidency he maintained the highest public approval ratings of any modern President. These numbers dipped somewhat in 1957–1958 (as a consequence of a series of events, including Sputnik and Little Rock), but bounced back again in 1959. Explanations for these numbers vary. John Mueller traces them to Eisenhower's wartime image and his relative inactivity as President (see his *War, Presidents, and Public Opinion*, 205–208). David Lanoue argues that Republican presidents have the advantage of a core group of supporters who do not abandon them when bad things happen during their presidency (see his "The 'Teflon Factor,'" 484). Kenneth Morris and Barry Schwarz suggest that Eisenhower retained public popularity because his image of equalitarianism and teamwork resonated spoke to the fears and hopes of a nation that had experienced twenty years of upheaval and was in the midst of a cold war (see their "Why They Liked Eisenhower.")

79. "The Curse of Indecision," *Reporter*, v. 17, Oct. 14, 1953, 13.

80. Quotes come from Everett Hughes, *The Ordeal of Power*, 125; and letter from Eisenhower to William Phillips, June 5, 1953, *Eisenhower Papers*, v. 14, 275.

81. On Eisenhower's view of communication as strategy, see Martin J. Medhurst, "Ike's Rhetorical Leadership"; and Fred I. Greenstein, *The Hidden-Hand Presidency*, 57–58.

82. Chalmers Roberts, "John F. Kennedy and the Press," 195.

83. For this interpretation of Kennedy's news meetings, see Elmer Cornwell, *Presidential Leadership*, 189, in which he writes, "The new administration accepted the conference institution as it was handed on to them, and took the logical next step in its evolution." Kennedy's press secretary Pierre Salinger is credited with advising the President to take this step. See Salinger, *With Kennedy*, 54–58. Other good discussions include E.R. Hutchison, "Kennedy and the Press"; Raymond Brandt, "Kennedy Expected to Expand Press Conferences," *St. Louis Post-Dispatch*, April 29, 1962; and Hugh Sidey, *John F. Kennedy, President*, 49.

84. See, respectively, "The Show-Biz Conference," *Time*, 78, November 17, 1961: 39; Ted Lewis, "Information or Persuasion?" *The Nation*, 192, February 11, 1961, 112; Russell Baker, "'Kennedy and Press' Seems a Hit; Star Shows Skill as Showman," *New York Times*, January 26, 1961, 12.

85. Alistair Cooke, broadcast on Sunday, January 29, 1961. A transcript of this broadcast can be found in the John F. Kennedy Library (JFKL) PR 18-2/B.

86. James Reston, "The Problem of Holding a Political Balance," *New York Times*, January 11, 1961.

87.   Robert Pierpoint, *At the White House,* 70.

88.   Tom Wicker, *On Press,* 112; Chalmers Roberts, *First Rough Draft,* 179; Helen Thomas, *Dateline,* 22, respectively. See also Harrison Salisbury, *A Time of Change,* 64–65.

89.   Quoted in Lewis J. Paper, *The Promise and the Performance,* 323–324.

90.   As David Halberstam put it, there was surely something to the notion that "Television loved [Kennedy]," that "he and the camera were born for each other...." Quotes come from Halberstam, *The Powers that Be,* 444; and Arthur Schlesinger, Jr., *A Thousand Days,* 658.

91.   My analysis is based on a sample of twenty press conferences, transcripts of which were taken from Public Papers of the Presidents series for President Kennedy [hereafter referred to as PPK]. This sample includes eighteen randomly selected press conferences plus the first press conference held on January 25, 1961, and the last press conference, held November 14, 1963.

92.   Worth Bingham and Ward S. Just, "The President and the Press," *The Reporter,* 26, April 12, 1962, 20.

93.   Elmer Cornwell, *Presidential Leadership,* 204–205.

94.   This sample consisted of the same eight newspapers as Chapter Two: *The New York Herald Tribune, The New York Times, The Washington Post, The Washington Evening-Star, The Kansas City Star, The Chicago Daily Tribune, The Los Angeles Times,* and *San Diego Union-Tribune.*

95.   This is confirmed by Rodger Streitmatter's larger study of news coverage of Presidents from Theodore Roosevelt to Ronald Reagan. Streitmatter found a constant increase in presidential news coverage to Kennedy's presidency, after which the quantity of news coverage stabilized. This implies that Kennedy represents the threshold of presidential dominance of the news. See Streitmatter, "Front Page From the White House."

96.   Elizabeth Keyes, "President Kennedy's Press Conferences as 'Shapers' of the News."

97.   Rodger Streitmatter, "Front Page From the White House."

98.   Discussions of Kennedy's preparation for his press conferences can be found in Pierre Salinger, *With Kennedy,* 137–138; Arthur Schlesinger, Jr., *The Thousand Days,* 657–658; Theodore Sorensen, *Kennedy,* 322–326; Elmer Cornwell, *Presidential Leadership,* 190; Joseph Loftus, "Preparation Key to New Sessions," *New York Times,* March 29, 1962; Alan Otten, "What Do You Think, Ted?" 5; and Mary McGrory, "The Right-Hand Men," 67.

99.   See the front page of the *Chicago Daily Tribune, The Los Angeles Times, The New York Herald Tribune, The Washington Post, The San Diego Union-Tribune, The New York Times,* and *The Kansas City Star* for February 16, 1961.

100. In a study of Eisenhower and Reagan press conference transcripts, Stephen Clayman and John Heritage find that in their questions reporters were much less deferential to Reagan than to Eisenhower. This finding seems to confirm a piece of conventional wisdom, namely, that in the aftermath of Watergate and Vietnam journalists have become more aggressive in their treatment of presidents. See Clayman and Heritage, "Questioning Presidents." While not disputing this conclusion, I think it is fair to say that, in the long view, White House reporters have treated presidents as mere

politicians—and not heads of state—at least since the advent of modern journalism in the progressive period. This means that while reporters may be more adversarial toward recent presidents, their general disposition has been toward confrontation rather than deference throughout the twentieth century.

101. To give a sense of the consistency of these three question types, only fifty-one of the 502 questions (9 percent of the total) were so ambiguous as to fall outside these three categories.

102. PPK, January 31, 1962, 92.

103. This finding is slightly lower than that found by Delbert McGuire, in a sample of eight Kennedy press conferences, counted an average of 18.9 topics per conference. However, given the much smaller number of press conferences in his sample, it is likely that my number is more accurate. Moreover, the average number of topics covered in McGuire's total sample, one that included 32 conferences spanning the Eisenhower, Kennedy & Johnson administrations, was 15.6, a number much closer to my finding. See McGuire, "Democracy's Confrontation," 642.

104. This analysis is based on a sample of twenty press conferences, transcripts of which were taken from PPK. This sample includes eighteen randomly selected press conferences plus the first press conference held on January 25, 1961, and the last press conference, held November 14, 1963.

105. PPK, August 30, 1961, 576.

106. This question-answer format constitutes the "adversarial" nature of the modern press conference. See, for instance, Carolyn Smith, *Presidential Press Conferences.*

107. PPK, March 21, 1963, 276.

108. PPK, April 21, 1961, 313. In this instance, the reporter recognized Kennedy's gambit, and succeeded in asking a follow-up question: "What I really meant, sir, was what do you plan to do if you don't get the tax cut?" Kennedy's response: "I plan to get the tax cut."

109. Theodore Sorensen, *Kennedy*, 328.

110. Quote found in Lewis Paper, *The Promise and the Performance*, 328.

111. This poll report can be found in "Polls-Public Reactions to President Kennedy during first sixty days of administration," POF #105, JFKL.

112. So as not to publicly appear overly interested in the broadcast of his press conferences, Kennedy's official policy was, as Salinger once put it to Robert Kintner, the President of NBC, to "merely say to the [television] representatives that the President is going to hold an evening press conference and he would be happy to make it available to TV networks should they want to carry it." Letter from Salinger to Kintner dated February 24, 1961, President's Official File (POF) 847, JFKL. From subsequent correspondence, however, it is evident that one of Salinger's duties was to negotiate with the networks for optimal broadcast times.

113. Letter from Reinsch to Salinger, dated February 5, 1962. White House Central File (WHCF) 849, January 1, 1962–March 20, 1962, JFKL.

114. Robert Pauley (Vice-President ABC Radio Network) to Pierre Salinger, dated April 20, 1961, WHCF 849, JFKL. Also see a letter from Clair Stout, representing owners of

several independent television stations, to Pierre Salinger, dated March 8, 1961, WHCF, 849.

115. The earliest studies of network TV journalism—completed in the late-1960s and 1970s—demonstrate that, if anything, TV reporters embraced the routines of professional journalism more than print journalists. See, for instance, Edward Epstein, *News From Nowhere*; and Herbert Gans, *Deciding What's News*.

116. See the front page of *The New York Times*, the *Los Angeles Times*, *The New York Herald Tribune*, and *The Kansas City Star*, for February 1, 1962.

117. Warren Unna, "U.S. to Accept Chinese Refugees," *Washington Post*, May 24, 1962, 1.

118. David S. Broder, "Referendum Farm Plan Offered," *Washington Evening-Star*, March 16, 1961, 1.

119. See Thomas Cronin, "An Imperiled Presidency"; Louis Koenig, *The Chief Executive*; Paul Light, *The President's Agenda*; Theodore Lowi, *The Personal President*.

120. See, for instance, Bruce Oppenheimer, "Congress and the New Obstructionism"; James Sundquist, *The Decline and Resurgence of Congress*; Jonathan Rauch, *Demosclerosis*; Larry Sabato, *Feeding Frenzy*; John E. and Paul E. Peterson, Eds., *Can the Government Govern*?

121. On Reagan's communication skills, see Mary E. Stuckey, *Playing the Game*; Michael Weiler and W. Barnett Pearce, Eds., *Reagan and Public Discourse in America*; Kurt Ritter and David Henry, *Ronald Reagan: The Great Communicator*; Kathleen Hall Jamieson, *Eloquence in an Electronic Age*, 117; Robert E. Denton, *The Primetime Presidency of Ronald Reagan*; and Mark Heertzgaard, *On Bended Knee*.

122. This term comes from Kiku Adatto, *Picture Perfect*.

123. This conclusion is born out by longer term evidence. During his first three years in office, Reagan gave an average of seven major (televised) addresses, a figure roughly comparable to that of President Kennedy. However, where Kennedy gave forty "minor" addresses per year, Reagan gave an average of sixty—a number that would continue to climb for presidents through the 1980s and 1990s. Data from Samuel Kernell, *Going Public*, 113. For an even longer comparative view, Franklin Roosevelt also gave an average of five major addresses, but fewer than ten minor addresses per year.

124. John Maltese, *Spin Control*.

125. Much of the following description comes from Jeffrey H. Birnbaum and Alan S. Murray, *Showdown at Gucci Gulch*.

126. Mary McGrory, "Has a Star Been Born," *Washington Post*, May 30, 1985, A2.

127. Peter T. Kilborn, "All Is Poised for Hints of Tax Plan," *New York Times*, May 13, 1985, A14.

128. Bill Peterson, "Lobbyists Line Up to Protect Oxen: dollars and reputations at stake at Ways and Means hearing," *Washington Post*, May 31, 1985, A19.

129. See, for instance, Stuart Taylor, "Certain Winners: Capital Lobbyists," *New York Times*, May 31, 1985, D16.

130. Sometimes, of course, these sources were contacted by reporters. Nearly as often, however, they sought media attention by holding meetings and press conferences, releasing press bulletins, and faxing publicity releases for their latest studies.

131. This strategy is outlined in W. Lance Bennett, *News*, 97. For assistance in outlining this strategy, Bennett consulted Mark Heertzgaard, *On Bended Knee*, 33.

132. On White House strategy, see Gerald M. Boyd, "Wisdom of the People Emphasized as President Sets Populist Strategy," *New York Times*, May 29, 1985, A17.

133. These numbers are in line with general trends in presidential addresses during the twentieth century. Samuel Kernell reports that while the number of major addresses given by presidents rose slightly over this period, the number of minor addresses increased dramatically, no more so than in Reagan's eight years in office. Samuel Kernell, *Going Public*, 113.

134. This counts, of course, only Reagan's speaking activities. His subordinates, principally James Baker and Donald Regan, also talked extensively to citizen groups, gave many press interviews, and appeared often on the Sunday morning network news shows.

135. These data were culled from the Public Papers of the Presidents series for Ronald Reagan [hereafter referred to as PPR], volume 1.

136. See, respectively, Leonard Silk, "Tax Fairness: What is It?," *New York Times*, June 12, 1985, D2; Mark Shields, "Jim Baker On His Own," *Washington Post*, May 13, 1985, A13; Hobart Rowan, "New Tax Rules, New Inequities," *Washington Post*, June 6, 1985, A27; David E. Rosenbaum, "Tax Plan to Reflect Political Realities, Regan Says," *New York Times*, May 10, 1985, D2; David S. Broder, "Waiting for Tax Reform; House Advantage; Senate Nightmare," *Washington Post*, June 2, 1985, C8; David C. Wilhelm, "Real Reform is Up to the Democrats," *New York Times*, June 2, 1985, D3; Ann Swardson, "Tax Reform Plan Seen Increasing Federal Deficit," *Washington Post*, June 11, 1985, D1; Ann Swardson and Dale Russakoff, "Tax-Revision Cornerstone Might Crumble," *Washington Post*, June 17, 1985, A1; Phil Gailey, "Poll Shows Most Americans See Reagan Tax Plan as Fair," *New York Times*, June 5, 1985, A1; Phil Gailey, "Roping in Political Advantages," *New York Times*, June 10, 1985, A16; Maurice Carroll, "Cuomo's Role in U.S. Tax-Plan Fight," *New York Times*, June 15, 1985, A27; Phil Gailey, "Risky Stand on Tax Plan," *New York Times*, June 21, 1985, A30; Leo C. Wolinsky, "California Loss Under Tax Plan Put at $3 Billion," *Los Angeles Times*, June 2, 1985, A14.

137. A finding which has been confirmed elsewhere. See, for instance, Frederic T. Smoller, *The Six O'clock Presidency*.

138. See Frederic Smoller, *The Six O'clock Presidency*; and Joseph S. Foote, *Television and Political Power*.

139. David S. Broder, "Opportunity Knocks: Rostenkowski to Answer Reagan on Taxes," *Washington Post*, May 28, 1985, A1; Jerry Knight, "Plugging Up Loopholes," *Washington Post*, June 3, 1985, F1; and Michael Wines, "Dedications Die Before Rates Are Cut," *Los Angeles Times*, June 1, 1985, A1.

140. See Richard Rosenblatt, "Plan Would Reduce Bills for 63%; Varies for Others," *Los Angeles Times*, May 30, 1985, A1; and Thomas Edsall, "Tax Plans Create Bizarre Alliances," *Washington Post*, May 21, 1985, A6.

141. See, for instance, David E. Rosenbaum, "Tax Effect on Family Assessed," *New York Times*, June 17, 1985, D1; and Phil Gailey, "Poll Shows Most Americans See Reagan Tax Plan as Fair," *New York Times*, June 5, 1985, A1.

142. On this trend in TV news, see Daniel Hallin, "Soundbite News."

143. Herbert Gans reports that as late as 1980 network reporters studiously ignored their viewers, claiming not to know who watched their reports, and more important, claiming not to care. See Herbert Gans, *Deciding What's News*, 230–241.

144. See, respectively, Joseph Berger, "New York Leaders Oppose Plan Vehemently," *New York Times*, May 29, 1985, A20; John M. Berry, "Sports Industry Boos Reagan Tax Proposal," *Washington Post*, May 31, 1985, D1; "Overhaul Proposal Draws Fire in High-Tax States," *Los Angeles Times*, May 29, 1985, A1; Robert Rosenblatt, "Business Fights for Capital Gains," *Los Angeles Times*, May 28, 1985, A1; David Hoffman, "Reagan Parades Simplification Plan Along 'Main Street America;'" *Washington Post*, May 31, 1985, A18; Tom Redburn, "Tax Battles Ahead But Leaders See Reform of System," *Los Angeles Times*, May 30, 1985, A1; Anne Swardson, "Congressional Reaction Mixed," *Washington Post*, May 29, 1985, A15; Hedrick Smith, "Fighting the Income Tax," *New York Times*, May 31, 1985, A1; Lou Cannon, "Second-Term Boost Sought," *Washington Post*, May 29, 1985, A1; and David S. Broder, "Tax Package Has Both Political Teams in There Pitching," *Washington Post*, May 30, 1985, A12.

145. On Reagan's remarks, see David E. Rosenbaum, "Tax Plan to Reflect Political Realities, Regan Says," *New York Times*, May 10, 1985, D2.

146. Tip O'Neill, for instance, responded to the President's statement by suggesting that less progressivity in the tax system would be a "great breach of faith" with the American people. And the Democratic Study group "blasted the Reagan plan for being more generous to well-off tax payers than to middle-income taxpayers, thereby making the system less progressive." Quotes in, respectively, Anne Swardson, "Packwood Optimistic On Tax Plan," *Washington Post*, May 10, 1985, G1; and Anne Swardson and Helen DeWar, "Baker Defends Tax Plans at Senate Hearings," *Washington Post*, June 12, 1985, F1. See also David C. Wilhelm, "Real Reform is Up to the Democrats," *New York Times*, June 2, 1985, D3; and Don Colburn, "The Health Insurance Tax: trimming the fringe," *Washington Post*, June 26, 1985, H7.

147. Bernard Weinraub, "Buchanan Sees Political Gain for GOP in Reagan Tax Plan," *New York Times*, May 17, 1985, D21.

148. See, for instance, Phil Gailey, "Politics of Taxation," *New York Times*, May 27, 1985, A35; Hedrick Smith, "Fighting the Income Tax," May 31, 1985, A1; David C. Wilhelm, "Real Reform is Up to the Democrats," *New York Times*, June 2, 1985, F3; Mark Shields, "The Democrats' Tax Test," *New York Times*, June 3, 1985, A13; Phil Gailey, "Poll Shows Most Americans See Reagan Tax Plan as Fair," *New York Times*, June 5, 1985, A1; Leonard Silk, "Reagan Bars a 4th Tax Rate," *New York Times*, June 8, 1985, D1; Phil Gailey, "Roping in Political Advantages," *New York Times*, June 10, 1985, A16; and Stephen Shuker, "Reagan's Tax Plan is Unfair," *New York Times*, June 12, 1985, A27.

149. Robert Entman, *Democracy Without Citizens*, 21.

150. Robert Entman, *Democracy Without Citizens*, 20.

151. In Robert Putnam's *Bowling Alone*, much of this terrain is covered. But see also John Hibbing and Elizabeth Theiss-Morse, Eds., *What Is It About Government that*

Americans Dislike?; Matthew Crenson and Benjamin Ginsberg, *Downsizing Democracy*; Kenneth Goldstein, *Interest Groups, Lobbying and Participation in America*; Margaret Conway, *Political Participation in the United States*; William Crotty, Ed., *The State of Democracy in America*; and Joseph S. Nye, et al., Eds., *Why People Don't Trust Government.*

Chapter Four

1. There is a growing literature on the Clinton presidency and national politics during the 1990s. Scholarly studies include Colin Campbell and Bert A. Rockman, Eds., *The Clinton Legacy*; Robert E. Denton and Rachel L. Holloway, Eds., *The Clinton Presidency;* Martin A. Levin, et al., Eds., *Seeking the Center*; James L. Sundquist, Ed., *Back to Gridlock?;* Bryan D. Jones, *The New American Politics*; Steven E. Schier, *The Postmodern Presidency;* Larry Sabato and Robert Lichter, *When Should Watchdogs Bark?* Thus far, however, journalists have written a more extensive first account of politics in this era. See especially Elizabeth Drew, *Whatever It Takes;* Elizabeth Drew, *Showdown*; Joe Klein, *The Natural*; Susan Schmidt, *Truth At Any Cost;* James B. Stewart, *Bloodsport;* Dan Balz and Ronald Brownstein, *Storming the Gates.*

2. For a comparison of Clinton's "going public" record with those of prior presidents, see Samuel Kernell, *Going Public,* Figures 4-2 and 4-3, 118 and 122, respectively.

3. For general studies of populism, see Michael Kazin, *The Populist Persuasion*; Ghita Ionescu and Ernest Gellner, Eds., *Populism;* Margaret Canovan, *Populism.* On the American populist movement of the late nineteenth century, see John D. Hicks, *The Populist Revolt*; and Lawrence Goodwyn, *Democratic Promise.*

4. The term "new social movements" has been coined by movement theorists to refer to movements of the 1960s forward which press particularly humanist, cultural, and nonmaterialist values. In the United States, the model for these movements was the Civil Rights Movement. Broadly, when theorists refer to NSMs in the United States, they mean such movements as the New Left; the Student Movement; the Women's Movement; the New Right-Evangelical Christian Movement; and the Environmental Movement—though one might note many others (such as the Nuclear Freeze Movement and the Chicano Movement). In this chapter I will draw my examples from early NSMs, including those for civil rights, women's rights, and the New Left, because it was in these movements that the basic vernacular of modern populism emerged.

5. Jurgen Habermas, "New Social Movements." For discussions of early NSMs and their emphasis on symbolic values, see Joseph R. Gusfield, *Symbolic Crusade*; Orrin Klapp, *Collective Search for Identity*; and Ralph H. Turner, "The Theme of Contemporary Social Movements."

6. Ronald Ingelhart coined the term "postmaterialist values." See his *The Silent Revolution.*

7. For a general history of how fears about the modern administrative state erupted in the late twentieth century, see Paul Edward Gottfried, *After Liberalism.*

8. On this transformation, see Mayer N. Zald and John D. McCarthy, "Appendix: The Trend of Social Movements in America: Professionalization and Resource Mobilization"; and Jean L. Cohen, "Strategy or Identity: New Theoretical Paradigms and Contemporary Social Movements," *Social Research*, 52, 1985, 665–715.

9.　Harry Boyte has argued that populism "grows from a sense of aggrieved "peoplehood,' as distinct from personhood...." In the introduction to Boyte and Frank Riessman, Eds., *The New Populism,* 8. While I take his point, it seems to me that populism in its modern variant is at least as much about personhood, in the sense that it imagines a politics flowing from personal life and convictions, and it is precisely this embrace of the personal that connects individuals to a larger conception of peoplehood.

10.　A few presidential candidates, such as Hubert Humphrey during the 1960 presidential campaign and Richard Nixon during the 1968 presidential campaign, have used formats that resemble the town hall meetings—but not sitting presidents. Moreover, these ancestors of the town hall meeting were much more scripted and formal than those initiated by President Carter.

11.　To give one a sense of the rarity of this development, only three other new forms of presidential communication were created in the twentieth century: the press conference (under Theodore Roosevelt and Woodrow Wilson); the nationwide broadcast (under Calvin Coolidge, Herbert Hoover, and Franklin D. Roosevelt); and the televised press conference (under Dwight Eisenhower and John F. Kennedy).

12.　See, for instance, Ernst Laclau, "Towards a Theory of Populism"; Ghita Ionescu and Ernest Gellner, Eds., *Populism*; Michael Kazin, *The Populist Persuasion*; Paul Taggart, *Populism*; and Margaret Canovan, "Two Strategies for the Study of Populism."

13.　Margaret Canovan, "Two Strategies for the Study of Populism," 552; and Michael Kazin, *The Populist Persuasion*, 1.

14.　As Westlind argues, "Due to the radical openness of the social field in which they are articulated, populist identities are only partially fixed through the construction of nodal points." In Westlind, *The Politics of Popular Identity,* 99.

15.　Critics complain that there is nothing especially "new" about these movements. Like earlier movements, they appear to have a class basis. They create organizational structures. They press grievances. They mobilize resources in ways similar to older movements. But one may accept this conclusion and still maintain that NSMs are distinctive. As Buechler suggests, "the newness" of NSMs is "not so much a quality of movements in isolation as it is a quality of the social structures to which [they have] respond[ed], and which they inevitably reflect." For critics, see Klaus Eder, *The New Politics of Class*; K.W. Brand, "Cyclical Aspects of New Social Movements"; Hank Johnston, Enrique Larana, and Joseph R. Gusfield, "Identities, Grievances, and New Social Movements"; and Craig Calhoun, "The Problem of Identity in Collective Action." Buechler's quote comes from his *Social Movements in Advanced Capitalism,* 50.

16.　NSM theorists have identified many provocations of this concern: the growth of an information society; the transformation of urban spaces and consumption patterns; the tendency of advanced capitalism to "colonize" the life-world with forms of instrumental reason; and the growth of a postindustrial, programmed society, among them. See, respectively, Alberto Melucci, *Nomads of the Present*; Manuel Castells, *The Power of Identity*; Jurgen Habermas, *Knowledge and Human Interest;* Jurgen Habermas, *The Theory of Communicative Action*; Alain Touraine, *The Voice and the Eye*; and Alaine Touraine, *Return of the Actor.*

17.　Alberto Melucci, "A Strange Kind of Newness," 112. On the importance of meaning and identity to NSMs, see also Melucci, *Nomads of the Present*; and Alain Touraine, *Return of the Actor.*

18. "A quest for personal fulfillment," Peter Clecak writes, "within a small community of significant others: this strikes me as the dominant thrust of American civilization during the sixties and seventies." In Peter Clecak, *America's Quest for the Ideal Self,* 9.

19. On commonalities across NSMs, see Hank Johnston, Enrique Larana and Joseph R. Gusfield, "Identities, Grievances, and New Social Movements"; Buechler, *Social Movements in Advanced Capitalism,* 45–511; and Rajandra Sing, *Social Movements, Old & New,* especially Ch. 4.

20. On the role of the Civil Rights Movement as a model for subsequent NSMs, see Stewart Burns, *Social Movements of the 1960s;* Doug McAdam, *Freedom Summer;* Doug McAdam, *Political Process and the Development of Black Insurgency, 1930–1970.*

21. Quoted in Stephen B. Oates, *Let the Trumpet Sound,* 79.

22. Quoted in Charles M. Payne, *I've Got the Light of Freedom,* 331.

23. Quoted in Carl Oglesby, Ed., *The New Left Reader,* 14.

24. Quoted in Sara Evans, *Personal Politics,* 104.

25. Quoted in Edward Morgan, *The 60s Experience,* 225.

26. Students for a Democratic Society, "The Port Huron Statement," 1964 (adopted at the founding convention of SDS held in Port Huron, MI, June 11–15, 1962).

27. Quoted in David Edwin Harrell, Jr., *Pat Robertson,* 30.

28. Philip Rieff, *The Triumph of the Therapeutic;* and Christopher Lasch, *The Culture of Narcissism.*

29. See T.J. Jackson Lears, "From Salvation to Self-Realization: Advertising and the Therapeutic Roots of Consumer Culture, 1880–1930."

30. See Rossinow, *The Politics of Authenticity.* In 1st Corinthians (11:21), "agape" or "love feast" is discussed in relation to the Lord's Supper as an occasion on which individuals come together to celebrate their relationship with God and one another. Stephen Oates reports that Martin Luther King Jr. was "transfixed" by the notion of agape. For him, it was "the kind of love [Jesus and Gandhi] meant—a disinterested love for all mankind, a love that saw the neighbor in everyone it met.... Agape was the love in Christ's teachings that took one to any length to restore the 'beloved community.'" Stephen B. Oates, *Let the Trumpet Sound,* 33. Many early NSM leaders, including King and many others, learned of "agape" through the writings of religion scholar Paul Tillich. See, for instance, Tillich, *The Courage to Be;* Tillich, *The New Being;* and Tillich, *Morality and Beyond.*

31. Brienes, *Community and Organization in the New Left,* 7. In this vein, see also Dominick Cavallo, *A Fiction of the Past.*

32. Quoted in Sarah Evans, *Personal Politics,* 53.

33. Sarah Evans, *Personal Politics,* 214.

34. Quoted in Charles M. Payne, *I've Got the Light of Freedom,* 93.

35. For a discussion of this point, see Andreas Schedler, *The End of Politics?*

36. "Consensus" historians of the 1950s especially gravitated to this view of populism. In the face of Joseph McCarthy's demagoguery, and with the memory of Huey Long and

Father Coughlin still resonant, these historians argued that populism's roots in feeling and communal tradition was essentially anti-intellectual and anti-liberal. Richard Hofstadter perhaps made this argument most forcefully. See his *The Age of Reform*; and *Anti-Intellectualism in American Life*.

37. Jean Cohen, "Strategy or Identity," 710.

38. Sara Evans, *Personal Politics*, 42.

39. Quoted in Payne, *I've Got the Light of Freedom*, 371.

40. John Mayer and Mayer Zald, "The Trend of Social Movements in America," 374.

41. On the history of the conservative movement, see Michael P. Federici, *The Challenge of Populism;* E. Ansell, Ed., *Unraveling the Right;* Walter Berman, *America's Right Turn;* Rob Boston, *The Most Dangerous Man in America?*; and Melvin I Urofsky and Martha May, Eds., *The New Christian Right*.

42. See Michael Oreskes, "For G.O.P. Arsenal, 133 Words to Fire," *New York Times*, September 9, 1990, 30.

43. Data for this section come from the Public Papers of the Presidents series for President Carter [hereafter referred to as PPC]; videotapes of several town meetings obtained from the Jimmy Carter Presidential Library; primary materials housed in the Jimmy Carter Library pertaining to the town meetings; and news coverage of the town meetings in *The New York Times, The Washington Post, The Los Angeles Times,* and ABC, NBC, and CBS network evening news broadcasts available at the Vanderbilt Television News Archives.

44. Material for this paragraph taken from Betty Glad, *Jimmy Carter;* and Peter G. Bourne, *Jimmy Carter*.

45. The program was announced on January 6, 1977, and organized under the Office of Public Liaison in the following weeks. For information on the initial organization of the program, see a memorandum from Rick Neustadt to Midge Costanza, dated January 25, 1977, Office of Public Liaison, Costanza, "People Program," Box 8; "Status of the People Program," a memo sent from Greg Schneiders to the president, dated February 8, 1977, in the Office of Public Liaison files under Costanza, "People Program," Box 8; and a memo from Jane Wales to Midge Costanza, dated January 27, 1977, also in the Office of Public Liaison Files under Costanza, "People Program," Box 8.

46. Joe McGinnis, *The Selling of the President, 1968*.

47. Quote comes from e-mail exchange with author, January 7, 2001.

48. Quoted in Edward Walsh, "The Making of a Presidential Trip," *Washington Post*, March 16, 1977, A1.

49. *New York Times*, July 5, 1980, 7.

50. The absence of television was not wholly intentional. Aides involved in the People Program tried to interest the networks in broadcasting the events. However, they were not willing to make the occasions television friendly. As Schneiders puts it, "The only reason the town hall meetings were not better media events is because we were not as sophisticated about these things as those who replaced us...." Schneiders e-mail communication, January 7, 2001. A memo from the Press Advance Office Files (Box 22, "4/25/79–2/26/79," NY Trip, Diagrams") appears to confirm Schneiders' memory. Canvassing the facilities chosen for the Portsmouth, NH, town meeting, this advance

person concludes that the "Lights [are] awful...Risers [are] unavailable. Power situation [is] marginal [and the] PA sucks."

51. However, ABC, the perennial third place network at the time, did agree to air a few of the town meetings on a tape-delayed basis, at 11:30 p.m., on the night they were broadcast.

52. For internal discussions of this issue, see "Town Meeting" memo to Tim Kraft and Tim Smith, dated February 17, 1977, in White House Central Files (WHCF), TR 8-1, Box TR-11, "1/20/77–1/20/81"; and WHCF-Trips, Box TR-11, "3/16/77-3/20/77."

53. Charles O. Jones has turned Carter's penchant for "doing the right thing" into the most persuasive theory of his presidency. According to Jones, Carter approached his role as a "trustee" of the people, someone obliged to do what was in the public's interest regardless of public opinion or the personal political consequences to himself. See Jones, *The Trusteeship Presidency.* Jones' interpretation is compatible with my own assertion, that in acting out of his personal convictions and political commitments, Carter displayed an essentially populist orientation.

54. Headlines come from, respectively, Laura Foreman, *New York Times*, July 22, 1977, A5; Helen Dewar, *Washington Post*, February 19, 1978, 1; and Don Irwin, *Los Angeles Times*, October 17, 1978, A8.

55. See, respectively, Edward Walsh, "Carter Stresses 'Family Planning' at Town Meeting," *Washington Post*, March 17, 1977, 1; Walsh, "President Presses to End 'Isolation,'" *Washington Post*, August 1, 1978, A6; David S. Broder, "Poll Finds Carter Popularity Soars: Weary President Campaigns," *Washington Post*, September 24, 1978, A1; Robert Shogan, "Carter Fields Questions in New England Town," *Los Angeles Times*, March 17, 1977, A1; and Eleanor Randolph, "Carter Urges Coal Over OPEC Oil in Kentucky Visit," *Los Angeles Times*, August 1, 1979, 1.

56. See, respectively, "Carter Pays New Hampshire a Campaign Type Visit," *Washington Post*, April 26, 1979, A2; Edward Walsh, "Carter Stresses 'Family Planning' at Town Meeting," *Washington Post*, March 17, 1977, A3; Steven R. Weisman, "President Predicts Interest-Rate Drop," *New York Times*, October 17, 1979, A24; and Don Irwin, "Carter Tests New Hampshire's Political Currents, Finds the Waters Lukewarm," *Los Angeles Times,* April 26, 1979, A8.

57. David Shaw, "Not Even Getting a 1st Chance," *Los Angeles Times*, September 15, 1993, A11.

58. David Shaw, "Not Even Getting a 1st Chance," *Los Angeles Times*, September 15, 1993, A11. Also see Jeffrey L. Katz, "Tilt? Did the Media Favor Bill Clinton, or Did George Bush Earn his Negative Coverage."

59. These reasons are outlined in Leslie Kaufman, "The Young and the Relentless," *American Journalism Review*, 15 (March, 1993), 15–30; Jonathan Alter, "The Manic-Depressive Media," *Newsweek*, February 8, 1993, 29.

60. See Elizabeth Drew, *On The Edge;* and Bob Woodward, *The Agenda,* for descriptions of the hectic early days in the Clinton administration.

61. Comments taken from Todd Gitlin, "Whiplash," *American Journalism Review*, 15 (April, 1993): 35; and Howard Kurtz, "First Days Offer Clinton 'Powerful Lessons,'" *Washington Post*, January 31, 1993, A1. Events surrounding Clinton's first major address to Congress on his economic plans, delivered on February 17, 1993, are

indicative of the spin cycle. Even before Clinton had delivered the address, Representative Robert Michel had already issued a typed rebuttal to the press. Based on leaks of his speech, lobbyists from every conceivable industry also had issued their opinions. After the speech, members of Congress and the media filled Statuary Hall, politicians eager to get their interpretation heard, and reporters there to record the moment. This is before the wave of talk shows, which began with Nightline that evening, went through the network morning shows the next day, and ended with interview shows on CNN and C-SPAN. See "Spin Cycle," *Washington Post*, February 19, 1993, C1.

62.   Sidney Blumenthal, "The Syndicated Presidency," *The New Yorker*, 69 (April 5, 1993): 42; & Walter Shapiro, No Mister President, I'm Brit, He's Wolf," *Esquire*, 120 (July 1993): 66.

63.   The first cohort of baby boomers entered national political office during the 1974 mid-term Congressional elections, when, partly as a result of party and electoral reforms, and partly as a consequence of public reaction against Richard Nixon, a large group of young Democrats won election. On the characteristics of this group and subsequent generations of politicians, see Burdett Loomis, *The New American Politician*.

64.   Richard Davis and Diana Owens, *New Media and American Politics*, 19. On mass media and populism more generally, see Jim McGuigan, *Cultural Populism*.

65.   This sense of the town hall format is confirmed by a focus group study of the 1992 presidential debates, where it was found that viewers saw the town hall format as "more democratic" than other formats, allowing for more "openness, honesty and personality exposure." John Meyer and Diana B. Carlin, "The Impact of Formats on Voter Reaction," 78.

66.   Sonia Livingstone and Peter Lunt, *Talk on Television*, 61 & 180. For other analyses of this television genre, see also Patricia Joyner Priest, *Public Intimacies*, especially Chapter 8; Gloria-Jean Masciarotte, "C'Mon, Girl: Oprah Winfrey and the Discourse of Feminine Talk"; Jane M. Shattuc, *The Talking Cure*; and Paolo Carpignano, et al., "Chatter in the Age of Electronic Reproduction."

67.   Quotes come from Richard Levine, "I Feel Your Pain: How to Host the Presidency in 12 Steps," *Mother Jones*, 18 (July/August, 1993), 24, 26; Lewis Lapham, "Notebook: Show and Tell," *Harper's*, 286 (April, 1993), 9; and James Kuhnhenn, "'Just Folks' Format Fits...For Now," *Kansas City Star*, April 7, 1994, A1, A13.

68.   George E. Condon, Jr., "Clinton Plans a Detroit Sales Pitch," *San Diego Union-Tribune*, February 4, 1993, A8. Don North, Channel 5 News Director in Kansas City, said that the "only condition they spelled out was that there were no conditions. It was our meeting. We could format it any way we wanted." Quoted in Barry Garron, "Just Another Story? Not at Channel 5," the *Kansas City Star*, April 6, 1994, C12.

69.   Robert E. Denton, Jr. and Rachel L. Holloway, "Clinton and the Town Hall Meetings," 31.

70.   Before the first town meeting in Detroit, there apparently was a minor tiff between the White House and the local station over exactly these kinds of considerations. See Berke, "Revival Meeting Tonight for Clinton the Populist," *New York Times*, February 10, 1993, A20. There was also a minor controversy over the fact that the White House planted audience members in a few town meetings. The controversy erupted when, during the April 7, 1994 town meeting, Clinton disclosed that he knew the first

questioner, Elaine Shaffer, and had written a letter to his wife some time before. See Steve Kraske, "This Time the Focus is on Healthcare," *Kansas City Star*, April 8, 1994, A1.

71.   John Freeman, "Town Hall Meeting with Clinton Will Be Local TV First," *San Diego Union-Tribune*, May 17, 1993, E6; Also see Richard L. Berke, "Revival Meeting Tonight For Clinton the Populist," *New York Times*, February 10, 1993, A20, for a similar discussion of the first town meeting held in Detroit.

72.   John Freeman, "Town Hall Meeting with Clinton Will Be Local TV First," *San Diego Union-Tribune*, May 17, 1993, E6

73.   Quoted in Barry Garron, "Just Another Story? Not at Channel 5," *Kansas City Star*, April 6, 1994, C12.

74.   And this is a conservative estimate. Because I did not have videotapes of every town meeting, I coded only for questions identifiable verbally rather than visually. For instance, while a question may not have indicated the social type of the person asking it, perhaps their race, gender, ethnicity, or some other obvious visual category did. I did not code for this kind of visual representativeness, hence my estimates are probably on the low side.

75.   However, not all the questioners represented, in the sense of embodied, a social type. Some represented actual groups: in Sacramento, a migrant rights activist asked a question about illegal immigration; in Cranston, Rhode Island, a commissioner of the New England Hispanic Civil Rights Commission asked a question about civil rights; the president of the South Dakota Farmer's Union asked a question during the April 8, 1994, meeting in Minneapolis; and a lobbyist for Montana Native-American tribes asked a question about racism and Native-Americans during the June 1, 1995, meeting in Billings. Such questioners obviously elided the sense that personal experience rather than professional qualifications would serve as the motive force of the town meeting discussions.

76.   Barry Garron, "Just Another Story? Not at Channel 5," *Kansas City Star*, April 6, 1994, C12.

77.   Tom Shales, "A Night in Neverland with the President and the King of Pop," *Washington Post*, February 11, 1993, D6.

78.   These data are taken from Television News Index and Abstracts, Vanderbilt Television News Archive, Nashville, TN. Data for network coverage of the June 2, 1995, town meeting were unavailable. However, the absence of these numbers does not significantly affect the overall findings.

79.   George Condon, "Clinton Plans Detroit Sales Pitch," *San Diego Union-Tribune*, February 4, 1993, A8.

80.   Dana Priest, "White House to Stump for Health Plan," *Washington Post*, February 6, 1993, A1; and "Clinton to Take Show to Detroit," February 4, 1993, A18; and Richard L. Berke, "Revival Meeting Tonight with Clinton the Populist," *New York Times*, February 10, 1993, A20.

81.   Dan Halz, "Railing at Critics, Touring Clinton Asks Public to Support Him," *Washington Post*, May 18, 1993, A8; David Lauter, "Clinton Calls for Tougher Gun Controls," *Los Angeles Times*, October 4, 1993, A3.

82.   Quoted in John Jacobs, "Clinton Tries the Oprah Approach," *San Diego Union-Tribune*, October 6, 1993, B9.

83.   See, for instance, John Meyer and Diana B. Carlin, "The Impact of Formats on Voter Reaction"; Michael Kates, "For Northside Couple, Clinton's Meeting Was 'Reassuring,'" *Chicago Daily Tribune*, February 11, 1993, 24; Robert W. Stewart, "Focus Group Gives Clinton's TV Pitch a Mixed Review," *Los Angeles Times*, February 11, 1993; Ronald W. Powell and Greg Moran, "Clinton's a Hit at Town Hall Meeting," *San Diego Union-Tribune*, May 18, 1993, A1; Staci D. Kramer, "Despite That 'Distraction,' Med Students Hail Clintons," *Chicago Daily Tribune*, March 16, 1994; Scott Canon and Matt Campbell, "Participants, Props Fill Clinton's Town Hall," *Kansas City Star*, April 8, 1994; and "Callers Rate President's Stop in KC," *Kansas City Star*, April 9, 1994

84.   Evidence of this was clear early on. See Thomas H. Edsall, "Survey Finds Consensus on Some Major Issues: But Clinton Actions also Evoke Unease," *Washington Post*, February 11, 1993, A18.

85.   Stephen Skowronek, *The Politics Presidents Make*.

Conclusion

1.   Raymond Williams, *Keywords*, 87.

2.   Jürgen Habermas, *The Structural Transformation of the Public Sphere*.

3.   Stephen Skowronek, *Politics Presidents Make*.

4.   The following genealogy of compassionate conservatism is based upon a Lexis-Nexis database search of major national newspapers and magazines from 1981 to the present. This search found over 600 references to the phrase in titles and first paragraphs of articles. Not surprisingly, over 400 of these references have occurred between 2000 and 2003.

5.   Quoted in Sheila Rule, "At Urban League, Mondale Derides Reagan Values," *New York Times*, July 22, 1981, A17.

6.   Quoted in John Herbers, "Party Looks Inward for Ways to Regain Majority," *New York Times*, November 8, 1984, A24.

7.   This is the general conclusion of Richard Davis and Diana Owens, *New Media and American Politics*.

Bibliography

Adatto, Kiku. *Picture Perfect: The Art and Artifice of Public Image Making*. New York: Basic Books, 1993.

Albertoni, Francesco. "The Powerless 'Elite': Theory and Sociological Research on the Phenomenon of Stars." In *Sociology of Mass Communications*, edited by Denis McQuail, 75–98. Middlesex, England: Penguin, 1972.

Aldrich, John. *Why Parties? The Origin and Transformation of Political Parties in America*. Chicago: University of Chicago Press, 1995.

Allen, Craig. *Eisenhower and the Mass Media: Peace, Prosperity, and Prime-Time TV*. Chapel Hill: University of North Carolina Press, 1993.

Alsop, Em Bowles. *The Greatness of Woodrow Wilson, 1856–1956*. New York: Rinehart & Co., 1956.

Alsop, Joseph, and Stuart Alsop. *The Reporter's Trade*. New York: Reynal, 1958.

Anderson, Quentin. *The Imperial Self: An Essay in American Literary and Cultural History*. New York: Knopf, 1971.

Ansell, E. Amy, ed. *Unraveling the Right: The New Conservatism in American Thought and Politics*. Boulder: Westview Press, 1998.

Baker, Ray Stannard. *Woodrow Wilson: Life and Letters*. New York: Doubleday, Doran & Co., 1937.

———. Papers. Library of Congress.

Ball, Terence. *Transforming Political Discourse: Political Theory and Critical Conceptual History*. Oxford: Basil Blackwell, 1988.

Balz, Dan, and Ronald Brownstein. *Storming the Gates: Protest Politics and the Republican Revival*. Boston: Little and Brown, 1996.

Barker, David. "'It's Been Real': Forms of Television Representation." *Critical Studies in Mass Communication* 5 (1988): 42–56.

Barkin, David. "Eisenhower's Secret Strategy: Television Planning in the 1952 Campaign." *Journal of Advertising History* 9 (1987): 18–28.

Barnouw, Erik. *History of Broadcasting in the United States*. 2 vols. New York: Oxford University Press, 1966–70.

Barry, David. *Forty Years in Washington*. New York: Beckman Publishers, 1974. First published 1924 by Little, Brown & Co.

Bazin, Andre. *What Is Cinema?* Translated by Hugh Gray. 3 vols. Berkeley: University of California Press, 1967–1971.

Beitzinger, A.J. *A History of American Political Thought*. New York: Dodd, Mead & Co., 1972.

Bell, Michael Davitt. *The Development of Romance: The Sacrifice of Relation*. Chicago: University of Chicago Press, 1980.

Bennett, W. Lance. "The Paradox of Public Discourse: A Framework for the Analysis of Political Accounts." *The Journal of Politics* 42 (1980): 792–817.

———. *News: The Politics of Illusion*. 3rd Ed. White Plains, NY: Longman, 1996.

Benson, Thomas W., ed. *American Rhetoric: Context and Criticism*. Carbondale: Southern Illinois University Press, 1989.

Berelson, Bernard, Paul Lazarsfeld, and William McPhee. *Voting: A Study of Opinion Formation in a Presidential Campaign.* Chicago: University of Chicago Press, 1954.

Berman, Walter. *America's Right Turn: From Nixon to Clinton.* 2nd Ed. Baltimore: Johns Hopkins University Press, 1998.

Bernays, Edward. "The Engineering of Consent." *Annals of the American Academy of Political and Social Science* 249 (1947): 113–120.

Best, Gary D. *The Critical Press and the New Deal: The Press Versus Presidential Power, 1933–1938.* Westport, CT: Praeger, 1993.

Bimes, Teri, and Stephen Skowronek. "Woodrow Wilson's Critique of Popular Leadership: Reassessing the Modern-Traditional Divide in Presidential History." *Polity* 39 (1996): 26–61.

Binkley, Wilfred. *Presidents and Congress.* New York: Vintage Books, 1962.

———. *The Man in the White House.* Baltimore: Johns Hopkins Press, 1958.

Birkhead, Douglas. "The Progressive Reform of Journalism: The Rise of Professionalism in the Press." In *Rhetoric and Reform in the Progressive Era*, edited by J. Michael Hogan, 113–144.

Birnbaum, Jeffrey H., and Alan S. Murray. *Showdown at Gucci Gulch: Lawmakers, Lobbyists, and the Unlikely Triumph of Tax Reform.* New York: Random House, 1987.

Bledstein, Burton J. *The Culture of Professionalism: The Middle Class and the Development of Higher Education in America.* New York: W. W. Norton & Co., 1976.

Blum, Joseph. *Joseph Tumulty and the Wilson Era.* Boston: Houghton Mifflin, 1951.

Blumenthal, Sidney. *The Permanent Campaign: Inside the World of Elite Political Operatives.* Boston: Beacon Press, 1980.

Bordwell, David. "Standardization and Differentiation: The Reinforcement and Dispersion of Hollywood Practices." In *The Classical Hollywood Cinema*, edited by David Bordwell, Janet Staiger, and Kristin Thompson, 96–112.

Bordwell, David, Janet Staiger, and Kristin Thompson, eds. *The Classical Hollywood Cinema: Film Style and Mode of Production to 1960.* New York: Columbia University Press. 1985.

Boston, Rob. *The Most Dangerous Man in America? Pat Robertson and the Rise of the Christian Coalition.* Amherst, NY: Prometheus Books, 1996.

Bourne, G. Peter. *Jimmy Carter: A Comprehensive Biography from Plains to the Post-Presidency.* New York: Simon and Schuster, 1997.

Bowie, Robert R. *Waging Peace: How Eisenhower Shaped an Enduring Cold War Strategy.* New York: Oxford University Press, 1998.

Boyte, Harry, and Frank Riessman, eds. *The New Populism: The Politics of Empowerment.* Philadelphia: Temple University Press, 1986.

Brace, Paul, and Barbara Hinckley. *Follow the Leader.* New York: Basic Books, 1992.

Brand, H. W. *T. R.: The Last Romantic.* New York: Basic Books, 1997.

Brand, Karl-Werner. "Cyclical Aspects of New Social Movements: Waves of Cultural Criticism and Mobilization Cycles of New Middle-Class Radicalism." In *Challenging the Political Order,* edited by Russell J. Dalton and Manfred Kuechler, 23–42.

Brantlinger, Patrick. *Bread and Circuses: Theories of Mass Culture as Social Decay.* Ithaca: Cornell University Press, 1983.

Brienes, Wini. *Community and Organization in the New Left: 1962–1968.* Westport: Praeger, 1982.

Brody, Richard A. *Assessing the President: The Media, Elite Opinion, and Public Support.* Stanford: Stanford University Press, 1991.

Brooker, Will, and Deborah Jermyn. *The Audience Studies Reader.* Routledge, 2003.

Brooks, Peter. *The Melodramatic Imagination: Balzac, Henry James, Melodrama and the Mode of Excess*. New Haven: Yale University Press, 1976.

Brown, Robert J. *Manipulating the Ether: The Power of Broadcast Radio in Thirties America*. Jefferson, NC: McFarland & Co., 1998.

Budick, Emily Miller. *Nineteenth-Century American Romance: Genre and the Construction of American Culture*. New York: Twayne Publishers, 1996.

Buechler, Steven. *Social Movements in Advanced Capitalism: The Political Economy and Cultural Construction of Social Activism*. New York: Oxford University Press, 2001.

Buehler, Daniel O. "Permanence and Change in Theodore Roosevelt's Conservation Jeremiad." *Western Journal of Communication* 62 (1998): 439–458.

Buenker, John, and Edward R. Kantowicz, eds. *Historical Dictionary of the Progressive Era, 1890–1920*. Westport, CT: Greenwood Press, 1987.

Burke, Kenneth. *A Rhetoric of Motives*. Berkeley: University of California Press, 1969.

———. "Literature as Equipment for Living." In *Perspectives by Incongruity*, 100–109. Edited by Stanley Edgar Hyman with the assistance of Barbara Karmiller. Bloomington: Indiana University Press, 1964.

———. *A Grammar of Motives*. Berkeley: University of California Press, 1969.

Burns, James MacGregor. *FDR: The Lion and the Fox*. New York: Harcourt, Brace, Jovanovich, 1956.

Burns, Stewart. *Social Movements of the 1960s: Searching for Democracy*. Boston: Twayne Publishers, 1990.

Butt, Archibald. *Taft and Roosevelt: The Intimate Letters of Archie Butt, Military Aide*. 2 vols. Port Washington, NY: Kennikat Press, 1971. First published 1930 by Doubleday, Doran & Co.

Calhoun, Craig, ed. *Habermas and the Public Sphere*. Cambridge: MIT Press, 1992.

———. "The Problem of Identity in Collective Action." In *Macro-Micro Linkages in Sociology*, edited by Joan Huber, 51–75. Newbury Park, CA: Sage, 1991.

Campbell, Angus, Gerald Gurin, and Warren E. Miller. *The Voter Decides*, Westport, CT: Greenwood Press, 1954.

Campbell, Angus, Philip E. Converse, Warren E. Miller, and Donald E. Stokes. *The American Voter*. Chicago: University of Chicago Press, 1976. First published 1960 by Wiley.

Campbell, Colin, and Bert A. Rockman, eds. *The Clinton Legacy*. New York: Chatham House, 2000.

Canovan, Margaret. "Two Strategies for the Study of Populism." *Political Studies* 30 (1982): 544–552.

———. *Populism*. New York: Harcourt, Brace, Jovanovich, 1981.

Cantril, Hadley. "The Invasion From Mars." In *The Processes and Effects of Mass Communication*, edited by Wilbur Schramm and Donald F. Roberts, 579–595. Urbana: University of Illinois Press, 1971.

Carpignano, Paolo, Robin Andersen, Stanley Aronowitz, and William DeFazio. "Chatter in the Age of Electronic Reproduction: Talk Television and the 'Public Mind.'" In *The Phantom Public Sphere*, edited by Bruce Robbins, 93–120. Minneapolis, MN: University of Minnesota Press, 1993.

Castells, Manuel. *The Power of Identity*. Malden, MA: Blackwell, 1997.

Cavallo, Dominick. *A Fiction of the Past: The Sixties in American History*. New York: St. Martin's Press, 1999.

Cavell, Stanley. *Senses of Walden*. New York: Viking Press, 1972.

Ceasar, James, Glen Thurow, Jeffrey Tulis, and James Bessette. "The Rise of the Rhetorical Presidency." *Presidential Studies Quarterly* 11 (1981): 158–171.

Chaffee, Stephen, and Joseph Hochheimer. "The Beginnings of Political Communication Research in the United States: Origins of the 'Limited' Effects Model." In *The Media Revolution in America and Western Europe*, edited by Everett M. Rogers and Francis Balle, 60–95. Norwood, NJ: Ablex, 1985.

Chalmers, David Mark. *The Muckrake Years.* New York: D. Van Norstrand Co., 1974.

Chaney, David. *Fictions of Collective Life: Public Drama in Late Modern Culture.* London: Routledge, 1993.

Charney, Leo, and Vanessa R. Schwartz, eds. *Cinema and the Invention of Modern Life.* Berkeley: University of California Press, 1995.

Chase, Richard. *The American Novel and Its Tradition.* New York: Doubleday, 1957.

Chernus, Ira. *Eisenhower's Atoms for Peace.* College Station, TX: Texas A & M University Press, 2002.

Chubb, John E., and Paul E. Peterson, eds. *Can the Government Govern?* Washington, D.C.: The Brookings Institution, 1989.

Clapper, Raymond. "Why Reporters Like FDR." *Review of Reviews* 1934 (June): 14–17.

Clayman, Steven, and John Heritage. "Questioning Presidents: Journalistic Deference and Adversarialness in the Press Conferences of U.S. Presidents Eisenhower and Reagan." *Journal of Communication* 52 (2002): 749–775.

Clayman, Steven. "Displaying Neutrality in Television News Interviews." *Social Problems* 35 (1988): 474–492.

Clecak, Peter. *America's Quest for the Ideal Self: Dissent and Fulfillment in the 60s and 70s.* New York: Oxford University Press, 1983.

Cmiel, Kenneth. *Democratic Eloquence: The Fight Over Popular Speech in Nineteenth-Century America.* New York: William Morrow & Co., 1990.

Cochran, Thomas. "Media as Business: A Brief History." *Journal of Communication* 25 (1975): 155–165.

Cohen, Jean L. "Strategy or Identity: New Theoretical Paradigms and Contemporary Social Movements." *Social Research* 52 (1985): 665–715.

Cohen, Jeffrey. *Presidential Responsiveness and Public Policy-Making: The Public and the Policies that Presidents Choose.* Ann Arbor: University of Michigan Press, 1997.

Cohen, Lizabeth. "Encountering Mass Culture at the Grassroots: The Experience of Chicago Workers in the 1920s." *American Quarterly* 9 (1986): 6–33.

Collin, Richard. "The Image of Theodore Roosevelt in American History and Thought, 1885–1965." PhD diss., New York University, 1966.

Condit, Celeste, and John Louis Lucaites. *Crafting Equality: America's Anglo-African Word.* Chicago: University of Chicago Press, 1993.

Conover, Pamela Johnson. "Presidential Influence and Public Opinion: The Case of the Iranian Hostage Crisis." *Social Science Quarterly* 63 (1982): 249–264.

Converse, Phillip. "The Nature of Belief Systems in Mass Publics." In *Ideology and Discontent,* edited by David Apter, 206–261. London: Free Press of Glencoe, 1964.

Conway, Margaret. *Political Participation in the United States.* 3rd Ed. Washington, D.C.: Congressional Quarterly Press, 2000.

Cook, James W. *The Arts of Deception: Playing with Fraud in the Age of Barnum.* Cambridge: Harvard University Press, 2001.

Cook, Timothy E. *Governing with the News: The News as a Political Institution.* Chicago: University of Chicago Press, 1998.

Corkin, Stanley. *Realism and the Birth of the United States.* Athens, GA: University of Georgia Press, 1996.

Cornwell, Elmer. "Presidential News: The Expanding Public Image." *Journalism Quarterly* 36 (1959): 275–283.

————. *Presidential Leadership of Public Opinion*. Westport, CT: Greenwood Press, 1965.

Crenson, Matthew, and Benjamin Ginsberg. *Downsizing Democracy: How America Sidelined Its Citizens and Privatized Its Public*. Baltimore: Johns Hopkins University Press, 2002.

Crockett, David. "George W. Bush and the Unrhetorical Rhetorical Presidency." *Rhetoric and Public Affairs* 6 (2003): 465–486.

Croly, Herbert. *The Promise of American Life*. New York: Macmillan, 1909.

Cronin, Thomas. "An Imperiled Presidency." *Society* 1980 (November/December): 57–64.

Crotty, William, ed. *The State of Democracy in America*. Washington, D.C.: Georgetown University Press, 2001.

Crunden, Robert. *From Self to Society, 1919–1941*. Englewood Cliffs, NJ: Prentice Hall, 1972.

————. *Ministers of Reform: The Progressives' Achievement in American Civilization, 1889–1920*. New York: Basic Books, 1982.

Cutright, Paul R. *Theodore Roosevelt: The Making of a Conservationist*. Chicago: University of Illinois Press, 1985.

Czitrom, Daniel. *Media and the American Mind: From Morse to McLuhan*. Chapel Hill: University of North Carolina Press, 1990.

Dahl, Robert. *A Preface to Democratic Theory*. Chicago: University of Chicago Press, 1956.

Dalton, Kathleen. "Why Americans Loved Teddy Roosevelt: or, Charisma Is in the Eyes of the Beholder." In *Our Selves/Our Past: Psychological Approaches to American History*, edited by Robert J. Brugger, 269–291. Baltimore: Johns Hopkins University Press, 1981.

Dalton, Russell J., and Manfred Kuechler, eds. *Challenging the Political Order: New Social and Political Movements in Western Democracies*. Oxford: Polity Press, 1990.

Darnton, Robert. "Writing News and Telling Stories." *Daedalus* 1975 (Spring): 175–194.

Davis W. Houck. *Rhetoric as Currency: Hoover, Roosevelt, and the Great Depression*. College Station, TX: Texas A & M University Press, 2001.

Davis, James W. *The American Presidency*. 2nd Ed., Westport, CT: Praeger, 1995.

Davis, Richard, and Diana Owens, *New Media and American Politics*. New York: Oxford University Press, 1998.

Day, Patricia, and Rudolf Klein. *Accountabilities: Five Public Services*. London: Tavistock, 1987.

de Cordova, Richard. *Picture Personalities: The Emergence of the Star System in America*. Urbana: University of Illinois Press, 1990.

Degler, Carl. *The Age of the Economic Revolution, 1876–1900*. Glenview, IL: Scott, Foresman, 1967.

Dekker, George. "The Genealogy of American Romance." *ESQ: A Journal of the American Renaissance* 35 (1989): 69–83.

Delia, Jesse G. "Communication Research: A History," In *Handbook of Communication Science,* edited by Charles E. Berger and Steven H. Chaffee, 46–50. Newbury Park, CA: Sage, 1987.

Denton, Robert E., Jr. *The Primetime Presidency of Ronald Reagan: The Era of the Television Presidency*. New York: Praeger, 1988.

Denton, Robert E., Jr., and Rachel L. Holloway. "Clinton and the Town Hall Meetings: Mediated Conversation and the Risk of Being 'In Touch.'" In *The Clinton Presidency: Images, Issues and Communication Strategies*, edited by Robert E. Denton and Rachel L. Holloway, 17–42. Westport, CT: Praeger, 1996.

Dewey, John. "Theodore Roosevelt." *Dial Magazine* 46 (1919): p. 115.

————. *Democracy and Education: An Introduction to the Philosophy of Education.* New York: The Free Press, 1966. First published 1916 by The Macmillan Company.

————. *The Public and Its Problems.* Athens, OH: Ohio University Press, 1927.

Doherty, Thomas. *Pre-Code Hollywood: Sex, Immorality, and Insurrection in American Cinema, 1930–1934.* New York: Columbia University Press, 1999.

Dorsey, Leroy, and Rachel Harlow. "'We Want Americans Pure and Simple': Theodore Roosevelt and the Myth of Americanism." *Rhetoric and Public Affairs* 6 (2003): 55–78.

Dorsey, Leroy. "Theodore Roosevelt and Corporate America, 1901–1909: A Reexamination." *Presidential Studies Quarterly* 25 (1995): 725–737.

————. "Preaching Morality in Modern America: Theodore Roosevelt's Rhetorical Progressivism." In *Rhetoric and Reform in the Progressive Era*, edited by J. Michael Hogan, 49–83.

————. "The Frontier Myth in Presidential Rhetoric: Theodore Roosevelt's Campaign for Conservation." *Western Journal of Communication* 59 (1995): 1–19.

Drew, Elizabeth. *Showdown: The Struggle Between the Gingrich Congress and the Clinton White House.* New York: Simon and Schuster, 1996.

————. *Whatever It Takes: The Real Struggle for Political Power in America.* New York: Viking Press, 1997.

Dyer, Richard. *Heavenly Bodies: Film Stars and Society.* New York: St. Martin's Press, 1986.

Edelman, Murray. "The Influence of Rationality Claims on Public Opinion and Policy." In *Public Opinion and the Communication of Consent*, edited by Theodore Glasser and Charles T. Salmon, 403–416. New York: Guilford Press, 1995.

————. *The Symbolic Uses of Politics.* Urbana: University of Illinois Press, 1985.

Eden, Robert. "Opinion Leadership and the Problem of Executive Power: Woodrow Wilson's Original Position." *Review of Politics* 57 (1995): 483–503.

Eder, Klaus. *The New Politics of Class: Social Movements and Cultural Dynamics in Advanced Societies.* Newbury Park, CA: Sage, 1993.

Edwards, George. *On Deaf Ears: The Limits of the Bully Pulpit.* New Haven: Yale University Press, 2003.

————. "Presidential Rhetoric: What Difference Does It Make?" In *Beyond the Rhetorical Presidency*, edited by Martin J. Medhurst, 199–217.

————. *The Public Presidency.* New York: St. Martin's Press, 1983.

Eisenach, Eldon. *The Lost Promise of Progressivism.* Lawrence, KS: The University Press of Kansas, 1994.

Ellis, Richard, ed. *Speaking to the People: The Rhetorical Presidency in Historical Perspective.* Amherst: University of Massachusetts Press, 1998.

Entman, Robert, and Andrew Rojecki. "Freezing Out the Public: Elite and Media Framing of the U.S. Anti-Nuclear Movement." *Political Communication* 10 (1993): 155–173.

Entman, Robert. "Framing: Toward Clarification of a Fractured Paradigm." *Journal of Communication* 43 (1993): 51–58.

————. *Democracy Without Citizens: Media and the Decay of American Politics.* New York: Oxford University Press, 1989.

Epstein, Edward J. *News From Nowhere: Television and the News.* New York: Random House, 1973.

Evans, Sara. *Personal Politics: The Role of Women's Liberation in the Civil Rights Movement and the New Left.* New York: Vintage Books, 1980.

Fairbanks, James D. "The Priestly Functions of the Presidency: A Discussion of the Literature on Civil Religion and Its Implications for the Study of Presidential Leadership." *Presidential Studies Quarterly* 11 (1981): 214–232.

Farrell, Thomas. "Knowledge in Time: Toward an Extension of Rhetorical Form." In *Advances in Argumentation Theory and Research*, edited by J. Robert Cox and Charles Arthur Willard, 123–153. Carbondale: Southern Illinois University Press, 1982.

Faulkner, Harold. *The Quest for Social Justice, 1898–1914*. New York, Macmillan, 1931.

Federici, P. Michael. *The Challenge of Populism: The Rise of Right-Wing Democratism in Post-war America*. Westport: Praeger, 1991.

Feffer, Andrew. *The Chicago Pragmatists and American Progressivism*. Ithaca: Cornell University Press.

Feuer, Jane. "The Concept of Live Television: Ontology as Ideology." In *Regarding Television: Critical Approaches—An Anthology*, edited by E. Ann Kaplan, 12–21. Los Angeles: American Film Institute, 1983.

Filene, Peter. "An Obituary for the Progressive Movement." *American Quarterly* 22 (1970): 20–34.

Filler, Louis. *The Muckrakers*. University Park, PA: Pennsylvania State University Press, 1968.

Fine, Robert. "FDR's Radio Chatting: Its Development and Impact During the Great Depression." PhD diss., New York University, 1977.

Fisher Fishkin, Shelley. *From Fact to Fiction: Journalism and Imaginative Writing in America*. Baltimore: Johns Hopkins University Press, 1985.

Foote, Joseph S. *Television and Political Power: The Networks, the Presidency, and the 'Loyal Opposition.'* Westport, CT: Praeger, 1990.

Fox, Harrison W., and Susan Webb Hammond. "The Growth of Congressional Staffs." In *Congress Against the President*, edited by Harvey C. Mansfield, 112–124. New York: Academy of Political Science, 1975.

Freidel, Frank. *Franklin D. Roosevelt: Launching the New Deal*. Boston: Little, Brown & Co., 1973.

Friedman, James, ed. *Reality Squared: Televisual Discourse on the Real*. New Brunswick: Rutgers University Press, 2002.

Gabriel, Ralph H. *The Course of American Democratic Thought*. 3rd Ed. Westport, CT: Greenwood Press, 1986.

Gaines, Jane, ed. *Classical Hollywood Narrative: The Paradigm Wars*. Durham: Duke University Press, 1992.

Galambos, Louis, and Daun van Ee, eds. *The Papers of Dwight D. Eisenhower. v.* 1, *The Presidency: The Middle Way*. Baltimore: The Johns Hopkins University Press, 1996.

Gamson, Joshua. *Claims to Fame: Celebrity in Contemporary America*. Berkeley: University of California Press, 1994.

Gamson, William, and Andrew Modigliani. "Media Discourse and Public Opinion on Nuclear Power: A Constructionist Approach." *American Journal of Sociology* 985 (1989): 1–37.

Gans, Herbert. *Deciding What's News: A Study of CBS Evening News, NBC Nightly News, Newsweek, and Time*. New York: Vintage Books, 1979.

———. *Democracy and the News*. Oxford: Oxford University Press, 2003.

Geertz, Clifford. *The Interpretation of Cultures*. New York: Basic Books, 1973.

———. "Deep Play: Notes on a Balinese Cockfight," Chapter 15 in *The Interpretation of Cultures*. New York: Basic Books, 1973.

Gerstle, Gary. "The Protean Character of American Liberalism." *American Historical Review* 99 (1994): 1043–1073.

Giddens, Anthony. *The Constitution of Society: Outline of a Theory of Structuration.* Berkeley: University of California Press, 1984.

Gillman, Howard. "The Constitution Besieged: TR, Taft, and Wilson on the Virtue and Efficacy of a Faction-Free Republic." *Presidential Studies Quarterly* 19 (1989): 179–201.

Glad, Betty. *Jimmy Carter: In Search of the Great White House.* New York: W. W. Norton & Co., 1980.

Goffman, Erving. "Radio Talk." Chapter 5 in *Forms of Talk.* Philadelphia: University of Pennsylvania Press, 1981.

Goldstein, Kenneth. *Interest Groups, Lobbying, and Participation in America.* Cambridge: Cambridge University Press, 2002.

Good, Howard. "The Journalist in Fiction, 1890–1930." *Journalism Quarterly* 62 (1985): 352–357.

Goodman, Ace. "Fireside Chitchat." *Saturday Review* 36 (1953): p. 31.

Goodwyn, Lawrence. *Democratic Promise: The Populist Moment in America.* New York: Oxford University Press, 1976.

Gottfried, Paul Edward. *After Liberalism: Mass Democracy in the Managerial State.* Princeton: Princeton University Press, 1999.

Gould, Lewis. *The Presidency of Theodore Roosevelt.* Lawrence: University Press of Kansas, 1991.

Graebner, Norman. "Eisenhower's Popular Leadership." *Current History* 39 (1960): 230–236.

Greatbatch, David. "Aspects of Topical Organization in News Interviews: The Use of Agenda-Shifting Procedures by Interviews," *Media, Culture and Society* 8 (1986): 441–456.

Greenstein, Fred. "Change and Continuity in the Modern Presidency." In *The New American Political System,* edited by Anthony King, 45–86. Washington, D.C.: American Enterprise Institute, 1977.

———. *The Hidden-Hand Presidency: Eisenhower as a Leader.* New York: Basic Books, 1982.

Griffith, Robert. "Dwight D. Eisenhower and the Corporate Commonwealth." *Journal of American Historical Review* 87 (1982): 87–122.

Gronbeck, Bruce E. "Rhetorical History and Rhetorical Criticism: A Distinction." *Speech Teacher* 24 (1975): 199–217.

Grossman, Michael, and Martha Joynt Kumar. *Portraying the President: The White House and the Media.* Baltimore: Johns Hopkins University Press, 1981.

Gunning, Tom. *D.W. Griffith and the Origins of American Narrative Film.* Urbana: University of Illinois Press, 1991.

Gusfield, Joseph R. *Symbolic Crusade.* Urbana: University of Illinois Press, 1963.

Habermas, Jürgen. *The Structural Transformation of the Public Sphere: An Inquiry Into a Category of Bourgeois Society.* Translated by Thomas Burger with assistance of Frederick Lawrence. Cambridge: MIT Press, 1989.

———. "New Social Movements." *Telos* 49 (1981), 33–37.

———. *Knowledge and Human Interests.* Translated by Jeremy Shapiro. Cambridge: Polity, 1987.

———. *The Theory of Communicative Action.* 2 vols. Translated by Thomas McCarthy. Boston: Beacon Press, 1984–1987.

Halberstam, David. *The Powers that Be.* New York: Dell Publishing Co., 1979.

Hallin, Daniel. "Soundbite News: Television Coverage of Elections, 1968–1988." Chapter 7 in *We Keep America on Top of the World: Television Journalism and the Public Sphere.* New York: Routledge, 1994, 133–152.

Halttunen, Karen. *Confidence Men and Painted Women: A Study of Middle-Class Culture in America, 1830–1870*. New Haven: Yale University Press, 1982.

Harrell, David Edwin, Jr. *Pat Robertson*. San Francisco: Harper and Row, 1987.

Hart, Roderick. *The Sound of Leadership: Presidential Communication in the Modern Age*. Chicago: University of Chicago Press, 1987.

Haskell, Thomas L. *The Emergence of the Social Sciences: The American Social Science Association and the Nineteenth Century Crisis of Authority*. Urbana: University of Illinois Press, 1977.

Hayes, Joy. "Radio Broadcasting and Nation Building in Mexico and the United States, 1925–1945." PhD diss., University of California, San Diego, 1994.

Hays, Samuel P. *Conservation and the Gospel of Efficiency: The Progressive Conservation Movement, 1890–1920*. Boston: Harvard University Press, 1959.

———. *The Response to Industrialism: 1885–1914*. Chicago: University of Chicago Press, 1957.

Heclo, Hugh. "The Executive Office of the President." In *Modern Presidents and the Presidency*, edited by Marc Landy, 65–82. Lexington, MA: D.C. Heath, 1985.

———. *A Government of Strangers: Executive Politics in Washington*. Washington, D.C.: The Brookings Institution, 1977.

Heertzgaard, Mark. *On Bended Knee: The Press and the Reagan Presidency*. New York: Farrar, Strauss, Giroux, 1988.

Henderson, Charles P., and Robert S. Alley, eds. *So Help Me God: Religion and the American Presidency: Wilson to Nixon*. Richmond, VA: John Knox Press, 1972.

Hendler, Glenn. *Public Sentiments: Structures of Feeling in Nineteenth Century American Literature*. Chapel Hill: University of North Carolina Press, 2001.

Herbst, Susan. *Reading Public Opinion: How Political Actors View the Democratic Process*. Chicago: University of Chicago Press, 1998.

Heritage, John. "Analyzing News Interviews: Aspects of the Production of Talk for an Overhearing Audience." In *Handbook of Discourse Analysis*, v. 3, edited by Teun van Dijk, 95–117. London: Academic Press, 1985.

Hess, Stephen. *The Washington Reporters*. Washington, D.C.: The Brookings Institution, 1981.

Hibbing, John, and Elizabeth Theiss-Morse, eds. *What Is It About Government that Americans Dislike?* Cambridge: Cambridge University Press, 2001.

Hicks, John D. *The Populist Revolt: A History of the Farmer's Alliance and the People's Party*. Minneapolis: The University of Minnesota Press, 1931.

Hiebert, Ray Eldon. *Courtier to the Crowd: The Story of Ivy Lee and the Development of Public Relations*. Ames, IA: Iowa State University Press, 1966.

Hilderbrand, Robert C. *Power and the People: Executive Management of Public Opinion in Foreign Affairs, 1897–1921*. Chapel Hill, NC: The University of North Carolina Press, 1981.

Hilmes, Michele. *Radio Voices: American Broadcasting, 1922–1952*. Minneapolis: University of Minnesota Press, 1997.

Hinckley, Barbara. *The Symbolic Presidency: How Presidents Present Themselves*. New York: Routledge, 1990.

Hinds, Lynn Boyd, and Theodore Otto Windt Jr. *The Cold War as Rhetoric: The Beginnings, 1945–1950*. New York: Praeger, 1991.

Hixson, Walter L. *Parting the Curtain: Propaganda, Culture, and the Cold War 1945–1961*. New York: St. Martin's Press, 1997.

Hoffmann, Karen. "'Going Public' in the Nineteenth Century: Grover Cleveland's Repeal of the Sherman Silver Purchase Act." *Rhetoric and Public Affairs* 5 (2002): 57–77.

Hofstadter, Richard. *Social Darwinism in American Thought.* New York: George Braziller, 1959.

———. *The American Political Tradition and the Men Who Made It.* New York: Vintage Books, 1954.

———. *The Age of Reform: From Bryan to F.D.R.* New York: Alfred E. Knopf, 1955.

———. *Anti-Intellectualism in American Life.* New York: Alfred E. Knopf, 1963.

Hogan, J. Michael, ed. *Rhetoric and Reform in the Progressive Era.* East Lansing, MI: Michigan State University Press, 2003.

———. "George Gallup and the Rhetoric of Scientific Democracy." *Communication Monographs* 64 (1997): 161–179.

———. "Introduction: Rhetoric and Reform in the Progressive Era." In *Rhetoric and Reform in the Progressive Era*, edited by J. Michael Hogan, ix–xxiv.

Horkheimer, Max, and Theodore Adorno. *Dialectic of Enlightenment.* Translated by John Cummings. New York: Herder and Herder, 1972.

Horton, Donald, and R. Richard Wohl. "Mass Communication and Parasocial Interaction: Observation on Intimacy at a Distance." In *Inter/Media: Interpersonal Communication in a Media World*, edited by Gary Gumpert and Robert Cathcart, 185–206. New York: Oxford University Press, 1979.

Howe, Frederic. *The Confessions of a Reformer.* New York: Charles Scribner's Sons, 1926.

Hughes, Emmett. *The Ordeal of Power: A Political Memoir of the Eisenhower Years.* New York: Atheneum, 1963.

Hutchison, E.R. "Kennedy and the Press: The First Six Months." *Journalism Quarterly* 1961: 453–459.

Ingelhart, Ronald. *The Silent Revolution: Changing Values and Political Styles Among Western Publics.* Princeton: Princeton University Press, 1977.

Ionescu, Ghita, and Ernest Gellner, eds. *Populism: Its Meanings and National Characteristics.* London: Wiedenfeld and Nicolson, 1969.

Irish, Marian D. "The Organization Man in the Presidency." *The Journal of Politics* 20 (1958): 259–277.

Iyengar, Shanto, and Donald Kinder. *Is Anyone Responsible? How Television Frames Political Issues.* Chicago: University of Chicago Press, 1994.

———. *News that Matters.* Chicago: University of Chicago Press, 1987.

Jackall, Robert, and Janice M. Hirota. *Image Makers: Advertising, Public Relations, and the Ethos of Advocacy.* Chicago: University of Chicago Press, 2000.

Jacobs, Lawrence, and Robert Shapiro. "Issues, Candidate, Image, and Priming: The Use of Private Polls in Kennedy's 1960 Presidential Election Campaign." *American Political Science Review* 83 (1994): 527–538.

———. "Presidential Manipulation of Polls and Public Opinion: the Nixon Administration and the Pollsters." *Political Science Quarterly* 110 (1995–96): 519–538.

———. *Politicians Don't Pander: Political Manipulation and the Loss of Democratic Responsiveness.* Chicago: University of Chicago Press, 2000.

Jamieson, Kathleen Hall. *Eloquence in an Electronic Age: The Transformation of Political Speechmaking.* New York: Oxford University Press, 1988

Johnson, Dennis W. *No Place for Amateurs: How Political Consultants Are Reshaping American Democracy.* New York: Routledge, 2001.

Johnston, Hank, Enrique Larana, and Joseph R. Gusfield. "Identities, Grievances, and New Social Movements." In *New Social Movements: From Ideology to Identity*, edited by Enrique Larana, Hank Johnston, and Joseph R. Gusfield, 3–35. Philadelphia: Temple University Press, 1994.

Jones, Bryan D. *The New American Politics: Reflections on Political Change and the Clinton Administration*. Boulder: Westview Press, 1995.

Jones, O. Charles. *The Trusteeship Presidency: Jimmy Carter and the United States Congress*. Baton Rouge: Louisiana State University Press, 1988.

Juergens, George. "Woodrow Wilson and the Press." *The Media*, edited by Kenneth Thompson, 168–184. New York: University Press of America, 1985.

———. *News from the White House: The Presidential-Press Relationship in the Progressive Era*. Chicago: University of Chicago Press, 1981.

Kahneman, Daniel, and Amos Tversky. "Choices, Values, and Frames." *American Psychologist* 39 (1984): 341–350.

Kaplan, Amy. *The Social Construction of American Realism*. Chicago: University of Chicago Press, 1988.

Kateb, George. "Walt Whitman and the Culture of Democracy." In *The Self and the Political Order*, edited by Tracy Strong, 208–229. New York: New York University Press, 1992.

Kazin, Michael. *The Populist Persuasion: An American History*. 2nd Ed. New York: Basic Books, 1998.

Kelley, Stanley, Jr. *Professional Public Relations and Political Power*. Baltimore: The Johns Hopkins Press, 1956.

Kernell, Samuel, and Matthew Baum. "Has Cable Ended the Golden Age of Television?" *American Political Science Review* 93 (1999): 99–114.

Kernell, Samuel. "Explaining Presidential Popularity." *American Political Science Review* 72 (1978): 506–522.

———. *Going Public: New Strategies of Presidential Leadership*. 3rd Ed. Washington, D.C.: Congressional Quarterly, Inc., 1997.

Kerney, James. *The Political Education of Woodrow Wilson*. New York: The Century Co., 1926.

Key, V.O. *The Responsible Electorate: Rationality in Presidential Voting, 1936–1960*. Cambridge: Harvard University Press, 1966.

Keyes, Elizabeth. "President Kennedy's Press Conferences as 'Shapers' of the News." PhD diss., University of Iowa, 1968.

King Davis, Oscar King. *Released for Publication: Some Inside Political History of Theodore Roosevelt and His Times, 1898–1918*. Boston: Houghton Mifflin Co., 1925.

King, Barry. "Stardom as Occupation," In *The Hollywood Film Industry*, edited by Paul Kerr, 154–184. London: Routledge, 1986.

Klapp, Orrin. *Collective Search for Identity*. New York: Holt, Rinehart and Winston, 1969.

Klaprat, Cathy. "The Star as Market Strategy: Bette Davis in Another Light." In *American Film Industry*, 351–376. Edited by Tino Balio. Madison: The University of Wisconsin Press, 1985.

Klein, Joe. *The Natural: The Misunderstood Presidency of Bill Clinton*. New York: Doubleday, 2002.

Kloppenberg, James. *Uncertain Victory: Social Democracy and Progressivism in European and American Thought, 1870–1920*. New York: Oxford University Press, 1986.

Koenig, Louis W. *The Chief Executive*. 6th Ed. Fort Worth, TX: Harcourt Brace College Publishers, 1996.

Kolko, Gabriel. *The Triumph of Conservatism: A Re-interpretation of American History, 1900–1916*. New York: The Free Press, 1963.

Kraig, Robert Alexander. "The 1912 Election and the Rhetorical Foundations of the Modern Liberal State." *Rhetoric and Public Affairs* 3 (2000): 363–395.

Krosnick, Jon, and Donald Kinder. "Altering the Foundations of Support for the President Through Priming." *American Political Science Review* 84 (1990): 497–512.

Kumar, Martha Joynt, and Michael B. Grossman. "Political Communications From the White House: The Interest Group Connection." *Presidential Studies Quarterly* 16 (1985): 92–101.

Laclau, Ernst. "Towards a Theory of Populism." Chapter 4 in *Politics and Ideology in Marxist Theory: Capitalism-Fascism-Populism.* London: New Left Books, 1977.

Lanoue, David. "The 'Teflon Factor': Ronald Reagan and Comparative Presidential Popularity." *Polity* 21 (1989), 481–501.

Larson, Arthur. *Eisenhower: The President Nobody Knew.* New York: Charles Scribner's Sons, 1968.

Lasch, Christopher. *The Culture of Narcissism: American Life in an Age of Diminishing Expectations.* New York: Norton, 1978.

Lawrence, David. *The True Story of Woodrow Wilson.* New York: George H. Doran Co., 1924.

Lazarsfeld, Paul, Bernard Berelson, and Hazel Gaudet. *The People's Choice: How the Voter Makes Up His Mind in a Presidential Campaign.* New York: Duell, Sloan and Pearce, 1944.

Le Bon, Gustav. *The Crowd: A Study of the Popular Mind.* Introduced by Robert K. Merton. New York: Viking Press, 1960.

Lears, T.J. Jackson. "From Salvation to Self-realization: Advertising and the Therapeutic Roots of Consumer Culture, 1880–1930," In *The Culture of Consumption*, edited by T.J. Jackson Lears and Richard Wrightman Fox, 1–38. New York: Pantheon Books, 1983.

Leff, Michael, and Fred Kauffeld, eds. *Texts in Context: Critical Dialogues on Significant Episodes in American Political Rhetoric* . Davis, CA: Hermagoras Press, 1989.

Leuchtenberg, William. *Franklin D. Roosevelt and the New Deal, 1932–1940.* New York: Harper and Row, 1963.

———. *In the Shadow of FDR: From Harry Truman to George W. Bush.* 3rd Ed. Ithaca: Cornell University Press, 2001.

Levin, Martin A., Marc Landy, and Martin Shapiro, eds. *Seeking the Center: Politics and Policymaking at the New Century.* Washington, D.C.: Georgetown University Press, 2001.

Light, Paul C. *Thickening Government: Federal Hierarchy and the Diffusion of Accountability.* Washington, D.C.: Brookings, 1995.

———. *The President's Agenda.* Baltimore: Johns Hopkins University Press, 1978.

Lim, Elvin. "The Lion and the Lamb: De-mythologizing Franklin Roosevelt's Fireside Chats." *Rhetoric and Public Affairs* 6 (2003): 437–464.

Link, Arthur. "What Happened to the Progressive Movement in the 1920s?" *American Historical Review* 64 (1959): 833–851.

Lippmann, Walter. *Public Opinion.* New York: The Free Press, 1997. First published 1922 by Harcourt, Brace & Co.

———. *A Preface to Morals.* New York: Macmillan, 1929.

Livingstone, Sonia, and Peter Lunt. *Talk on Television: Audience Participation and Debate.* London: Routledge, 1994.

Loomis, Burdett. *The New American Politician: Ambition, Entrepreneurship, and the Changing Face of American Politics.* New York: Basic Books, 1988.

Lowi, Theodore. *The Personal President: Power Invested, Promise Unfulfilled.* Ithaca: Cornell University Press, 1985.

Lowry, Edward. *Washington Close-Ups; Intimate Views of Some Public Figures.* Boston: Houghton Mifflin Co., 1921.

Lumley, Frederick. *Measurement in Radio*. Columbus, OH: Ohio State University Press, 1934.

Lustig, Jeffrey. *Corporate Liberalism: The Origins of Modern American Political Theory, 1890–1920*. Berkeley: UC Press, 1982.

Maltese, John. *Spin Control: The White House Office of Communications and the Management of Presidential News*. 2nd Ed. Chapel Hill, NC: The University of North Carolina Press, 1994.

Maney, Patrick. *The Roosevelt Presence: A Biography of Franklin Delano Roosevelt*. New York: Twayne Publishers, 1992.

Manoff, Robert Karl. "Writing the News (By Telling the 'Story')." In *Reading the News*, edited by Robert Karl Manoff and Michael Schudson, 197–229. New York: Pantheon, 1986.

Mansfield, Harvey, Jr. *Taming the Prince: The Ambivalence of Modern Executive Power*. New York: The Free Press, 1989.

Marbut, F.B. *News from the Capital: The Story of Washington Reporting*. Carbondale, IL: Southern Illinois University Press, 1971.

March, John, and Johan Olsen. *Democratic Governance*. New York: The Free Press, 1995.

Marchand, Roland. *Advertising the American Dream: Making Way for Modernity, 1920–1940*. Berkeley: University of California Press, 1985.

Marcosson, Isaac. *Adventures In Interviewing*. New York: John Lane Co., 1920.

Masciarotte, Gloria-Jean. "C'Mon, Girl: Oprah Winfrey and the Discourse of Feminine Talk." *Genders* 11 (1991): 81–110.

May, Henry F. *The End of American Innocence: A Study of the First Years of Our Own Time, 1912–1917*. New York: Alfred E. Knopf, 1959.

May, Lary. *Screening Out the Past: The Birth of Mass Culture and the Motion Pictures Industry*. New York: Oxford University Press, 1988.

McAdam, Doug. *Freedom Summer*. New York: Oxford University Press, 1988.

McAdam, Doug. *Political Process and the Development of Black Insurgency, 1930–1970*. Chicago: University of Chicago Press, 1982.

McArthur, Benjamin. *Actors and American Culture, 1880–1920*. Philadelphia: Temple University Press, 1984.

McCoombs, Maxwell. "Agenda-Setting Research: A Bibliographic Essay." *Political Communication Review* 1 (1976): 1–7.

McCormick, Robert. "The Discovery that Business Corrupts Politics: A Reappraisal of the Origins of Progressivism." *American Historical Review* 86 (1981): 247–274.

McElvaine, Robert. *Down and Out in the Great Depression: Letters From the 'Forgotten' Man*. Chapel Hill, NC: University of North Carolina Press, 1983.

McGeary, M. Nelson. *Gifford Pinchot: Forester, Politician*. Princeton: Princeton University Press, 1960.

McGee, Michael Calvin. "A Materialist's Conception of Rhetoric." In *Explorations in Rhetoric: Studies in Honor of Douglas Ehninge,* edited by Ray E. McKerrow, 23–48. Glenview, IL: Scott Foresman, 1982.

———. "In Search of 'The People': A Rhetorical Alternative." *Quarterly Journal of Speech* 61 (1975): 235–249.

McGerr, Michael. *The Decline of Popular Politics: The American North, 1865–1928*. New York: Oxford University Press, 1986.

McGinnis, Joe. *The Selling of the President, 1968*. New York: Trident Press, 1968.

McGrory, Mary. "The Right-Hand Men." In *The Kennedy Circle*, edited by Lester Tanzer, 58–81. Washington, D.C.: Luce, 1961.

McGuigan, Jim. *Cultural Populism*. London: Routledge, 1992.

McGuire, Delbert. "Democracy's Confrontation: The Presidential Press Conference, I." *Journalism Quarterly* 44 (1967): 638–644.

———. "Democracy's Confrontation: The Presidential Press Conference, II." *Journalism Quarterly* 45 (1968): 31–41.

McWilliams, Wilson Carey. "Standing at Armageddon: Morality and Religion in Progressive Thought." In *Progressivism and the New Democracy*, edited by Sidney Milkis and Jerome M. Mileur, 103–125.

Medhurst, Martin J. "Ike's Rhetorical Leadership: An Interpretation." In *Ike's War of Words: Rhetoric and Leadership*, Martin Medhurst, 287–297.

———. *Dwight D. Eisenhower: Strategic Communicator*. Westport, CT: Greenwood Press, 1993.

———. *Ike's War of Words: Rhetoric and Leadership*. East Lansing, MI: Michigan State University Press, 1994.

———, ed. *Beyond the Rhetorical Presidency*. College Station, TX: Texas A & M University Press, 1996.

———. "Introduction: A Tale of Two Constructs: The Rhetorical Presidency versus Presidential Rhetoric." In *Beyond the Rhetorical Presidency*, edited by Martin J. Medhurst, xi–xxv. College Station, TX: Texas A & M University Press, 1996.

Medhurst, Martin J., and H. W. Brands, eds. *Critical Reflections on the Cold War: Linking Rhetoric with History*. College Station, TX: Texas A & M University Press, 2000.

Medhurst, Martin J., Robert L. Ivie, Philip Wander, and Robert L. Scott, eds. *The Cold War as Rhetoric: Strategy, Metaphor, and Ideology*. Rev. Ed. East Lansing: Michigan State University Press, 1997.

Melucci, Alberto. "A Strange Kind of Newness: What's 'New' in New Social Movements?" In *New Social Movements: From Ideology to Identity*, edited by Enrique Larana, Hank Johnston, and Joseph Gusfield, 100–130. Philadelphia: Temple University Press, 1994.

———. *Nomads of the Present: Social Movements and Individual Needs in Contemporary Society*. London: Hutchinson Radius, 1989.

Meyer, John, and Diana B. Carlin. "The Impact of Formats on Voter Reaction." In *The 1992 Presidential Debates in Focus*, edited by Diana Carlin and Mitchell S. McKinney, 69–84. Westport, CT: Praeger, 1992.

Mickelson, Sig. *From Whistle Stop to Soundbite: Four Decades of Politics and Television*. New York: Praeger, 1989.

Milkis, Sidney, and Jerome M. Mileur, eds. *Progressivism and the New Democracy*. Amherst: University of Massachusetts Press, 1999.

Miller, William Lee. "Can Government Be Merchandised?" *The Reporter* 9 (October 27, 1953): 11–16.

Mills, C. Wright. *The Power Elite*. New York: Oxford University Press, 1956.

Miroff, Bruce. *Icons of Democracy: American Leaders as Heroes, Aristocrats, Dissenters and Democrats*. New York: Basic Books, 1993.

Moe, Terry. "Presidents, Institutions, and Theory." In *Researching the Presidency: Vital Questions, New Approaches*, edited by George Edwards, John Kessel, and Bert Rockman, 337–56. Pittsburgh: University of Pittsburgh Press, 1993.

Morgan, Edward. *The 60s Experience: Hard Lessons About Modern America*. Philadelphia: Temple University Press, 1991.

Morris, Kenneth, and Barry Schwarz. "Why They Liked Eisenhower: Tradition, Crisis, and Heroic Leadership." *The Sociological Quarterly* 34 (1993): 133–151.

Mott, Frank L. *The News in America*. Cambridge: Harvard University Press, 1965.

Mowry, George E. *The Era of Theodore Roosevelt: 1900–1912*. New York: Harper and Row, 1958.

———. *Theodore Roosevelt and the Progressive Movement*. NY: Hill and Wang, 1946.

Mueller, John E. *War, Presidents, and Public Opinion*. New York: Wiley and Sons, 1970.

Munson, Wayne. *All Talk: The Talkshow in Media Culture*. Philadelphia: Temple University Press, 1993.

Neale, Stephen. *Cinema and Technology: Image, Sound Colour*. London: MacMillan, 1985.

Nelson, Thomas, and Donald Kinder. "Issue Frames and Group-Centrism in American Public Opinion." *The Journal of Politics* 58 (1996): 1055–1078.

North, Douglass. *Institutions, Institutional Change, and Economic Performance*. Cambridge: Cambridge University Press, 1990.

Novak, Michael. *Choosing Our King: Powerful Symbols in Presidential Politics*. New York: MacMillan, 1974.

Nye, Joseph S., Philip D. Zelikow, and David C. King, eds. *Why People Don't Trust Government*. Cambridge: Harvard University Press, 1997.

Oates, Stephen B. *Let the Trumpet Sound: The Life of Martin Luther King, Jr*. New York: Harper and Row, 1982.

Oglesby, Charles, ed. *The New Left Reader*. New York: The Grove Press, 1969.

Oppenheimer, Bruce. "Congress and the New Obstructionism: Developing an Energy Program." In *Congress Reconsidered*, edited by Lawrence C. Dodd and Bruce Oppenheimer, 275–295. Washington: Congressional Quarterly, 1981.

Oravec, Christine. "Science, Public Policy, and the 'Spirit of the People': The Rhetoric of Progressive Conservation," In *Rhetoric and Reform in the Progressive Era*, 85–112. Edited by J. Michael Hogan. East Lansing, MI: Michigan State University Press, 2003.

Otten, Alan. "What Do You Think, Ted?" In *The Kennedy Circle*, edited by Lester Tanzer, 3–28. Washington, D.C.: Luce, 1961.

Page, Benjamin, and Robert Shapiro. "Presidential Leadership of Public Opinion." In *The Presidency and Public Policy Making*, edited by George Edwards, Steven Shull, and Norman Thomas, 22–36. Pittsburgh: University of Pittsburgh Press, 1985.

Pan, Zhongdong, and Gerald Kosicki. "Framing Analysis: An Approach to News Discourse." *Political Communication* 10 (1997): 55–75.

Paper, Lewis J. *The Promise and the Performance: The Leadership of John F. Kennedy*. New York: Crown Publishers, 1975.

Park, Robert. "Introduction." In *News and the Human Interest Story*. By Helen McGill, xi–xxiii. Chicago: University of Chicago Press, 1940.

Park, Robert. *Society: Collective Behavior, News and Opinion: Sociology and Modern Society*. Edited by Everett Cherrington Hughes, et al. Glencoe, IL: Free Press, 1955.

Parry-Giles, Shawn. "Militarizing America's Propaganda Program, 1945–55." In *Critical Reflections on the Cold War*, edited by Martin J. Medhurst and H. W. Brands, 95–133.

———. *The Rhetorical Presidency, Propaganda, and the Cold War, 1945–1955*. Westport, CT: Praeger, 2002.

Payne, Charles M. *I've Got the Light of Freedom: The Organizing Tradition in the Mississippi Freedom Struggle*. Berkeley: University of California Press, 1995.

Perkins, Frances. *The FDR I Knew*. New York: Harper and Row, 1946.

Pierard, Richard V., and Robert D. Linder. *Civil Religion and the Presidency*. Grand Rapids, MI: Academic Books, 1988.

Pierpoint, Robert. *At the White House: Assignment to Six Presidents*. New York: Putnam, 1981.

Pika, Joseph. "Interest Groups and the Executive: Presidential Intervention." In *Group Politics*, edited by Allan Crigler and Burdett Loomis, 298–321. Washington, D.C.: Congressional Quarterly Press, 1983.

Pinchot, Gifford. *Breaking New Ground*. Introduced by James Penick Jr. Seattle: University of Washington Press, 1947.

Pinkett, Harold T. *Gifford Pinchot: Private and Public Forester*. Urbana: University of Illinois Press, 1970.

Pitkin, Hannah. *Wittgenstein and Justice: On the Significance of Ludwig Wittgenstein for Social and Political Thought*. Berkeley: University of California Press, 1972.

Pollard, James. *The Presidents and the Press*. New York: Macmillan, 1947.

Ponder, Stephen. "'Publicity in the Interest of the People': Theodore Roosevelt's Conservation Crusade." *Presidential Studies Quarterly* 20 (1990): 547–555.

———. *Managing the Press: Origins of the Media Presidency, 1897–1933*. New York: St. Martin's Press, 1999.

Price, Vincent, David Tewksbury, and Elizabeth Powers. "Switching Trains of Thought: The Impact of News Frames on Readers' Cognitive Responses." *Communication Research* 24 (1997): 481–506.

Priest, Patricia Joyner. *Public Intimacies: Talk Show Participants and Tell-All TV*. Creeskill, NJ: Hampton Press, 1995.

Pringle, Henry. *Theodore Roosevelt: A Biography*. New York: Harcourt, Brace & Co., 1931.

Putnam, Robert. *Bowling Alone: The Collapse of American Civic Life*. New York: Simon and Schuster, 2000.

Quandt, Jean. *From the Small Town to the Great Community: The Social Thought of Progressive Intellectuals*. New Brunswick, NJ: Rutgers University Press, 1970.

Ragland, James. "Franklin D. Roosevelt and the Man in the Street: A Study in Public Opinion." Master's Thesis, Stanford University, 1951.

Ragsdale, Lyn. "The Politics of Speechmaking, 1949–1980." *American Political Science Review* 78 (1984): 971–984.

———. "Presidential Speechmaking and the Public Audience: Individual Presidents and Group Attitudes." *Journal of Politics* 49 (1987): 704–736.

———. *Vital Statistics on the Presidency*. Rev. Ed. Washington, D.C.: Congressional Quarterly, 1998.

Ranney, Austin. *The Doctrine of Responsible Party Government: Its Origins and Present State*. Urbana, IL: The University of Illinois Press, 1962.

Rauch, Jonathan. *Demosclerosis: The Silent Killer of American Government*. New York: Random House, 1994.

Rechner, Peter. "Theodore Roosevelt and Progressive Personality Politics." *Melbourne Historical Journal* 8 (1969), 43–58.

Ricci, David. *The Transformation of American Politics: The New Washington and the Rise of Think Tanks*. New Haven: Yale University Press, 1993.

Rieff, Phillip. *The Triumph of the Therapeutic: Uses of Faith After Freud*. Rev. Ed. Chicago: University of Chicago Press, 1987.

Riker, William. *The Art of Political Manipulation*. New Haven: Yale University Press, 1986.

Ritchie, Donald. *Press Gallery: Congress and the Washington Correspondents*. Cambridge: Harvard University Press, 1991.

Ritter, Kurt, and David Henry. *Ronald Reagan: The Great Communicator*. New York: Greenwood Press, 1992.

Ritter, Kurt, and Martin Medhurst. *Presidential Speech-Writing: From the New Deal to the Reagan Revolution and Beyond.* College Station, TX: Texas A & M University Press, 2003.

Rivers, William. *The Other Government: Power and the Washington Media.* New York: Universe Books, 1982.

Roberts, Chalmers. "John F. Kennedy and the Press." In *The Media*, edited by Kenneth Thompson, 181–193. Lanham, MD: University Press of America, 1985.

Roberts, Chalmers. *First Rough Draft: A Journalist's Journal of Our Times.* New York: Praeger, 1973.

Rodgers, Daniel. "In Search of Progressivism." *Reviews in American History* 10 (1982): 113–132.

Rogers, Everett M., and James W. Dearing. "Agenda-Setting Research: Where Has It Been, Where Is It Going?" In *Media Power in Politics*, edited by Doris Graber, 68–86. Washington, D.C.: CQ Press, 2000.

Rohr, John A. *To Run a Constitution: The Legitimacy of the Administrative State.* Lawrence, KS: University Press of Kansas, 1986.

Rollins, Alfred B. *Roosevelt and Howe.* New York: Alfred A. Knopf, 1962.

Roosevelt, Nicholas. *Theodore Roosevelt: The Man as I Knew Him.* New York: Dodd, Mead & Co., 1967.

Roosevelt, Theodore. *Autobiography.* Edited by Wayne Andrews. New York: Scribner and Sons, 1958.

Ross, Dorothy. *The Origins of American Social Science.* New York: Cambridge University Press, 1991.

Ross, Edward. *Social Control: A Survey of the Foundations of Order.* Cleveland: Press of Case Western Reserve University, 1969. First published 1901 by Macmillan Company.

Rossinow, Douglas. *The Politics of Authenticity: Liberalism, Christianity, and the New Left in America.* New York: Columbia University Press, 1998.

Rossiter, Clinton. *The American Presidency.* 2nd ed. Baltimore: The Johns Hopkins University Press, 1987.

Rosten, Leo C. *The Washington Correspondents.* New York: Harcourt, Brace & Co., 1937.

Rouse, Morleen Getz. "Daytime Radio Programming for the Homemaker, 1926–1935." *Journal of Popular Culture* 12 (1978–79): 315–327.

Ryfe, David. "'Betwixt and Between': Woodrow Wilson's Press Conferences and the Transition Toward the Modern Rhetorical Presidency." *Political Communication* 16 (1999): 77–93.

Sabato, Larry. *The Rise of Political Consultants: New Ways of Winning Elections.* New York: Basic Books, 1981.

———. *Feeding Frenzy: How Attack Journalism Has Changed American Politics.* New York: Free Press, 1991.

Sabato, Larry, and Robert Lichter. *When Should Watchdogs Bark? Media Coverage of the Clinton Scandals.* Washington, D.C.: Center for Media and Public Affairs, 1994.

Sadler, David Francis. "Theodore Roosevelt: A Symbol to Americans, 1898–1912" PhD diss., University of Minnesota, 1954.

Salinger, Pierre. *With Kennedy.* New York: Doubleday & Co., 1966.

Salisbury, Harrison. *A Time of Change: A Reporter's Tale of Our Times.* New York: Harper and Row, 1988.

Scannell, Paddy. *Radio, Television and Modern Life: A Phenomenological Approach.* Oxford: Blackwell, 1996.

Schattschneider, E. E. *The Semisovereign People*. New York: Holt, Rinehart and Winston, 1960.

Schedler, Andreas. *The End of Politics? Explorations into Modern Anti-Politics*. London: MacMillan Press, 1997.

Scheufele, Dietram. "Framing as a Theory of Media Effects." *Journal of Communication* 49 (1999): 103–122.

Schiappa, Edward. *Defining Reality: Definitions and the Politics of Meaning*. Carbondale: Southern Illinois University Press, 2003.

Schier, Steven E. *The Postmodern Presidency: Bill Clinton's Legacy in American Politics*. Pittsburgh: University of Pittsburgh Press, 2000.

Schlesinger, Arthur, Jr. *A Thousand Days: John F. Kennedy in the White House*. New York: Fawcett Premier Books, 1965.

———. *The Coming of the New Deal*. Boston: Houghton Mifflin, 1959.

Schmidt, Susan. *Truth At Any Cost: Ken Starr and the Unmaking of Bill Clinton*. New York: HarperCollins, 2000.

Schudson, Michael. *Discovering the News: A Social History of American Newspapers*. New York: Basic Books, 1978.

———. *The Power of News*. Cambridge: Harvard University Press, 1995.

Schumpeter, Joseph. *Capitalism, Socialism, and Democracy*. 3rd Ed. New York: Harper, 1950.

Scott, Marvin, and Stanford Lyman. "Accounts." *American Sociological Review* 33 (1968): 46–62.

Scott, Walter. "Institutions and Organizations: Toward a Theoretical Synthesis." In *Institutional Environments and Organizations*, edited by Walter Scott, John Meyer and Associates, 55–80. Thousand Oaks, CA: Sage, 1994.

Searle, John. *Speech Acts: An Essay in the Philosophy of Language*. Cambridge: Cambridge University Press, 1969.

Sewell, William. "A Theory of Structure: Duality, Agency, and Transformation." *American Journal of Sociology* 98 (1992): 1–29.

Sharon, John. "The Psychology of the Fireside Chat." B.A. Thesis, Princeton University, 1949.

Shattuc, M. Jane. *The Talking Cure: TV Talk Shows and Women*. New York: Routledge, 1997.

Shi, David. *Facing Facts: Realism in American Thought and Culture, 1850–1920*. New York: Oxford University Press, 1995.

Sidey, Hugh. *John F. Kennedy, President*. New York: Atheneum, 1963.

Sies, Daniel. "The Presidency and Television: A Study of Six Administrations." PhD diss., University of Cincinnati, 1978.

Sigal, Leon. *Reporters and Officials: The Organization and Politics of Newsmaking*. Lexington, MA: D.C. Heath, 1973.

Sigelman, Lee. "Gauging the Public Response to Presidential Leadership." *Presidential Studies Quarterly* 10 (1980): 427–433.

Simpson, Christopher. *Science of Coercion: Communication Research and Psychological Warfare, 1945–1960*. New York: Oxford University Press, 1994.

Sing, Rajandra. *Social Movements, Old and New*. Thousand Oaks, CA: Sage, 2001.

Sklar, Martin. *The Corporate Reconstruction of American Capitalism, 1890–1916: The Market, the Law, and Politics*. Cambridge: Cambridge University Press, 1988.

Skowronek, Stephen. *The Politics Presidents Make: Leadership from John Adams to Bill Clinton*. 2nd Ed. Cambridge: Belknap Press, 1997.

————. *Building a New American State: The Expansion of National Administrative Capacities, 1877–1920*. Cambridge: Cambridge University Press, 1982.

Smith, Carolyn. *Presidential Press Conferences: A Critical Approach*. New York: Praeger, 1990.

Smith, James Allen. *The Idea Brokers: Think Tanks and the Rise of a New Policy Elite*. New York: Free Press, 1991.

Smoller, Frederic T. *The Six O'clock Presidency: A Theory of Presidential Press Relations in the Age of Television*. Westport, CT: Praeger, 1990.

Smulyan, Susan. "'Radio Advertising to Women in Twenties America': A Latchkey to Every Home." *Historical Journal of Film, Radio, and Television* 13 (1993): 299–314.

————. *Selling Radio: The Commercialization of American Broadcasting, 1920–1934*. Washington: Smithsonian Institution Press, 1994.

Smythe, Ted Curtis. "The Reporter, 1880–1900: Working Conditions and Their Influence on the News." *Journalism History* 7 (1980): 1–10.

Sontag, Susan. *On Photography*. New York: Dell, 1977.

Sorensen, Theodore. *Kennedy*. New York: Harper and Row, 1965.

Spalding, John W. "1928: Radio Becomes a Mass Advertising Medium." *Journal of Broadcasting* 8 (1963–64): 31–44.

Sparrow, Bartholomew. *Uncertain Guardians: The News Media as a Political Institution*. Baltimore: Johns Hopkins University Press, 1999.

Spellman, Robert L. "Cooperation on a Secondary Story: Oscar King Davis and the President." *Studies in Newspaper and Periodical History* 1993: 117–134.

Steffens, Lincoln. *The Autobiography of Lincoln Steffens*. New York: Harcourt, Brace and World, 1958.

Stein, Henry A. "Theodore Roosevelt and The Press." *Mid-America* 54 (2) 1972: 94–107.

Stewart, James B. *Bloodsport: The President and His Enemies*. New York: Simon and Schuster, 1996.

Stockbridge, Frank. "How Woodrow Wilson Won His Nomination." *The Current History Magazine* 1924 (July): 561–572.

Stott, William. *Documentary Expression and Thirties America*. New York: Oxford University Press, 1973.

Strasser, Susan. *Satisfaction Guaranteed: The Making of the American Mass Market*. New York: Pantheon, 1989.

Streitmatter, Roger. "Front Page from the White House: A Quantitative Study of Personal News Coverage from Teddy Roosevelt to Ronald Reagan." PhD diss., The American University, 1988.

————. "The Impact of Presidential Personality on News Coverage in Major Newspapers." *Journalism Quarterly* 62 (1985): 66–73.

Stuckey, Mary E. *Playing the Game: The Presidential Rhetoric of Ronald Reagan*. New York: Praeger, 1990.

————. "'The Domain of Conscience': Woodrow Wilson and the Establishment of a Transcendent Political Order." *Rhetoric and Public Affairs* 6 (2003): 1–24.

Stuckey, Mary, and Frederick J. Antczak, "The Rhetorical Presidency: Deepening Vision, Widening Exchange." *Communication Yearbook* 21 (1998): 405–444.

Sundquist, James L., ed. *Back to Gridlock?: Governance in the Clinton Years*. Washington, D.C.: Brookings Institution, 1995.

————. *The Decline and Resurgence of Congress*. Washington: Brookings, 1981.

Susman, Warren. "The Culture of the Thirties." Chapter 9 of *Culture as History: The Transformation of American Society in the Twentieth Century*. New York: Pantheon Books, 1973.

Sussman, Leila. *Dear FDR: A Study of Political Letter-Writing*. Totowa, NJ: The Bedminster Press, 1963.

"A Symposium: 'Neustadt's *Presidential Power* Twenty Years Later: The Test of Time.'" *Presidential Studies Quarterly* 11 (1981): 341–363.

Taggart, Paul. *Populism*. Buckingham: Open University Press, 2001.

Tebbel, John, and Sarah Miles Watts. *The Press and the Presidency: From George Washington to Ronald Reagan*. New York: Oxford University Press, 1985.

Thomas, Helen. *Dateline: White House*. New York: Macmillan, 1975.

Thompson, Charles. *Presidents I've Known and Two Near Presidents*. Freeport, NY: Books for Libraries Press, 1929.

Thompson, John A. *Reformers and War: American Progressive Publicists and the First World War*. Cambridge: Cambridge University Press, 1987.

Thomson, Charles A.H. *Television and Presidential Politics: The Experience of 1952 and the Problems Ahead*. Washington, D.C.: The Brookings Institution, 1956.

Tietge, David J. *Flash Effect: Science and the Rhetorical Origins of Cold War America*. Athens, OH: Ohio State University Press, 2002.

Tillich, Paul. *Morality and Beyond*. New York: Harper and Row, 1963.

———. *The Courage to Be*. New Haven: Yale University Press, 1952.

———. *The New Being*. New York: Scribner and Sons, 1955.

Touraine, Alain. *Return of the Actor: Social Theory in Postindustrial Society*. Translated by Myrna Godzich. Minneapolis: University of Minnesota Press, 1988.

———. *The Voice and the Eye: An Analysis of Social Movements*. Translated by Alan Duff. Cambridge: Cambridge University Press, 1981.

Trilling, Lionel. *The Liberal Imagination: Essays on Literature and Society*. New York: Viking, 1950.

Truman, David. *The Governmental Process: Political Interests and Public Opinion*. New York: Alfred E. Knopf, 1962.

Tucher, Andie. *Froth and Scum: Truth, Beauty, Goodness, and the Ax Murder in America's First Mass Medium*. Chapel Hill, NC: University of North Carolina Press, 1994.

Tulis, Jeffrey. *The Rhetorical Presidency*. Princeton: Princeton University Press, 1987.

Turner, Kathleen, ed. *Doing Rhetorical History: Concepts and Cases*. Tuscaloosa: University of Alabama Press, 1998.

Turner, Ralph H. "The Theme of Contemporary Social Movements." *British Journal of Sociology* 20 (1969): 390–405.

Urofsky, I. Melvin, and Martha May, eds. *The New Christian Right: Political and Social Issues*. New York: Garland Publishers, 1996.

Vidich, Arthur, and Stanford Lyman. *American Sociology: Worldly Rejections of Religion and Their Directions*. New Haven: Yale University Press, 1985.

Weid, Clyde P. *The Nemesis of Reform: The Republican Party During the New Deal*. New York: Columbia University Press, 1994.

Weiler, Michael, and W. Barnett Pearce, eds. *Reagan and Public Discourse in America*. Tuscaloosa: University of Alabama Press, 1992.

Weinberg, Arthur, and Lila Weinberg, eds. *The Muckrakers*. New York: Simon and Schuster, 1964.

Weinstein, James. *The Corporate Ideal in the Liberal State, 1900–1918*. Boston: Beacon Press, 1968.

Westlind, Dennis. *The Politics of Popular Identity: Understanding Recent Populist Movements in Sweden and the United States*. Lund: Lund University Press, 1996.

Weyl, Walter. *The New Democracy: An Essay on Certain Political and Economic Tendencies in the United States*. New York: Macmillan, 1912.

White, Graham. *FDR and the Press*. Chicago: University of Chicago Press, 1979.

White, Hayden. *Tropics of Discourse: Essays in Cultural Criticism*. Baltimore: Johns Hopkins University Press, 1978.

White, James Boyd. *When Words Lose Their Meaning: Constitutions and Reconstitutions of Language, Character, and Community*. Chicago: University of Chicago Press, 1984.

White, Morton. *Social Thought in America: The Revolt against Formalism*. New York, Viking Press, 1949.

White, William Allen. *The Autobiography of William Allen White*. New York: Macmillan, 1946.

Wicker, Tom. *On Press*. New York: The Viking Press, 1975.

Wiebe, Robert. *The Search for Order, 1877–1920*. New York: Hill and Wang, 1967.

Williams, Raymond. *Keywords: A Vocabulary of Culture and Society*. New York: Oxford University Press, 1976.

Wilson, Woodrow. *Congressional Government: A Study in American Politics*. Boston: Houghton Mifflin, 1913.

———. *Constitutional Government in the United States*. New York: Columbia University Press, 1908.

Windt, Theodore. "Presidential Rhetoric: Definition of a Discipline of Study." Introduction to *Essays in Presidential Rhetoric*. 2nd Ed., edited by Theodore Windt and Beth Ingold. Dubuque, IA: Kendall/Hunt Publishers, 1987.

Winfield, Betty. *FDR and the News Media*. Urbana: University of Illinois Press, 1990.

Wittgenstein, Ludwig. *Philosophical Investigations*. 3rd Ed. Translated by G. E. M. Anscombe. New York: Macmillan, 1958.

Wittner, Lawrence. *Cold War America: From Hiroshima to Watergate*. New York: Praeger, 1974.

Woodward, Bob. *The Agenda: Inside the Clinton White House*. New York: Simon and Schuster, 1994.

Wuthnow, Robert, ed. *Vocabularies of Public Life: Empirical Essays in Symbolic Structure*. New York: Routledge, 1992.

Young, Roland. "Woodrow Wilson's Congressional Government Reconsidered." In *The Philosophy and Policies of Woodrow Wilson*, edited by Earl Latham, 201–213. Chicago: University of Chicago Press, 1958.

Zald, Mayer N., and John D. McCarthy. "Appendix: The Trend of Social Movements in America: Professionalization and Resource Mobilization." In *Social Movements in an Organizational Society*, edited by Mayer N. Zald and John D. McCarthy, 337–392. New Brunswick, NJ: Transaction Publishers, 1987.

Zarefsky, David. "Presidential Rhetoric and the Power of Definition." Paper presented at the Conference on the Public Presidency, College Station, TX, January 7–10, 2004.

Zelizer, Barbie. "'Saying as Collective Practice: Quoting and Differential Address in the News." *Text* 9 (1989): 369–388.

Index

POLITICAL COMMUNICATION

FRONTIERS IN

General Editors
Lynda Lee Kaid and Bruce Gronbeck

At the heart of how citizens, governments, and the media interact is the communication process, a process that is undergoing tremendous changes as we embrace a new millennium. Never has there been a time when confronting the complexity of these evolving relationships been so important to the maintenance of civil society. This series seeks books that advance the understanding of this process from multiple perspectives and as it occurs in both institutionalized and non-institutionalized political settings. While works that provide new perspectives on traditional political communication questions are welcome, the series also encourages the submission of manuscripts that take an innovative approach to political communication, which seek to broaden the frontiers of study to incorporate critical and cultural dimensions of study as well as scientific and theoretical frontiers.

For more information or to submit material for consideration, contact:

BRUCE E. GRONBECK
Obermann Center for Advanced Studies
N134 OH
The University of Iowa
Iowa City, IA 52242-5000

LYNDA LEE KAID
Political Communication Center
Department of Communication
University of Oklahoma
Norman, OK 73109

To order other books in this series, please contact our Customer Service Department:

        (800) 770-LANG (within the U.S.)
        (212) 647-7706 (outside the U.S.)
        (212) 647-7707 FAX

Or browse online by series:
        WWW.PETERLANGUSA.COM